Dear J.P.,

It's Not About Me!
- An Autobiography

Confessions of a Recovered Outlaw Addict
– *from Living Hell to Living Big*

I DO HOPE YOU ENJOY
READING THIS AS MUCH AS
I ENJOYED LIVING (MOST OF)
IT! STAY JOLLY,

Ian Young

IAN

It's Not About Me!

First published in 2013 by Anoma Press
48 St Vincent Drive, St Albans, Herts, AL1 5SJ, UK
info@anomapress.com
www.anomapress.com

Book layout by Sophie Norman
Profile photography courtesy of Joel Dyer
Original artwork 'Image of Hell' attributed to a follower of Bosch c.1516

Printed on acid-free paper from managed forests. This book is printed on demand to fulfill orders, so no copies will be remaindered or pulped.

Printed and bound by TJ International Ltd, Padstow, Cornwall

ISBN 978-1-908746-86-3

This book is available online and in all good bookstores.

It's Not About Me!

-An Autobiography

Confessions of a Recovered Outlaw Addict
– *from Living Hell to Living Big*

Ian Young

www.ianyoung.co
www.itsnotaboutme.co

Warning:

This book contains adult themes such as detailed drug use and alcoholism, sex and wanton lust, crime and disorder, profanity and absolute recklessness. Please kindly desist from reading this book if you are too easily offended.

Disclaimer:

The opinions I've expressed in this book are my own. Please do not take offence if you disagree with any of them. They're based upon my own experiences and therefore likely to be different to your own. They are not meant to upset anyone, although some of them may be upsetting. They are not meant to influence you, although some of them may do so. They are not meant to cause disruption to your current values, although some of them may indeed affect the way you view yourself, your values and how you interact with the rest of the planet. Although I mean to put my point across, because of my experiences, my views could be considered by some to be extreme. Personally, I'd like to think of them as accurate and forward thinking. If you disagree, that's OK. If you agree, that's OK. If you're not sure, that's OK. This is just a book, albeit it is my book, and therefore it is written from my perspective. This book is relevant and personal to me. I hope it is to you too.

Dedication:

This book is dedicated to the memory of my Father, who absolutely, definitely taught me right from wrong, lest I never forget that. His influence on me goes beyond words and years.

Thanks:

I must say thank you to a number of people who have helped me through this book writing process and through my life so far:

My wonderful wife, always cheerful and humble in spirit and kind, and who surprisingly has stood by me without seeking a divorce due to my snoring... yet. Emma, I love you! Thank you for allowing me to practice being second, and thank you for being my jump up and down friend.

To my Mum for never letting go of me. A most honourable task, excellently executed.

To Rabbi Debbie Young-Somers for being you and having the decency to believe in me when others had lost hope.

To my Grandfather Michael Sherbourne, an all round top bloke, charming, witty, sensitive and someone who embodies the spirit of selfless service. It's never about him.

To Russell Sedman for being my closest friend and confident for so many years. It's always a pleasure figuring things out with you.

To Nicholas Lynn for being here and there throughout. I salute you.

To Kent Coleman, for continually reminding me it's all about God, and it's never about me.

To Sukhi Wahiwala for being such a friend, brother, mentor and spiritual dude. And then, for allowing me to share your family – I am Uncle Ian.

To Paul Vernon, who knows how to have a great time, even if we do get the timing wrong – every time. Cheers for being such an inspiring friend, teacher, confident and partner. Fun is always on the agenda.

To Gavin Cooper for services rendered through those light and dark years. My original business mentor and the man I always know I can absolutely trust for an honest answer. I'm grateful to you.

To Steve Bedlam, for being you and always letting everyone else be themselves. You are the nicest guy I've ever had the pleasure to grow old alongside. Kindly have a drink to our good health on my behalf please mate.

To Césario Fernando, mon manager formidable a l'époque, et mon Frère sous toutes. Merci, mon gar! Tu as toujours pensé moi et me faites sortir de la merde – chaque fois! Je t'embrasse très forte pour être toujours las pour moi. Gros bisous comme d'hab. La Salle putain D'Anglais – D.J. Nerate. Tu es toujours bienvenu chez nous!

To all the Spiral Tribe ~ SP23 rules. We know who we are and what we achieved. Details will be revealed in a different book one day. Some of the very best days of my life. Proof that tribal life works. Utopia? TBC.

To everyone involved in Sober Services. Thank you. I can't do it with out you.

To Mindy Gibbins Klein AKA The Book Midwife, for continually encouraging to finish this bloody thing, and then for permitting me to be published, promoted, printed, and distributed under her fine reputation – I hope I haven't ruined it with my filthy stories?

And finally, to God, for allowing me to show up and play full out. AHO!

CONTENTS

It's Not About Me!

Part 1. ADDICTION – *the early years*
"So the Story goes a little like this..."

Part 2. ADDICTION – *the later years*
"My Self-imposed exile"

Part 3. ADDICTION – *The Dying Years*
"Being the person I never wanted to be"

Part 4. RECOVERY – *Rehab & The Early Years*
"and...breathe"

Part 5. RECOVERY – *Onwards & Upwards*

"Life's in session and I'm showing up"

Epilogue: A final word from Ian

Afterword: The 12-Step Programme (Formal explanation)

WHAT'S THIS BOOK ALL ABOUT THEN?

Hello, and thanks so much for investing your time in my book. It's an absolute honour for me to be able to present my story to you, but it will truly become valuable if you or someone you love actually benefits from it.

So, with that in mind, please pass this book on to other people you believe may benefit from it, and feel free to contact me personally if I can be of any assistance whatsoever.

Please don't feel it's necessary to try any of the stupid things I did yourself; because even though I, a complete amateur, was able to carry them out, there is no reason, to believe that you're also going to be impenetrable. Do remember that people die doing the very same stuff I was doing. I have friends who lost their lives to their addiction, so please, just take my word for it and enjoy the story.

Furthermore, this book can be easily read in two different styles. You can read it through as an autobiography and hopefully enjoy the journey I take you on. Or you can use it as a reference guide to assist you in understanding how best to help someone struggling with addiction, or even recovery. There are descriptions and examples contained within this book which can be used and understood by someone either on a personal level or as a friend watching out for someone else and their addictive illness, to enable them to stop and to stay stopped.

And I guess finally, I want to point out that this isn't a book attempting to scare people against drugs and partying. Although I have found it necessary to stop to remain stopped, I sincerely enjoyed a great deal of my journey into the depths of my addiction. This is not an anti-drugs book. But it most certainly is a pro-recovery book.

Thank you for paying attention and taking the time to find out what the hell happened to me.

Ian Young
November 24th 2012

It's Not About Me!

PREFACE

I am here to tell you that it has been my experience that you can stop drinking and stay stopped. That you can stop smoking marijuana and stay stopped. That you can stop smoking Crack and stay stopped. That you can stop snorting Heroin and stay stopped. That you can stop injecting Cocaine and stay stopped (yeah, I know, wrong way around – but we'll talk more about that later).

It is my experience, that given enough pain and distress, we reach a breaking point. We reach a point where we become willing to do just about anything to beat our debilitating habits. The good news is that there's nothing uncomfortable or unpleasant about the process. I've experienced this process first hand. I have used the steps on myself and I have implemented the changes successfully in the lives of my clients.

This process was developed as a direct response to my own experiences and this book is about not only the process itself but also the journey I took to get here.

I know first hand that you can stop snorting or shooting Heroin, that you can stop injecting Cocaine, and that you can stop drinking and stay stopped. I went through the addiction and the fight with each of these substances, and I have stayed stopped – permanently! I don't take prescription drugs recklessly – even the ones that make me feel nice and fuzzy, and then send me bananas when

It's Not About Me!

I mix them with booze. I don't smoke Cannabis – even though it grows out of the ground and could be considered one of Mother Earth's gifts for us. Mind you, anyone smoking skunk needs to know that there is nothing natural or organic about it – that it is completely genetically modified ganja! I don't do any of that anymore because I made a commitment to myself and I made it work. If I can get this message across in the book to those of you who are scared about making such a radical change in your life, then I'll be a happier person. More than anything else, this book is to help you understand that you have it in you to stop, given the right tools and beliefs. That it is your choice to tap into these belief systems, and that even though they may sound airy-fairy, they could save your life. Only you have the ultimate power to make that choice, although maybe I can help you too.

When you are stuck in the middle of your addiction, it feels impossible to get out of it. You feel trapped, and even trying to quit feels hopeless. Addiction is a horrible and destructive behaviour that completely destroys the essence of your life. More than anything I want to show you that as well as recovering from addiction, you can be reborn and your life can change in ways that you would have never imagined. Your life can be whatever you dream it to be. I am certain that I can offer a guarantee to a successful recovery. As long as you are prepared to do what I have done; if you are ready to say no, if you are ready to take control of your own life, I can help you and I can guarantee that if you do what I've done, you'll get what I've got – freedom from addiction. There's nothing here in this programme that is unachievable; none of it is difficult. The hardest part is the first step and that is admitting to yourself that you are ready to change and then moving to a place of abstinence and surrender. Once you are truly ready, the rest is easy.

If you do what I have done, you will get what I have got. I guarantee it.

This book is not a step-by-step addict's guide to kicking the habit, though it can certainly help. This book is about laughter, and life and inspiration. It is designed to help those who have recovered from addiction to stay on track, to remain inspired and to continue to move in the right direction. This book is designed to help family members understand the process of recovery. This book is full of ideas and reminders of the help that exists right outside your door.

This book is my life story, my path, the good, the bad and the ugly. By giving an account of my story I allow you, the reader, to get into my world, my addictions and my path to recovery. This will not only help addicts understand and forge their own path but it's also designed for loved ones, mine included, to understand a world that seems so far away from their own experiences.

This book is hope. Hope for the future of every addict. Hope for recovery. Hope for forgiveness.

This book is many things, but above all, it is a damn good yarn, if I do say so myself. It is not just a lesson, it is a story and I am sure it is one that you are going to enjoy.

The book is broken up into the four eras of my life; before addiction, my growing addiction including some of my biggest challenges living as an addict, my early recovery and the lessons I learnt, and finally, some of my thoughts and attitudes based on my current perspective.

When I look back on my life, it is easy to separate it into these particular eras. Each of these periods had a different feeling to me. I was a different person during each time, my wants and needs were different, and my actions, behaviours and attitudes were certainly different too. Each era reflects elements of the human condition that all people, addicts or not, will be able to connect with personally. There is the first part where I was just growing up. My life was a lot of fun, I was a popular kid, and I was a nice guy at school. I had lots of friends. I was cheeky and popular and fun to be around and this led me to soft drugs and into the gateway to harder substances. My teenage years were filled with me switching identities, trying to figure out who I was and what I wanted. My personality and behaviours evolved from fun-loving hippie, to punk to raver. I began travelling, left school and my friends and I created some pretty magical moments during that period of my life.

The stories of the earliest part of my life outline my character and my behaviours and show exactly where some of my issues formed and why. There are the very first glimpses of my addictive personality and tendencies long before I started using heavy drugs. We will take a look at the early warning signs that could have been picked up had someone known what they were looking for. Even as a teenager I was selfish and had self-centred attitudes that quickly sent me down the wrong path. I began to manipulate and lie and cheat to get my own way, and from this behaviour, the addict was born.

In the second part of this book, addicts and their families will be able to recognise behaviours, attitudes and painful realities that everyone who deals with addiction will have to face at one time or another. During this dark period of my life, I thought I was in control. I thought I was having the time of my life, but slowly I was destroying myself, one day at a time, with my addictions. I started using needles and my behaviour began to truly affect the people in my life who I cared about. I became ashamed and guilty regarding my own actions. I did things that I was not proud of. I did things for my addiction that, without drugs, I never would have done. This part of the book is a truly emotional journey of the life of an addict; my focus in life was just to get another hit and it took me across Europe, across the world running from my problems and chasing the next high.

The story ends with my returning back to London, dishevelled, extremely addicted and in pain and completely alone. When I returned to London I had successfully alienated myself from my friends, my family and everyone who had ever supported me. I was alone. I was addicted to hard drugs and, after a few overdoses, sadness and intense emotional pain, I finally realised that the choices I was making were killing me.

The third section of the story is my journey to recovery. It was not an easy journey but it is a true story of hope and transformation. During this section of the book you, the reader, will come with me through the early days of recovery, the slip-ups, the revelations, the fears and the disbelief, and move through these to finally finding a reason to become sober and the motivation to do so. You will read as I reinvent my life, discover meaning and spirituality and discover true meaning in a world without drugs.

The third section begins with me writing a letter to God in late November 2000 and beginning the process of recovery. My sober date is March 16th 2001, so it took me a few months before I truly became sober, but once I did, I have remained sober ever since.

The final section of the book is all about life today and the lessons I teach in the work I do with addicts and their families. I talk about the freedom of this lifestyle and the difficulties that we all come up against in the journey towards freedom from addiction. We will talk about spirituality to a deeper extent and explore the new attitudes and behaviours I have adopted personally to make not only my life but also the world around me a more positive place to exist.

At the end of the book is a full explanation of each of the steps in the 12-Step recovery programme. I have included this explanation to help addicts and families of addicts to understand the steps that we take towards a successful recovery.

My whole life story is one that explores the issues related to addiction and drug abuse. But it is the story of my journey to recovery that is the most profound, and this is what I think will bring hope and motivation to those struggling with their own personal recovery from addiction. Since my first day of sobriety I have had some of the most amazing experiences, all of which I could never have imagined. I have had incredible work experiences, trips around the world and amazing opportunities to meet incredible, inspiring people along the way. It was in recovery that I decided that working in this industry, helping other people to recover was what I wanted to do with my life. And, for the past ten years+, I have done exactly that. I am so blessed to have had the opportunity to touch the lives of so many people and help wonderful people get clean and open up the world of experiences that life has in store for each of them personally.

That is my mission in life and it continues to drive and inspire me every day to stay on my chosen path.

My background

My journey is a story of travel, counterculture, survival and hedonism. It is one of going against the grain and doing things differently. It is one full of adventure, mystery and for a few years the ultimate defeat, which I was of course able to rise from and conquer life once again, like a phoenix. But in my early years as a teenager and a twenty-something I was just trying to have fun and live life by my own rules. My lifestyle was anything but conventional. Regardless of the fact I had been raised as a part of a very conventional English family, I branched out in an incredibly different direction. I didn't reside within society. I lived completely outside the boundaries of society and the law. I was an outlaw, and proud of it.

I was an extreme character, to say the least. I never really operated within the bounds of reasonable behaviour, which most youth operate within. When I changed my life around and became sober after a thirteen-year stretch with active and constant addiction, I did so at the start of the new millennium. At this point, life took on a whole new direction for me: every day I woke up with a purpose and meaning in my life. Now here I am, well over ten years later, in the perfect place where I feel inspired to tell the story of my life as an addict as well as the important stories of before and after.

I fraternise in 12-Step Fellowships and have done so since they helped me get clean and sober in early 2001, but I do not often share my story there particularly these days as I my attendance and personal recovery programme has me sharing stories and lessons to be learnt about recovery. I don't find it too useful to tell my stories of hedonism and active addiction to people trying to learn how to stop. I believe they benefit more from my stories of healthy living and recovery principles. I am constantly asked about my story. People seem drawn to the outrageousness of my previous life and after enough asking, I relent here in the pages of this book and happily share my story with everyone who asked and everyone who wants to hear it. Now feels like the right time.

I came from a dark place and turned my life around. It is as if now, looking back on where I have been, I managed somehow to transport myself to a completely different world. My current life just doesn't resemble my previous one. This difference and turnaround makes it a story of hope. It is a story that shows every person that it is possible to rebalance our karma. It is possible to draw a line in the sand, step over it and start our lives again. This book's purpose is to show that it is possible to stop using, and stay stopped. Even more importantly, it is possible for an addict to get a quality of life beyond anything you could have imagined. The power is in your hands. All you have to do is make the right choices to change and life is yours for the making.

Where I am now

I have been drug and alcohol free since early in 2001. And once my spirit was freed from my chronic addictions, I have dedicated my life to helping others to achieve the same freedom from addiction and other damaging behaviours that I have experienced myself. I have opened and founded two different residential rehabilitation centres, which I am very proud of, and I have gone on to build a number of separate companies. My proudest achievements are Sober Services Ltd, a company that helps people attain and maintain their recovery through professional services, and Living Big - a growing forum and community for people who offer professional help to other people, but get caught up trying to do their own sales and marketing, since it detracts from their actual passion. Living Big allows them the freedom to just focus on the coaching/mentoring/ training/ therapeutic involvement and removes their obligation to go chasing business. I also speak and present at seminars and conventions, being fully trained and able to deliver accelerated learning to large audiences. As you may be able to tell, I've managed to keep myself very busy!

My most cherished skill is, however, my ability to stay sober and the gift to be able to pass this skill on to other addicts and help them to transform their own lives. Since I learnt how to stop drinking/drugging and to stay stopped i.e. permanent recovery, I have been able to pass this on to others and I consider it a privilege and a beautiful way to spend the days of my life.

Why I am writing this book?
"We're on a mission from God" (Jake Blues, circa 1980)

Over the past twelve or so years I have developed my own sense of both global and community responsibility. My personal mission is to co-create humour and harmony in everyday life through laughter and love. I am also a strong advocate for bringing about change in others so that they may have an even better quality of life. So, I bring value to others, mainly through my abilities as a 'connector supreme'. By this I mean that I connect people together and bring about positive changes in everyone's lives. These missions are only achievable when I am fit both spiritually and emotionally. I can only achieve my greatest goals when I am at peace with myself so that I can focus my energy on improving the quality of the lives of others, realising that, in the grand scheme of things, it really is not about me!

I have been asked time and time again to tell my story right from the very beginning. I am often fond of just telling the good parts – from when I began to recover from my addiction and moved into the solution of living a happier life. I speak frequently about the methods I have used to remain drug free and sober. However, I have never actually told the whole story of how I got there, warts and all.....until now!

What makes you so special?

But before I go on, please know this: I don't believe I'm anyone special, or in some way more important than the next person trying to stop using. I don't think there's anything extraordinary about me. But, I do think I have an outrageous story; I had a very unique and great adventure that I travelled along during my time drinking and using. It was certainly the type of madness that if made into a film would always leave you guessing what could possibly happen next, as the tale becomes more and more insane.

Yet, there's nothing special about me. The only thing that separates me form the next person is that I have gotten off my arse, rather tentatively, and decided I'm going to take some action and write a book. Once the decision was made, I started to write it all down. It was a slow and arduous process that I continued to commit myself to even when I really ought to have been doing something else, like earning money and getting a real job.

The reason I am writing this book is not because I think there is anything special about me, but rather to satisfy all of the people who asked me to tell it. I can also see the potential value that others could gain from reading a story like mine and finding their own inspiration to get clean within its pages. There is inspiration in the pages of this book for parents who are looking for guidance. Addicts looking to get clean, partners who fear for their loved ones, a person looking to learn new ways to improve their own quality of life are also all appropriate readers for this story. I feel very lucky and fortunate to have the time to write it down and the resources to put it together and share this story with the people around me.

I don't think I am special, but I do think I have a special story.

Personal Disclaimer

I need to make a disclaimer here. I am a member of the 12-Step Fellowships, but I don't speak on behalf of them. I will not be naming anyone else by his or her correct or full names unless previous permission has been granted. After all, they are called the Anonymous Fellowships for a reason.

This is because two of the twelve traditions of the 12-Step Fellowships refer to anonymity. The 12th tradition suggests anonymity as a spiritual principle, which is kind of why this book is titled "It's not about me!" I will discuss this more later on. But it is the 11th tradition that talks about anonymity at the level of press, radio, TV and films, which clearly includes books like this. This is to allow for the safety of members who may still struggle with the stigma associated with addictions.

You know a lot of people are quite precious about their anonymity and that's cool. I fully respect that. But, in my case, anyone who ever met me when I was drunk, or came across me while I was stoned, or crossed my path while I was high, knew there was something wrong with me, even if they didn't recognise the signs that I was an alcoholic and a drug addict. Everyone could tell that I was messed up in some way. So, now to have the opportunity to inform people that I've recovered from that illness is actually something I'm quite proud of. I have no shame and I see no stigma attached to that whatsoever. In fact, I use my experience to see how I can help the next person who's looking for someone to 'understand' them. I do, however, appreciate that many other people want to be more discreet about their past and current situations. They do want to keep that information private, and they don't want to have it disclosed to their employer, friends or family. For me, I'm an open book; I don't have any qualms about telling anyone I was a drug addict but I'm no longer a drug addict. I think that's beautiful.

I have an outstanding memory of walking down the high street just drooling on downers, barbiturates, alcohol and glue (that's something that's guaranteed to put you into zombie mode). It is really not very beautiful!

Yet I seem to remember it so very vividly. So when people talk about anonymity... well, let's just say that I've since returned to that town and I truly have no qualms about my anonymity. Everyone in that town who ever saw me walking down the high street drooling can see me today as I walk along that same high street carrying myself with dignity and pride. And I can tell anyone who's even remotely interested that today I'm a recovered drug addict. These people remember what I was like when I was using and now they see me today, a responsible member of society. I have broken my anonymity, not at the level of press, radio, television and film but under that level, at the level of a town centre. I was never ashamed of my recovery or my prior addictions. I have never hidden my story. Because of this, people who know my family have referred people to me who need help, knowing that I have already managed to recover. I have been able to help people achieve their own breakthroughs and help them get on their path to recovery. All of this is because I'm never ashamed to say I was a junkie and now I'm clean. Everyone's anonymity will mean different things to them personally. I won't judge anyone else's choices on this matter; honestly it's not important to me. What is important to me is that I have no problem with my own.

Before I continue, I do need to point out that I genuinely and sincerely believe that my journey into healthy living and healthy behaviours began with, and were supported by, my 12-Step work. The 12-Steps are a process that blew me away. I was amazed at their simplicity and ability to teach me a new way of living. They started with teaching me the principles of complete abstinence, a clear fast track towards stopping drinking and drugging, and supported me through the process every step of the way. The 12-Steps helped me to continue my journey by encouraging me to carry their message of recovery and by teaching me that performing acts of kindness towards others is a positive way to maintain my own recovery.

Without the 12-Step programme, I honestly believe that I never would have been able to transform my life into the healthy, happy one that it is. I may have stopped using or stopped drinking but I don't think I ever would have recovered my mental, emotional or physical health. If I had managed to stop using without this process, I am sure that I would have been miserable about it. Certainly, as far as I am concerned, my whole journey relies on the words of the 12-Step Fellowships. It is what I will suggest as a solution for anyone and everyone looking to conquer their addictions.

It is not necessarily, however, the solution for everybody. I know there are many people who struggle with the 12-Step programmes, particularly with dependence on the spiritual dimension. I feel the need to emphasise that there are certainly other solutions and not everybody needs to find a place of abstinence. Abstinence is only necessary in certain cases. However, although it may not be necessary for everybody, there is no dispute that abstinence never harmed anyone and that 12-Step programmes will benefit anyone whether they're addicted or not. Much of my work these days is non 12-Step work. These days I spend more time working with people who need some sort of leverage or imagination or encouragement with which to make changes in their lives. I provide this without going to some of the extreme measures that are employed using the 12-Step recovery programme. That said, the 12-Step programme has never hurt anyone who took it seriously. It is a very good programme that is bound to improve the quality of life of the participant.

IAN YOUNG

The 12-Step programme for me was the vital first stage of my recovery. But after I became sober, I discovered many other processes and programmes which I have found very useful too. I stand before you today, not just a product of the recovery available through the 12 step programmes, but very much the sum total of a great many different personal development experiences, most notably NLP – Neuro Linguistic Programming, which I have found helped me with a great deal of other parts of my character outside of my addiction. I'll always enjoy considering myself a work in progress.

It's Not About Me!

Part 1.
ADDICTION
– the early years

"So the story goes a little something like this..."

1. **Growing up** - daydreaming my life away

I am a raver in recovery. I am the type of guy who likes to dance to very loud Techno music and take very strong psychedelic drugs. Plenty of them! I'm pretty sure that I am one of the early ravers to recover. I am undoubtedly within the first generation of ravers in recovery.

You might wonder what this even means. I don't blame you. The story starts a long way back, back at the beginning, before I became a raver at all. That's the only way we can get back to how I started my process of recovery.

I was born 9 November 1971, at about teatime. It was a cold and windy night and I distinctly remember thinking to myself, this is going to be fun! It was a quick birth. I was ready to take on the world. My mother was home in time for supper, and I had arrived, ready for the crazy things my life was about the throw at me.

I have very few memories of being a child. Well, to be fair, it is probably the same amount of scattered memories as most adults. I do remember a couple of key moments, however, like my indescribable attachment to an inflatable beach ball, and the insurmountable loss of surrendering it to the fast-flowing river.

I spent a lot of my early childhood on the Peter Pan ward of the Great Ormond Street Hospital. The Peter Pan ward was a children's ward designed for children who were destined never to grow up. It wasn't me who was sick, though, it was my big brother Mark. I have vague memories of my brother Mark, who passed away from Leukaemia when he was four and I was only three. I remember us being dressed up as Tweedledum and Tweedledee out of Alice in Wonderland. I'm not sure who was which character, but I loosely recollect climbing through chairs piled on top of one another so as to make a small cave and to escape the adults' wrath for some mischief I was likely to have caused, but was fully prepared to deny. Actually, I think I was dressed up as a Womble during this episode, which is kind of funny because one of my nicknames when I grew up, and was living rough, was Orinoco; the Womble who used to make good use out of the things he found.

After me came my sister, only ten months later, and the fight began for attention. My sister was also born sick, though not terminally. She was born with water on the brain - hydrocephalus. So there I was, between two children who demanded my parent's full attention. I started to fix my attention on things rather than on people. I became attached to things and would throw unnecessary tantrums if I couldn't get my own way.

2. **First drink, first kiss. – First drunk, first vomit.**

I didn't have my first alcoholic drink until I was about nine, which isn't too bad for an alcoholic of my type. It was the night of Halloween. I was living in a small village in France, after my father had moved the family there with his job.

The first time I had a drink, I didn't get drunk. I had a can of beer that was shared between three of us. I also had my first cigarette that evening, which we shared between three of us. And I had my first kiss with a girl. I didn't share this. There was no way I was going to share her! I wanted her all to myself. She made me feel wonderful and so grown up. Actually, it wasn't just a kiss, it was a snog – for those of you who don't know, a snog is a rather passionate embrace with a girl using tongues and, needless to say, I was very proud of myself having achieved such a feat at age nine. I guess it was a combination of the beer (which didn't get me drunk) and the cigarette (which I never inhaled) and the girl (which I never shared), which left me feeling fantastic.

I did like to show off, and this was great ammunition. I didn't have too much to brag about at the time, so this was really important to me. I was the first guy in my class to kiss a girl and smoke a cigarette (without inhaling) and have a drink (though to be fair, I didn't even like the taste and I didn't get drunk).

Looking back on it all now, I can see that it was nothing less than a miracle that I managed to stay sober from the age of nine to the age of eleven. In fact, I'm more than a little proud of my childish self during those two years, considering I wasn't able to get two years sober again until I was in my early thirties.

So, at eleven I picked up a drink again, only this time wasn't at all like the first. This time I actually consumed a decent amount of booze, certainly enough to get wasted. My parents held an annual party, and my favourite aunty was there. She was the cute one and I decided that getting drunk was sure to impress her. She was certain to be proud of how masculine and mature I was...or so I thought at the time. So, I got drunk with her, (though she didn't really get drunk) and I kept drinking until I vomited all over myself, and the kitchen floor. Much to my surprise, my auntie didn't seem very impressed with my attempts to show off. My Mum had to tidy me up and put me to bed. Not so mature or masculine after all. I felt so embarrassed. Here I was trying to show off to my favourite auntie and all I had done was humiliate myself completely. If only I had learnt that lesson at that stage. Clearly, I wasn't ready to learn because more of the same was to follow...

You see when I was nine, I had already had my first drink and I connected my first drink to my first kiss. And it occurred to me that I liked being kissed. I still do. I still have this thing about being kissed by women, although these days I reserve that luxury for my wife. I am much better behaved these days. But, what I found was that drinking led to me getting lucky with girls and, the way I saw it, that meant that drinking could only be a good thing.

I was a child raised in the 70s and 80s, and thus a true member of the 'Television Nation'. What I saw on TV and in magazines was inspiring, intriguing and fully engrossing. Hippies, with their values of freedom of expression, freedom of sex, freedom of intoxication, freedom of washing, were not only exciting but also enchanting. I was obsessed. I was sure the hippies knew what was going on and I wanted to be a part of it. I was really excited by that whole

Woodstock experience and I remember my father turning me on to the music of the era. I just tripped out watching the Hammer man himself, Alvin Lee, from Ten Years After playing the fastest blues guitar I'd ever heard during "I'm Going Home". Then the drum solo by the eleven year old kid playing "Soul Sacrifice" with Santana was awesome. It all blew my mind. I tried to imagine what it would be like to be able to perform, to achieve something amazing like that. I wanted exactly what that kid had. I knew that the eleven year old kid up on that stage was getting exactly what I wanted.

It must be safe for me to do what he's doing; I thought to myself, I'm eleven too, after all. If I were doing what he was doing, then I would get what he was getting. And, really to be honest, I had no idea what this kid was getting, I could only imagine. So imagine I did. And did it feel good! I started my own kind of research and, sure enough, I discovered that surprise, surprise, hippies did drugs. My train of thought was indeed one of an eleven year old yearning for fame and freedom, and I decided that not only would getting my hands on some drugs be a good thing, but also it was necessary for me to live the fancy-free life of a hippie. If I could get drugs and become a hippie, I would get free love just like they promised in the Gospel according to Woodstock. Then I would be just like that eleven year old Santana drummer, and life would be perfect.

From there, it all began.

3. Secondary school: a babysitting service

I was mischievous. I started messing around at school. I was always playing the fool, although I rather considered myself to be the jester of any class I was in. The way I saw it, school was a babysitting service so that my parents could go to work. I never saw school as a chore or something I didn't enjoy. In fact, I made damn sure that I did enjoy it.

I took this attitude of, 'hey let's have a laugh, this is school, let's enjoy ourselves'. And every day I had fun and enjoyed myself with my friends. Studying, as far as I was concerned, was out of the question. It didn't really seem like it was going to be much fun, and thus was not an important part of my school life. I still don't understand people who say they didn't have a good time at school. School for me was so exciting, so much fun, and I was at an all boys' school! I was having all of this fun without the temptation of girls! Well, for the first few years at least.

In the UK, at age eleven you go to a bigger school called secondary school. By the time I got to secondary school, it was clear to my class and teachers that my attitude and behaviour were not pleasant. I was always getting it on with the teachers, winding them up by asking continual inconsequential questions until they got more and more frustrated with me. My behaviour just got worse and worse while I continued to have more and more fun. Some people say that school is the best years of your life, and that certainly was my experience. School was great fun...for me anyway...my teachers I'm sure weren't having the wonderful time that I was.

I was a bully and a brat. And, really, with all this fun I was having I didn't learn much of anything at all. I would spend my time teasing the other kids. I was the class clown and the class bully. As I progressed through school, year after year, there would be a fresh selection of kids to tease in the year below. A favourite trick of mine would be to take the younger boys and throw them through the tuck-shop window like a ram raider, where you drive a car into a shop window and run off with all the goods. Well I would launch the younger boys through the window and, in the confusion, steal armfuls of sweets.

I got real hands-on learning in the field of black market economies when I started up my own lucrative business in luncheon vouchers. We were given these vouchers to buy our lunch with and I used to buy and sell these tickets to those who wished to buy sweets and candy instead of school dinners. I would buy £1 worth of vouchers for 70p and then I would sell them at greatly inflated prices. I had so many vouchers in my pockets at any given time that I was completely free to eat whatever I wanted, whenever I wanted, in whatever quantity I felt at the time. So I did. I ate and I ate and I ate. And I was happy... until I turned a little pear shaped. A quick lesson to anyone who aspires to be a dealer of any sort: Don't consume your own product unnecessarily! This is just as true for luncheon vouchers as it is for Cocaine or Girl Guide cookies or anything else you may be trying to sell. Regardless of my over consumption most of the time I had sufficient cash left over to go down to the pub. The town I went to school in, St. Albans City has the most pubs per square mile than anywhere in the country, so drinking was a buyers' market and the landlords were largely happy enough to serve us, despite us being in our school uniforms.

It's Not About Me!

I would go down there with one or two other rebellious mates, spending my luncheon voucher profits on pints of lager and the slot machines during my lunch break from school. I loved those slot machines, the ones with the little pieces of fruit just waiting to line up and make me rich. They kept me amused so long as I had enough money to keep playing. It took me a while to realise that this slot-machine lunchtime entertainment was an expensive habit. It seemed always to be demanding money and never paid out any amount that was decent enough to merit retiring. So, eventually, I realised what a waste of money it really was and I gave it up. Fortunately, since then, gambling has never been an issue for me. However, risk taking with my own life...well that's certainly been a concern.

Coincidently, I began to swiftly develop an interest in solvents; things like Evo-stik glue and Tipex thinners, anything that I could shoplift or pick up cheaply and easily from high street shops. So, I had started off fairly slowly but firmly in the drug game. I had started with glue sniffing. Glue sniffing was followed soon after with nail polish remover and various industrial-strength thinners and varnishes. Sniffing glue and other solvents became a much more acceptable way for me to waste my time, as far as I was concerned. It gave me oblivion and obliteration and it felt good. It was a perfect way to daydream through my classes. It was the perfect way to get through my evenings. It was perfect at weekends. It was perfect any day of the week, at any time. I loved sniffing thinners. I always wanted to invent a pill that gave you the same effects as thinners did, but lasted longer – say a few days. I just loved the way the world seemed to spin past you and leave you feeling invisible. It was perfect for me.

But, there comes a point in every young man's life when he starts thinking about sex. And I was by no means an exception to that rule; in fact, I was more like a bold, underlined statement of how young men are sure to behave if they are not adequately restrained. I was a quick learner when it came to both substances and girls. It didn't take me more than a few moments to figure out that drinking alcohol gave me a courage and confidence around girls that sniffing solvents couldn't match. I was very good at drinking; it was one of my primary skills as a teenager and came hand in hand with becoming the life and soul of a party. The charismatic party animal in me was very good at attracting the company of a young girl and this always led to a very successful mutual participation in the throes of teenage love.

I do remember on one School Disco occasion, mixing a litre and a half of various alcohols that I nicked from my parent's drink cabinet. There must have been more than a dozen varieties. A friend and I drank a fair portion of it before we went in and sipped it throughout the rest of the evening. I have a vague recollection that, at some point, I was found under the school's stage in the hall, with my trousers down and rolling around with a girl, both of us drunk beyond reasonableness. Who said school couldn't be fun?

But it wasn't all girls and booze for me. I was still well and truly excited by making school my playground and my teachers suffered because of it. At some point in the 4th Form - aged around fifteen - I made it a mission of mine to try and make the Economics teacher cry on a daily basis. I became nasty and vindictive. I became a darker person and I revelled in my own personal enjoyment by seeing others hurting. This was not really very hippie of me. The love and peace element was certainly missing when it came to my attitude in many things. Perhaps I had the definition of what it meant to be a hippie a little confused. Free love and drugs at this stage in my life were not only my activities; they were my motivation on a day-to-day basis.

4. Bullying behaviours – early addictive signs

I was expelled from school at the age of sixteen, just before my O-level exams. They let me come back to sit the exams, but I was suspended until then and told not to come into school at all. Although they couldn't prove anything, they assumed (correctly) that I had built and ignited a fire in the 5th form block and were trying to build a case against me. Fortunately for me, they had no real evidence. My friends and I had gone through a stage where we set off the fire alarm every day. This often happened just prior to our Economics class, which we weren't too keen on attending, but Economics didn't receive exclusive attention with this prank, as there were other classes we didn't want to attend, so they weren't ignored.

After almost two weeks of this daily false alarm, the school decided to turn the alarm off altogether. Surely you can see our motivation here. We made sure that they'd learn the lesson by actually building a fire this time. It started in a wastepaper basket and it grew. Actually, it grew much faster than we had ever anticipated and before we knew it, it was out of control. We ran down the stairs screaming fire, but no one believed us. The teachers assumed it was another prank. Anyway, cutting a short story shorter, they knew I was behind this anti-authority campaign, but they had no proof. So they tried to build their case. They couldn't suspend me for the fire because they had no proof. So they used another technical legality to get me out of the school basing their claims on my absenteeism. I hadn't actually attended 'Sports and Exercise' for three years. I had better things to do than attend Sports classes! Most Wednesday afternoons, when we were meant to be attending 'Sports and Exercise' classes I was in the Public Houses playing slot machines and drinking lager. By this point, I had begun messing around with amphetamines, and was enjoying myself far too much to care about playing football or running relays.

I was very proud of my three-year absenteeism record. It may just go to show how unpopular I was with the teachers, considering they would openly prefer me being absent. My parents, on the other hand were not proud at all of this record or the fact that I had been expelled.

When the news reached my parents that I wasn't welcome back at school, I was given an ultimatum: 'Get a job, get into college or get out of our house'. I knew my parents had my best interests at heart and that they loved me dearly, but I had driven them mad (mad furious, not mad crazy). They had been offered various explanations to justify my chaotic and disruptive behaviour. These explanations included ADHD (Attention Deficit Hyperactivity Disorder), Dyslexia and other learning disorders, but I truly believe I was a healthy young boy who was simply lacking inspiration, direction and motivation. I require the stimulus of something I'm interested in to pay attention to it. I simply don't pay attention to something I'm not interested in; even if you tell me it's for my own good. These are character traits that I still carry today. Give me something I'm interested in and I'll commit 100% to it. Leave me with something of no consequence to me and I'll only participate at the minimum level required. So, when my parents gave me this ultimatum, it seemed obvious to me that I needed to leave home and prove to them that I could live, support and survive by myself without them and their help.

They told me in no uncertain terms to get a job, go to college or leave home. That was more reason than I needed. I virtually walked straight out the front door and didn't turn back. Really, I genuinely cannot blame my parents. They did the best that they could. I don't blame them for being traditional, strict and opinionated, especially since they were justifiably so when trying to look after a brat like me. But a kid like me doesn't think about things like this at the time, so

I just thought, "Screw you, I'll show you", and walked out the door.

Leaving school was a good thing for me, the other pupils, the teachers and possibly for society at large. I had been a brat and definitely a bad influence on others. Before I knew it, with the freedom of a school-free life, I was well and truly living the hippie lifestyle I had always dreamed of. And then I discovered LSD, you can't get much more hippie than that. I was now sixteen years old and using Cannabis, psychedelics and amphetamines daily. I was still drinking most days as I had been since the ripe young age of fourteen. I had begun smoking pot a few years before with my neighbour, an American kid, and his older sister. Now, for a couple of years, I had been drinking on a daily basis, and do you know what? It made me feel really good. Really damn good indeed. Everything was good for me, or so I thought. Things didn't stop there, of course. Not only was I taking drugs on a daily basis, I was also getting it on ever so regularly with the fairer sex.

5. Sixteen and out in the world

At fifteen I was successfully attracting girls and experimenting with 'lovemaking', although there was not a great deal of love involved. I will not go into all the details here (it would be rude), but I did get myself a reputation as someone who would not be with the same girl twice. I broke a fair few teenage hearts and hurt many more. In fact, retrospectively, my behaviour towards girls was very poor. I used and abused. I was obnoxious and arrogant. I played hard to get, but I was actually very easy. Virginities were stolen and never treated with any sort of respect. For me, it was more like a trophy. I owe many female souls various types of amends, though so far, God has seen it fit to keep me out of their line of vision, probably for their benefit rather than mine. But it felt like such fun at the time!

I was a bad boy, living the hippie dream, and then I discovered that punks did more drugs than hippies!

The first place I went to live when I left home was an abandoned cowshed in the middle of a field of nettles. I moved in with a couple of other disgruntled drug using friends all about the same age. There was no glass in the windows, no electricity, no water, in fact there were zero amenities whatsoever. Fortunately for us, it was summertime and warm. I was now one of the unofficial homeless statistics. I say unofficial because I never registered as being homeless. I was of 'No Fixed Abode', but I refused to register anywhere. So I was homeless and no one knew or cared; my parents cared, of course, but I didn't consider them much during this time. I was a self-taught squatter! I was rapidly adding to my life skills! As I'm sure you can appreciate, I started off in this cowshed with the most humble beginnings. It was a pretty low bar to set for oneself, and the bar stayed pretty low for quite a while. But this really is down to perspective, and this is in hindsight, looking back at my living conditions and the situations I was getting myself into. At the time, however, I still believed I was having the best days of my life.

We lived by firelight and slept on the floor in unwashed sleeping bags, enjoying the liberty of doing whatever we wanted, whenever we wanted. We partied every day and every night. I began exploring the delights of LSD and handpicked Magic Mushrooms. I became a punk because I figured that punks did more drugs than hippies and that was definitely the road I wanted to walk down. We certainly cared more about being intoxicated than our general health, but then what teenager doesn't. As I was approaching seventeen and feeling immortal...I just wanted to get high... all the time!

Now I was a full blown punk. Punks do more drugs than hippies, right? I was particularly fond of amphetamines (also referred to as Speed) and drinking... yes, alcohol. My love affair with alcohol had been progressing steadily all this time. It seemed like the answer to all daily problems – particularly boredom. Drinking amused me in times when no other amusement was available, and yet it also seemed to make situations even more amusing when I wasn't bored. Boozing just worked when other pastimes failed. And, now at seventeen I was an everyday lover of the stuff. I drank because I could, because I loved it, because I wanted to. I was a free man and I was a punk. I had a rainbow-dyed Mohican and I spent each day dressed in combat boots, scruffy, torn black (never blue) jeans and old jumpers I found lying around.

Being such an arrogant young punk, I was not only loud and outspoken but also rebellious and constantly seeking amusement from any source. Since my parents had told me to get out of the house if I wasn't going to get a job or go to college, now that I had a home (of sorts) I decided to enrol in college...to really show them.

6. Student Politics and Poll Tax rioting

I was accepted into the St. Albans City College of Further Education aged seventeen.

I used to go to college tripping on psychedelics and off my head on various narcotics. Often drunk, I didn't really take college very seriously. It was a place for me to learn how to start selling drugs, which was a good way for me to support myself, and seemed much more punk than any kind of job I could think of. I wasn't someone who just rested on my laurels. I was always someone who went out and got stuff done. I needed to earn some money but I wasn't prepared to 'work for the man' (I'm still not) and so I made it happen. I began by dealing Cannabis resin – hashish.

I treated college just like I treated school – as a playground for my own entertainment. On the second day of my second week (after Fresher's week) I was elected Vice-President of the College Student Union. Maybe it was because they liked my attitude. Maybe it was because they liked my energy. Maybe it was because they liked my drugs. Maybe it was because they were desperate for people to volunteer and participate. Maybe it was because I was the only candidate? Whatever the reason, I was very proud of myself when I was elected as the Vice-President of the Union of Students at St. Albans College.

Needless to say, studying was never really a focal point of my time at college. College was like school, I had so much fun but I really didn't get a whole lot of schoolwork done, especially when you consider just how chaotic my life squatting and drugging was. College was a platform for my drug dealing, social networking (all long before the rise of Facebook – why didn't I think of that?) and a place I could stay warm and dry. I did actually get myself a real job as a 'Dinner Man' for a couple of terms. I used to peel potatoes and clean the tables. It supplemented my income a little, but better than that, it allowed me to network with my potential clients while cleaning their tables. A year later I was elected as the President of the College and soon afterwards, I was elected to a larger platform as the Student Union President of the Greater Area of Colleges, which was Hertfordshire at the time.

I had begun attending the National Union of Students events and conferences. I, of course, bought my own kind of ethos and naive worldly view. I started telling other students about the Libertarian Socialist Division which was my own personal political theory and was, you may not be surprised to discover, largely (entirely) based on the thought processes that had occurred to me while under the influence of LSD. The Libertarian Socialist Division was all about taking LSD. LSD politics are very logical and humanist in nature and I was sure they would change the world. Most people, however, missed the connection. I don't think they saw the reference to hallucinogenic drugs, taking my political party title at face value. At the Annual Conferences, frequent NUS events and demos, I was always both vocal and apparently popular. The hot topic of the time (1989-1990) was a debate on the students' rights to a financial grant, instead of a loan, which the Tory Thatcher government was pushing through Parliament (my sister is still paying off her student loan twenty years later). It is not all that dissimilar to debates currently occupying the hearts and minds of students across the country, except these days students are squeezed considerably more, unless financially supported by their family.

I arrived at these events and conferences and preached my own rhetoric of Libertarianism. Libertarianism is a political standpoint that mixed equality with freedom and was a really nice combination of my hippie and punk belief systems. Ultimately, it believes in the right of the individual to make their own life choices and it empowers its citizens to make the right choices. That's where it could be considered as flawed. Libertarianism has never been able to work in a free-market economy because too many traders will take advantage and profit from the libertarian, who would naively expect everyone to be treated fairly, simply because they were a fellow human being. Libertarianism fails because it believes in the inherent goodness of man, dismissing the way that most people will take advantage of someone who appears to be playing too fairly. I believed and desired equality and freedom for all, but in a way that was more than slightly anarchic, since I actively went out of my way to try to remain at the top of whatever food pile I was standing on. I won support quickly and started making friends in esteemed places within the student political community. At the time, the most powerful groups running student politics were the NOLS (National Union of Labour Students) and a group called 'Left Unity', which was largely made up of the Trotskyites. Ironically enough, the Trotskyites missed the point all together and started backing me as some sort of student candidate who would carry their Principles. They thought that I was some kind of political front man who was going to change the student society for the better and turn everyone into a Communist.

They had missed the point. They missed the fundamental point of my views.

ADDICTION – *the early years*

I had no political affiliation at all, in any way. I was all about libertarianism which is all about empowering individuals to be whoever they want and do whatever they please as long as it in no way harms another individual. The Trotskyites, however, were about Totalitarian Socialism. I absolutely conflicted with totalitarianism. Totalitarianism is where the state has absolute power to force you to do the right thing and make the right choices. I was far too romantic for that! My beliefs were all about saying anything goes as long as you don't get in my way or infringe on my space. This is very much an addict's train of thought. Anything goes as long as you stay out of my way. It's a very selfish way to think but is delivered with such panache that it makes you think it is completely free and selfless. Looking back, it seems almost amazing to see how Libertarianism totally suited me at the time. The point is, I directed myself towards this road of anarchy and threw myself down it head first. I had the backing of one of the largest student political groups with a good deal of power and authority in the Student body around the country at the time. The fact that these Trotskyites missed the most dynamic part of my whole theory and gospel amazed me and amused me to no end. I went along with them because I loved the attention and was happy to play along while the whole time considering myself to be a free thinker and a member of no group but my own. My motto was much like the motto of Groucho Marx who said, "I don't care to belong to a club that accepts people like me as members."

While my political career as an anarchist and spokesman for the student body was flying along, my housing situation really didn't change. It just evolved along with everything else in my life. I moved squats frequently because we were always being busted or evicted from this place or that and every now and again we would come across somewhere more suitable for our needs so we would just pick up and move. The first Winter I spent squatting was the first time in my young life that I never bathed or fully removed my underwear. For three solid months it was quite simply too cold for me to face bathing. We never had hot water and we didn't have any furniture, so we were freezing all the time. If we did happen to stumble across a place that had electricity connected, we would run an electric bar heater and huddle around it, practically on top of it just to try to thaw out. With the cold, the rain and the sleet, bathing in cold water was not on the top of my things to do.

I was always getting myself arrested. Mostly it was for drunk and disorderly behaviour. The police would let me sleep off the booze and throw me back out onto the street in the morning. Often I got arrested when I'd dropped

It's Not About Me!

Acid because I'd be off exploring somewhere that was definitely out of legal boundaries. Building yards, private gardens, public service offices were all so tempting when I was tripping, just to climb over the gate and explore the mystical world that my mind created for me was too much fun to refuse. With all this in mind, it's not hard to imagine that I was on first name terms with quite a few of the local Bobby, who regarded me as harmless to the general public. They knew I was only a danger to myself and would lock me up until I'd straightened out a bit and then get rid of me.

Regularly the police would raid our squats to see what they could turn up, and there were often more than of a dozen of us living together. Out of twelve squatters, at any given time, the police would almost always find at least one of us holding something that we just shouldn't have. One day, very early in the morning, we were busted, and a few of us were hauled off for theft. We had nicked some of the larger candles out of St. Alban's Abbey Cathedral to use as light in our power-less home. You would have thought they could have been a little more sympathetic to our cause and given us a break. We were just kids trying to survive and live with a little luxury in our otherwise bare bones life. However, they busted us anyway...apparently you are not supposed to steal from a cathedral, even if you are living on the poverty level. Go figure.

Anyhow, the Police knew where I was living and they kept noticing me to be missing whenever they busted our squat whilst I was in my office at the college. One day they raided our squat and, once again, I wasn't there. They asked a few questions and they determined that I was the President of the local college Student Union. They knew that there was a fair amount of drug dealing going through the squats that we were living in and so they took a closer look at my activities. Once they found out that I had my own office in the College Student Union buildings where I was currently serving up drugs (mostly Cannabis, LSD and some Ecstasy) from, the wheels began turning. It was only a matter of time until my world started to be rocked, too. I found myself being asked to leave the employment of the Student Union by the Principal on behalf of the College Board of Directors. It was my first serious job and, amazingly, it was my last until I got sober − over 13 years later. I figured I was done with real jobs. I was done with the system and I just walked away from it all. I felt like I had been cheated by it all and I was feeling really let down. It felt like society was kicking me when I was just trying to do my best and make a difference. After all, Hashish is a drug of peace not war, and I was a big supporter of peace. Furthermore, surely everyone understood the magical qualities of LSD ingestion and the profound message of love associated with MDMA (Ecstasy) tripping. These were acceptable drugs ~ surely. Since we were getting stoned first and last thing every day, surely you can agree that we weren't hurting anyone else, aside form our own brain cells? Libertarianism, right? Really, we weren't causing any trouble. We were just busy with ourselves, spending our days thinking up plans for a perfect world and daydreaming about anarchy and freedom for all. No one ever got into a fist-fight because they were too stoned. Getting stoned on hash could be considered to be the ultimate way to control a crowd. Everyone becomes placid and unthreatening. It's a drug of relaxation. No one gets violent on LSD. Everyone turns inward and begins to reflect upon ways to improve the world. And how can anyone challenge the absolute love felt and displayed by those whilst turned on to Ecstasy? It's beyond me. At least, back in those 1989 days that's how I felt.

Anyhow, I fell on my sword to protect the good name of the College and to avoid prosecution – these were the only terms offered to me by the Principal. There was no negotiation. I leave quietly or they would allow the Police to charge me. I left blazing with resentment and the unfairness of it all ad the way they had treated me. After all, wasn't I doing a great job? Didn't they appreciate me and what I was doing for them? I was blind to my own part in this affair, and I blamed the Police, the state, the College, the system, society, everyone else I could think of. Stubbornly, I turned to crime to stick it to them and became involved in a credit card 'kiteing' crew. This meant travelling to various supermarkets and using stolen debit or credit cards for buying a few items like bottles of spirits and cigarettes, and then taking £50 cash back. The system was very different in those days and there was no chip and pin. You didn't need a four-digit number – just a signature; easy money and yet another skill to add to my ever expanding set. I didn't do any of the actual in-store crimes, because I looked far too suspicious – I had a Mohican that was growing into dreadlocks. My part in the scheme was investing the money collected into drugs, which we then sold. Well, we sold some of them; the ones we didn't consume first.

I walked away from society aka 'The System' and became more and more militant. I began my life as an outlaw. I got involved with the Anti-Poll tax movement and began demonstrating. That's where things became ugly. Trafalgar Square, March 1990 and I'm in the thick of it. You can see me in some of the photos that circulated amongst the media, in the background whilst a woman shoves a piece of scaffolding through a Police car window with South Africa House nearby beginning to smoulder. History has shown us what happened that day and I won't go into

It's Not About Me!

all the details but what I will say is that I attended a further demonstration later that year, demanding the release of those previously arrested during the Trafalgar Square riots. This demonstration was held in Brixton and, as we marched past Brixton prison where some of those people accused after the previous riot were being held, we heard cheers from inside. I had dropped Acid that day (as I often did) and had been (fortunately) recorded on video that afternoon while I stared at trees looking dazed and confused. And then just as the action exploded it happened. I was dragged out of the demonstration by two Police officers and charged with rioting. I was so stoned I could barely walk, let alone riot!

In reality, the cops were scared and they grabbed the first guy they could to get themselves out of harm's way and out of the riot (that's my story anyway). When we got away from the violence, they were both very nice guys and, to this day, I don't hold any resentment towards them for what happened next. They wanted to get out of a volatile and increasingly nasty situation, and I was an easy way out for them, so they took it. I can't blame them for that. I was held in a cell with six or seven other freaks and outcasts. One person had a small piece of hash, one had some skins (rolling papers), one had some tobacco and someone else had a lighter. So much for the searches before they locked us up. I guess they were a little busy that day or perhaps they knew it would make us happy and docile - probably not. Smoking a few tugs on a joint helped me cope with my Acid trip, which had become very interesting indeed. I was released to 'no fixed abode' in the middle of the night, charged with being a public nuisance and rioting. So, now I was in a position where I had to prove my innocence. Thankfully, an old friend of mine was now working at a law firm and they wanted to help me. So my Solicitor (funded by legal aid) got his hands on the film of me wandering around like a bit of a zombie and used it to prove that I was not at all violent or aggressive as the charges stated. There was a two-minute time lapse between the time stamp on the video and the time I was charged with rioting and, to be fair, I have caused more than a little trouble in less than two minutes in the past, but they couldn't prove that either. When I had my day in court, I couldn't prove that the charges had been trumped up but, given the evidence, the judge couldn't find me guilty or rioting. Instead, I was handed down a fine of £50 on some other grounds (which I don't ever recall paying) and bound over to keep the peace for six months (the very minimal term possible).

The time I spent in the extreme end of politics introduced me to many different kinds of people and some pretty intense situations. Out of all of the weird and wonderful people I met, I found that I identified most with the New Age Travellers, or the Peace Convoy as they were also known, and other Anarchist Squatters from London and other cities. As I started to socialise more and more in these circles I found that again I started to evolve. My musical tastes changed from punk to dub and then to something else entirely. I discovered Techno music. And this is (cutting a long story short) how I became a raver. After all, ravers do more drugs than punks. Much more drugs. Not only more drugs, but raver drugs are more fun...so again, I evolved and metamorphosised, changing myself. I evolved and I dove headfirst into the psychedelic nocturnal life of a raver.

So, rewinding back just a little to when I was first coming into London and being exposed to a much larger anti-establishment and counterculture than just the band of punks and squatters I knew in St. Albans, there we're a couple of places I frequented every week. These places were to turn me on to the next stage of my development.

The first was the Whirl-Y-Gig. This was a club predominantly attended to by people aged 16-23 and was clearly established and run by some genuine real old-school hippies. The decoration was entirely psychedelic with kaleidoscopic lights and cushions all over the floor instead of chairs. The music was from all around the world, and it built and built into the evening, peaking for the final couple of hours with solid house music from around the world with clear ethnic sounds. The final part of the evening involved lying under a giant parachute with the light show reflected on our faces. It was at this moment that people either went into their hallucinogenic experiences, or ended up snogging with the nearest person. I loved it. They turned their back on us smoking spliffs and taking LSD or Ecstasy (Es). In fact, I was the resident LSD dealer and I virtually cornered the market every week since most people sold hash or Es. I loved it and I was there at the beginning every Saturday evening, and as it finished at midnight, I would then headed on to another party with a merry band of newly-made friends and acquaintances, normally with a new girlfriend for the evening.

The other place I'd frequent was the George Robey Pub in Finsbury Park (now closed) to see live bands. This was another counterculture urban hippie venue. The bands I saw included the Ozric Tentacles and Radical Dance Faction – RDF. These were underground bands that came from the London squats and the free festivals in the summer – the very culture I was embracing. The Ozrics also had a seriously hardcore psychedelic following, so I made it my duty to attend as often as possible with LSD for sale.

In fact, I was gaining quite a reputation as a prolific LSD retailer, alongside my partner in crime, Andy who also hailed from the St. Albans squatting scene and had been living with me (or vice-versa) since that very first cowshed in the field of nettles.

But there was someone who stood out to me as one of the nicest guys I ever met. His name is Steve Bedlam and, at his request, I'm going to limit some of the details of his business and our interaction, but I will say this – he is still the nicest guy on the scene. Ever so popular with everyone, he deserves the name 'Mr. Nice Guy'. Well we met on the North London scene, and mainly grew to know one another because he could never believe how cheaply I could score LSD trips by the hundreds and thousands. Let me be very clear, Steve never took any drugs harder than puff, skunk or alcohol. He simply didn't. But he was always at the very centre of the underground scene, keeping the peace and talking to the Police whenever they turned up. He was the patron saint of the party scene, and there are far too many examples to begin mentioning his contribution to our drug culture without his actual participation in our hedonism. He was just there for the vibe. So Steve has been a constant companion of mine since we first met in 1990.

7. **Spiral Tribe** - Ravers take more drugs

I've got plenty of stories about my life as a New Age Traveller and Techno Traveller with the Spiral Tribe and attached to various other counter-culture communities, gangs, crew and possees, and my memories of those squatting and travelling years are always really positive. They were some of the very best years in my life. However, for the purposes of this book I don't want to be glamorising those years of chaos living as an outlaw too much. So what I've chosen to do is to reveal to you some of the episodes and examples of my years of absolute (perceived) freedom travelling and enjoying myself by any means necessary. I have purposefully held back on revealing too many details of the weekly party scene and the public nuisance that we most certainly were. I hold my own memories very dear to me, but it wouldn't be fair to start inspiring and motivating that anarchic lifestyle to you, the reader. It doesn't fit in with what this book is attempting to achieve. Just know that I/we had a wonderful time; but that it's not for everybody.

Ravers did more drugs than anyone I knew and I wanted to become a raver. So I did, and honestly the transition was pretty straightforward. From my experience, mixing with different groups of cultures and partying with them, raver drugs were certainly the most fun. When I was using these drugs I felt on top of the world, I felt amazing, I felt invincible, important, powerful, and confident. I felt like anything was possible and I couldn't consider the option or the possibility of going out without the fantastic fun these drugs promised and successfully brought me. I dedicated myself to these 'designer' drugs and I certainly couldn't imagine my life without them. I loved the feeling of being high, it was the most like 'myself' I had ever felt, and the whole world seemed like the most incredibly beautiful place, filled with possibilities. In fact, it actually is if we ever stop to look at it.

I'll tell you a secret here. The real reason people use drugs is because they love the way these drugs make them feel. That's right... the effect drugs have on them. Drugs make us feel wonderful. If they didn't, why would we do them? We will dive further into this topic later on, but for now all that is relevant is that I loved what I was doing...and I felt amazing.

I don't need to tell you in too much detail about why participating in a rave is so fulfilling, but just in case you've never had the experience personally, imagine the camaraderie you get from attending any sort of local community event, or a club or fellowship, and enlarge that feeling by 100%. Then throw in the pleasant feeling you may have experienced when you're slightly tipsy or merry, and exaggerate that by 100%. And just for good measure, imagine yourself staring at a fireworks show and times those visual experiences by 100%. Maybe, just maybe this will begin to help you see the appeal of being at a rave. I found it so appealing that I decided to live there, in the rave. All the time.

I was messing about with Ecstasy and somehow ended up at the Stonehenge Free Festival in 1991 in Longstock – or rather on some land near the village of Longstock, close to the 'Stones'. We hadn't been able to party at the Stones for a couple of years, since the Police had come on site and battered the hell out of travellers, their buses and their vans, destroying whole families and convoys of peaceful, loving hippie-type New Age Travellers, also known during that stage of cultural evolution as the Peace Convoy. These were the same types you'd see at CND (The Campaign for Nuclear Disarmament) rallies and occupational protests such as Greenham Common, or the guys who lived in trees when forests were being threatened with destruction. This was an absolute travesty, and I hope the Police who were involved in this devastation feel ashamed. Their violence and behaviour was similar to soccer violence, without the other side fighting back; totally unacceptable and dreadful behaviour. This was known as the Battle of the Beanfield, though there was no actual battle. It was desecration and annihilation by the coppers. This was overshadowed by the Police violence in dealing with the striking miners, but in the travelling community it goes down as part of our struggle with society and is yet another example of Margaret Thatcher's legacy of heavy-handed Police violence. That said, I'm not personally attached to any political party enough to want to promote one over the other. I've always been a Libertarian and this seems to have stuck with me right the way through to today. Live and let live – just don't give anyone else a hard time protecting your own right to do what you want to do. Be thoughtful to others and allow them to be thoughtful to you.

And so it was at this festival, running along in a small valley, that up on the side of a hill, stood a pyramid. There was nothing in this pyramid. It had no sides to it. It wasn't a tent. It was just the frame. It was the frame of a giant pyramid. And it served absolutely no purpose at all when it started raining. In fact, I couldn't see how it served any purpose at all, any time, until I sat in it. At the bottom of the hill was the Spiral Tribe Sound System and, sitting in this pyramid structure, I heard Techno music and, for the first time, I connected with it. I connected with the music and the earth and the moon and the stars, and I had a full-blown spiritual experience, albeit of the chemically induced type. I was immediately a dedicated follower of something so wonderful that gave me sonic rushes so warm and comfortable, I felt safe in this hallucinated state, as if in a protected bubble.

I needed to know more about this. What was that I'd just experienced? Returning back to my squat (now demolished and turned into a shopping mall) in South East London, I knew I had had some sort of transformation and I liked it. I had progressed from squatting in empty houses while I developed the art of breaking into much larger buildings, which could hold communes. My first big one in London was the Midland Bank on Peckham High Street. These were such fun days. We would take speed and go down for a few days into the old vaults to try to play thrash punk music on guitar, bass and drums. It must have sounded awful! I loved Peckham, and would wander around the streets in the middle of the night tripping on Acid. The local gang members, also lurking around the 'unsafe' streets would refer to me as "White Rasta" because of my dreads and my brazenness. Nothing seemed to faze me or spook me, least of all the gang members. We had mutual respect for one another.

ADDICTION – *the early years*

So there I was with my newfound interest and desire to connect further with this sound system that had had such a transformative effect on me. I had been attending their 'Spiral Tribe' parties since that first exposure to them in the Summer of June '91, and specifically now back in London at their squat in North West London's Maida Vale 'The Green House' on Chippenham Road and then after their eviction into Grittleton Road.

After we hosted a large underground Punk Rock free party (all of our parties, raves, festivals and later Technivals, were always free i.e. no entrance fee – entry was welcome to absolutely all) we were violently evicted by a few hundred riot Police, resulting in a number of hospitalised injuries and incarceration of dogs, we moved up the road from Peckham into the Lewisham Library on Lewisham Way (ironically in New Cross). It seemed like the time had come for me to take that next step in my metamorphosis – punk to raver, by opening my squatted doors to the Spiral Tribe. Those who were at this party will never forget it. It's one of those party legends. The whole place was spray-can decorated in fluorescent ultraviolet paint, and lit by black guns (UV Lights) and terror strobes. It was the biggest Spiral Tribe party in London to date, and probably the biggest illegal party in London ever, for its era. It went off in a big way; absolutely hedonistic and hardcore. The place was still slammed and rocking Monday morning. It was my first exposure to anything like it. These guys knew how to take drugs seriously. I was in heaven. That weekend I had been intoxicated on a variety of designer drugs and met a whole new community of people, who, although they dressed differently to me, completely shared in my values and principles. These were my kind of people. I had found my Tribe.

I became part of the notorious Spiral Tribe. We had a terrible reputation for turning the music up very loud and never turning it off, or down, regardless of how many times we were asked. We were anarchic and had a strong 'fuck society' attitude. We were children of a revolution, we loved Ecstasy, amphetamines, LSD and basically any other mind-altering chemical (notably Ketamine) we could get our hands on, our mouths around, or up our nostrils. We built up strong attitudes towards the reformation of society and the greater world. We developed our own core values and beliefs. We had a fascination with the number 23. The number 23 is the number of chaos theory. It is known in counterculture circles, and I was exposed to it and its significance through the new age movement. It is like a code to connect with other likeminded people. It is used like a secret handshake to connect with people who live unconventionally and may share alternative and/or counterculture principles, although this would just be the beginning of an explanation, so I'm going to stop now before we get side-tracked by the psychic occult and magic sides of its understanding.

Thus begun my career as the squat provider for Spiral Tribe. I would get into old warehouses, factories, police stations, fire stations, banks, theatres, cinemas, libraries, schools, pubs, restaurants...any place that was abandoned and of fair enough size was fair game as far as I was concerned. Large abandoned spaces were my forte. We would break in on a Saturday afternoon and by Saturday night there would be three or four thousand people ready for a long weekend party. We would move out on Tuesday or Wednesday, either that week or sometimes even the next, depending upon Police pressure, once everyone had left, crawling back to wherever it was they spent their weekdays, while I returned to the 'New Cross Posse' and my own family of squatters. On Thursday and Friday we would go scouting for somewhere new, bust in and move right in on Saturday once again. Then all my friends would turn up that evening, before the Police knew what was going on, and again, I'd be up and running for at least the next three days, so high I sought no sleep, just more and more narcotics, to enable me to maintain my place as LSD and various other 'pick n mix party pack' drugs retailer. When the music went off sometime on Monday night or Tuesday morning I would look for somewhere to sleep. I found myself falling into this pattern of waking up on Thursday and going to sleep on Tuesday and sleeping for 36 hours, completely missing Wednesday every week.

I maintained this pattern fairly easily during the warmer months. Looking back now, it is hard, even for me, to imagine how I managed to maintain this lifestyle and for so long. However, I did, largely (entirely) through the use of amphetamines, psychedelics and every now and again some Cocaine. Wintertime was different, the days were cold and short, and the nights were long and colder. The best way to illustrate this would be by telling you about the Roundhouse. The Roundhouse is a very famous London venue where many of the greatest bands have played. Bands such as The Doors, Jimi Hendrix, Pink Floyd, The Who, Rolling Stones, Led Zeppelin, Hawkwind, The Clash, etc., and us. I happened to know a few of the Camden Crusties who had gone into the Roundhouse to keep warm. They had lit a small fire and were dossing there. I had a better idea. I had a bigger idea. I had an outrageous idea for them. It was the week before Christmas 1991, so I suggested that we bring the Spiral Tribe Sound System in and have a party. This party was to run from 21st December to 3rd January! It went on and on and on. It was non-stop.

Christmas rolled into the regular weekend crowd, which then rolled straight through into the New Year's bash before beginning to run its course. I'd spend eight hours awake and then I'd get four hours sleep. Then I would party for eight and then crash for four. I'd be high for eight, zone out for four, and the cycle would continue for the entirety of the party. I had found a completely new zone to exist in, and it worked so long as I was in a venue with no natural light. That occurred fairly frequently in the winter since the places we partied in had long since been abandoned and, to keep the cold out (a little), we would cover the windows. This also added to the psychedelic atmosphere we produced. It is not easy to maintain a lifestyle like this but I did it for a few months, virtually surviving on just the drugs washed down with booze and an occasional slap-up meal or kebab. That kept me warm, awake and happy, day and night during the winter months.

It was at a party in Brewery Road, Kings Cross that I first tried Cocaine. I have heard about people who buy a quarter gram and it lasts them a week. This has never been my experience. A quarter gram never lasted me more than one snort, unless someone else was making the lines. At that point, Cocaine was something quite different to anything I'd ever played with before. I noticed that as soon as I had a little taste, I wanted more immediately. I wanted more and more...one taste was never enough. No drug had ever had this effect on me before. It was, to coin a phrase "totally addictive immediately." I knew this drug was dangerous because of the instant craving for more that it gave me. I also saw what it did to the personalities of the people I was using it with. They became greedy and self-centred, almost immediately. Although I didn't like what I saw in other people, I knew that I loved it. I knew that I wanted more if it. I knew that I wanted Cocaine in my life and I figured I was going to need a lot of it to keep me happy. Fortunately, for a while, I wasn't exposed to it very frequently, so my first few experiences became distant fond memories.

8. Absolute BEDLAM

It was December 1991 when Steve put me together with a few other mates and we discussed an alternative Sound System. You see, Spiral Tribe was built by ravers who joined the alternative underground culture. Bedlam was formed by members of this alternative culture who were falling in love with raving and wanted to bring a slightly different feel to the scene. And we did - in a massive way! The impact we had on the ever-growing underground scene was like throwing petrol on the fire - everything grew and everyone benefitted.

Bedlam and the Spirals were always on extremely great terms which each other (we still are) - often joining up at the same location and providing a second rig to the other group's parties. We were joined like two tribes. The Bedlam boys chased the Spiral girls. The ravers came to party with both Sound Systems and there was complete synergy.

Because I was involved with the central core members of both Sound Systems, I found myself in a very informed and connected position. This was the best of both worlds, especially for a dealer like I was. I had access to buy and sell drugs from both circles and it wasn't long before the UK's larger drug barons became interested in what we were doing and the markets we opened up for them. We were very clearly the centre of the designer drugs industry in the UK. We were its biggest supporters and biggest customers. People were developing new drugs; new exciting drugs, and they would bring them to us. We were willing guinea pigs for trial and error, and we would happily test any designer drug that came our way. We were always given more than sufficient amounts of test product and, depending on our reactions, we would then happily introduce them to the UK market. Product Tester – another skill acquired.

So, I've actually had the privilege of testing a number of different psychedelics and I would be interested to see if anyone reading this book has ever tried some of these quite random drugs that were on the market for very short periods of time. Has anyone ever heard of DOET – Do It? DOET was a designer drug that was only released on one occasion (in sugar lump form), and you were either there or you weren't (20,000 of us were there that weekend). However, a whole flurry of a genre of Techno music called "Do It Music" was released shortly after their experiences at this particular festival. DOET is a derivative of DOM. Have you ever heard of that? DOM is somehow related to STP. Anyone tried that one? STP is a manipulated derivative of DMT. DMT comes from the bark of a certain Australian tree and sends you into the cosmos for about fifteen minutes of spectacular hallucinations. It is an intense trip. For a quarter of an hour, one would be transported to a completely different planet. Then as soon as the time was up, you would wake, back on earth, stone cold sober. This allows a person to do lots and lots of it which, of course I sought to do and indeed did. This is why it has the nickname "Business Man's Lunch" because it's such a short though intense experience. DMT was a drug used on a small scale in the 60s and 70s but forgotten about largely in the 80s. Well we resurrected it for a while. You may have heard of 2CB, a delightfully trippy experience lasting about six hours. Or the various incantations of MDMA, such as MDA, MDEA, MEMA, etc. I tested all of them. I tested and retested them, plenty of times. Then we get to Ketamine. Ketamine had been around briefly in the USA in the late 60s and early 70s but had never really taken off. I was involved in the new Ketamine experiments, the UK's own special mix. And, every now and then Ketamine would be mixed with Cocaine for that extra special combination. When we got to play with that, we called it "Calvin Klein," C for Cocaine and K for Ketamine. This is how we spent our days - being the guinea pigs for drug experimentation. . It was like our job, and we took it very seriously; we saw it as community service!

I was now in London during the colder months and travelling in buses and converted lorries as part of the festival scene during the warmer months. In the winter we'd squat in these huge venues, often with our vehicles inside of the warehouses, hosting these enormous raves. In the summer we would go out to the Countryside finding fields where we would put on these massive free festivals for ravers to come and enjoy what we loved most in the world − drugs and loud Techno music. There was a whole new generation of subcultures being born right there and then. We were definitely the first generation of the Techno Traveller. Which, if you're not familiar with the term, is an evolution from the Punk Travellers or Peace Convoy who had come before us but had come after the Hippie Travellers or New Age Travellers, who incidentally had evolved from the original Beatniks. Each of these bands of merry, drug-taking followers had similar outlooks on life but the evolution was found in musical style, dress codes and drugs of choice. More often than not, we all played together in harmony, after all, we believed in free love, free expression and freedom in general. We were not only anarchist in our thinking, but we were actually anarchists in our living, although I ought to point out, just in case I'm giving you an image of a stereotypical anarchist here, we were not one of those groups you'd see rioting and fighting the Police during some politically motivated demonstration, although I guess some were, but mostly we just lived outside of society and tried to keep ourselves to ourselves. More Libertarians than Anarchists.

These incredible illegal festivals developed minds of their own and were eventually known as Technivals once we hit mainland Europe − a huge free-enterprise marketplace designed for fun, drug selling and drug using. Honestly, they were

It's Not About Me!

an amazing place to party, play and dance. Many people say the festivals were about the music. Indeed, I used to say that, as an effort to justify the carnage we were actually making to ourselves and the neighbouring villages or communities. I guess in so many ways they were. But this sort of music needs one thing to be truly enjoyed: Drugs. These festivals were about the drugs, no questions asked. Any raver who tells you raves are about the music is bullshitting you. It was always about the drugs. It was about finding more drugs, better drugs. It was about ensuring we never ran out of drugs. It was about making sure everyone was sorted so that on the off chance I didn't have what I needed, someone would be there to supply me with my good-time enhancement. We were as co-dependent about our drug use as we were hardcore. And this drug use just escalated as the festivals evolved quickly from parties that lasted four or five days to parties that were lasting weeks at a time. It was so much fun. It was crazy. It was insanity and we loved it. Undeniably it wasn't fun for everyone, and certainly there were more than a few casualties along the way; that's the nature of risk and living on the edge. But thankfully for me, I wasn't one of them (yet). I still felt invincible. I was all about having a good time, and that was one thing I certainly had no trouble achieving.

This is how I lived from the age of nineteen and it went on into my early twenties. I was throwing parties, taking drugs, selling drugs, and moving drugs around. I was testing drugs, studying drugs promoting drugs, and I loved every minute of it. Sex and drugs, and drugs and sex followed by new drugs, new sex, and then more of the same again. I moved house every week and I would have about 4,000 to 6,000 friends over every weekend. During the summer we would throw massive festivals and in the winter we hibernated, warm and high in London.

On May 1, 1992 we threw one of the most amazing parties I ever went to. We had more than 20,000 party people – an assortment of ravers, punks, hippies, and various other alternative culture or non mainstream folks, all getting high, spread across a few fields, dancing, playing, laughing, loving and peaking (a drug term meaning to be at the top of a narcotic's influence). It was phenomenal. It was amazing; our festival party was four times the size of the local population of Lechlade, the village next to us. Lechlade is a small market town on the River Thames in Gloucestershire at the southern edge of the Cotswolds. It was here that we experimented with DOET, which is such a profound psychedelic drug that you remain high for three or four days without sleep. It was the most amazing party. I couldn't have imagined topping it. Until a few weeks later, that is. During the end of May, we had almost 40,000 people partying on Castlemorton Common in Worcestershire at the foot of the Malvern Hills. It was quite an incredible experience to be a part of the primary convoy of 150 vehicles driving out from a few sites around the A46 and Monmouthshire. Together we drove onto the site and turned around only to see a second convoy of 100 vehicles approaching from the opposite direction. Moments later a third convoy of more than 250 vehicles arrived. Now, if that isn't exciting for a compulsive partier, I don't know what is. It was spread across the front pages of all the national magazines and newspapers. We were famous, or at least infamous. We had arranged the largest free festival ever in the UK and I knew that I was going to get arrested for it. I didn't care. It was my duty to get arrested. I was so proud of what we had created! With all the press we were getting, it was clear that the police and society wanted some form of retribution. By this time, there were more and more Sound Systems setting up and joining the Free Party circuit. The Bedlam Sound System was made up of some of the more alternative elements of Spiral Tribe. We were the squatters who turned to raving, rather than the ravers who took to squatting. But we were still very close to the Spirals, spiritually, politically and emotionally. Most weeks we would combine our parties so that there would be two different rigs (Sound Systems) running – and even bigger, more outrageous parties, and we did the same during the Festival months in the Summer – making these huge Mad Max style gatherings, self governing and united at the same time. It was profound.

At this time I was driving an ex-Library Ford bus which we converted so that it carried our entire rig (we used the tailgate lift to raise the heavy speakers up and down) and still left space for a few of us to sleep. Since I was the driver, I was the obvious target for them. I was an easy target and it was pretty convenient to pin the whole event on me since I was in possession of the sound system. When I drove off the festival site with my mate Eddie, we both knew the Police were going to arrest us. I knew I would be held responsible. I didn't even bother putting up a fight. During this time I was known as a 'crusty raver' because of my bum-length dreadlocks and my aversion to bathing. We had just previously been squatting at an abandoned refuse tip near Monmouth in Wales, after having been escorted by the Police in that vague direction at the end of the Lechlade Festival a few weeks earlier. It was an amazing spot where we used to drop Acid and go in search of the 'dragon myth' regularly. It had a river that we dammed and turned into a swimming pool. We were fortunate because there had been an impressive heat wave that summer so we all had the chance to swim and have a wash every now and then. I guess what I am saying is that really, I wasn't as crusty as I could have been. I had bathed a couple of weeks previously.

Anyway, about thirty people were arrested in my convoy. We were all charged with something or other. We were charged with whatever they could pin on us. I remember I shared a cell that night with someone who had the same birthday as me, from the Conspiracy Sound System. Before now, whenever I had been arrested (about thirty five times) I had given a false name. And I never carried any form of ID. This time, for some reason unbeknownst to me, I decided to give them my real name. I think I figured they would actually do the research for a change and find out who I was. Maybe I was being overly paranoid. Maybe I was overemphasising the importance of my heinous crime (being part of an organising commune of folks who liked to find spaces for people to party is pretty heinous, right?). But, for some reason, I kinda relented and gave them my real name.

After being held for a long day, I was strangely released on bail to one of my squat addresses in Hackney. London Fields at that time was a small part of Hackney that had been left to rot, where we squatted - effectively there were three full street blocks that were occupied by squatters and vehicles containing travellers. My bail conditions were such that I had to sign in at Holloway Police Station on Mondays, Wednesdays and Saturdays. I knew it was likely that I would be getting a custodial sentence since we were still being blasted as Public Enemy No.1 by the press. The press was having a field day calling us dirty ravers and blaming us for damaging the countryside. We were the talk of the media and were slandered by the tabloids. The charge was 'Conspiracy to Breach the Peace.' This was a heavy-duty charge at the time with a sentence of up to sixteen years. It had been suggested that our bad behaviour was on par with that of terrorists.

Clearly, I wasn't too concerned. When out on bail, the party continued, although the police presence was increased considerably. They were trying to stop the party, so more and more incidents of police violence emerged as we began defending our community. We started bringing our sound rigs to parties knowing that the Police were going to impound them. We got round that by simply hiring them under different false names – often using the name of one of the policemen that had harassed us! It was our form of revenge. After the party, we would simply leave the rigs for the police to impound and skip out quickly once it had 'come on-top' and the police began making arrests. I always hoped the policeman returning the rigs to the hire company turned out to be the name we had used to hire them; little things.

Despite having to sign in at the police station on Holloway Road three times a week, I would still stay where my rave family was parked and head out of town or into London for the parties. I would just hitchhike back and forth as necessary and would work around it; it was not like I had anything better to do anyway. I would pick up and pay for my LSD (I was selling thousands of tabs each week) while back in London, and then get back out to the party to sell it. Times were tough and all this messing around with the police was terribly inconvenient, but I was selling more Acid than ever and the intensity of our parties never let up – the Acid kept the pace going and we were still changing venues every week without fail. But, faced with a heavy jail sentence at the end of the summer, I knew I needed to make a decision. There was one thing I was even more scared of than waking up without drugs, and that was waking up in prison – possibly without drugs! I have never actually been to prison, although I've been arrested and spent many nights in Police cells. I realised that summer that I wasn't prepared to do any sort of prison time. That decision was made easier for me when a particular festival site had been split up by the Police into three separate events, all just few miles from each other, based around Romsey, a small market town in the county of Hampshire. I managed to get smuggled between all three of the sites (I needed to pick up the money owed to me for some LSD credit I'd extended to someone) and, while at the largest of the three sites, I witnessed a recycling plant being set alight by a small minority of the ravers. This broke my heart, conflicted with my morals and crushed some of my principles. Devastated by this, I made a decision that I don't regret at all. I got onto someone's bus that was heading to Europe for a festival in Holland.

I didn't want to go to prison and so I skipped my bail and left the country.

Simple.

Now I do not know how many of you will identify with this but if you are an Englishman and you need to go into rapid exile in Europe, there is really only one logical destination. That destination is Amsterdam. There is no other obvious location – the weather's the same, there's already a massive British ex-patriot community there, they speak English and you can smoke ganja openly on the streets. It's even sold in shops. This deserved my close attention.

It's Not About Me!

Part 2.
ADDICTION
– *the later years*

"My self-imposed exile"

1. Amsterdam, Berlin, Amsterdam, Milano, Amsterdam, Paris, Amsterdam, etc.

I don't know how much you know about European geography, but when going into exile from the British Isles into Europe, the trick is to head towards more pleasant climates, or at least not be exposed to any further unnecessary rain. If you really have to leave England straight away, then it is probably essential you get the hell out of Great Britain altogether, and that means crossing the English Channel. Once you cross the Channel, you are officially on the European mainland and so long as you keep your gob shut, it's not too much bother to blend in. For a drug user like me, there was only one destination that came to mind and only one place to which I would head to once I'd made the decision to skip my bail. It was my turn to go on pilgrimage. Where to? Well Amsterdam, of course.

The weather in Holland is just like England, except slightly less rainy and cloudy. Holland is flat and famous for its windmills. This implies wind, which is indeed the case, since it's flat. So there was no point getting my hopes up. It certainly didn't have the climate of Spain or Southern France. But what it did have that no other location offered were drug laws that suited me to a tee. Yes, ladies and gentlemen, the drug laws, the drug availability and the opportunity to use drugs openly on the streets and in their cafes (coffee shops) were such a draw to me, that there never really was any other option, no matter what the weather. So, needless to say, I landed myself in Amsterdam, after getting myself a lift out of the England on a hippie bus, leaving one festival in Romsey, Hampshire for another one in the outskirts of Amsterdam. They offered me a space on their bus and I said, "Yes please." I actually used my own passport to leave (it wasn't checked) and once over there I got myself a fake one made using the help of a friend who owed me a favour after I let him off and helped him out when earlier that year a deal for a quarter kilo of weed went wrong and he lost my money. I won't mention his name, but he knows I was very grateful to be able to travel around on his passport for a few years, and I know he was grateful I didn't give him too hard a time for getting burnt himself with my money doing that skunk deal. Win, win.

From the moment I arrived in Amsterdam, I began developing new skills. I landed in the city with nothing but the clothes on my back and my first night was spent sleeping (or trying to) with nothing but a cement bag and potato sack for shelter. I was freezing. The cold was such a shock to my system that I realised pretty quickly I was going to have to change my approach in order to survive. By the second night, I had gathered seven old blankets and I found some shelter from the wind between two out-of-service buses. I had already been pretty self-sufficient, having lived as a squatter for so many years, but Holland presented a new challenge and I immediately adjusted to becoming a true survivor – rough sleeper or otherwise.

It immediately dawned on me that I had landed in a drug dealer's Mecca. I was quickly introduced to an incredible network I had previously been unaware of. There were an amazing number of people who were just like me, in some sort of self-imposed exile, not just in this brilliant city, but actually travelling across the whole of Europe. These people had already established themselves as traffickers of all kinds of drugs and were making some healthy money in the process. I was suitably impressed. I settled in very quickly to my new playground – Western Europe, with Amsterdam as my office. Amsterdam is a pretty special place, particularly geographically. It seems as if it is designed as the perfect running location, with a port and roads heading out through Europe to a whole host of other capitals and major cities. Belgium, France and Germany were obvious neighbours, but Spain, Italy, Switzerland, Austria, etc. were all within easy access.

I went on to meet some astonishing people in Amsterdam, who seemed drawn to my energy and vice-versa. One such guy was heading to Berlin so I decided to explore a bit more of this unknown European mainland, and I hitched a ride with him. We rode around in an East German Trabant, which basically is a two-stroke engine car that was built to provide Communist countries, but mainly East Germany, a car to give to the population that was state approved. These state-approved cars had a notoriously long waiting list; some people went without transport for years before receiving one of these less than luxurious pieces of machinery. It's basically little more than a petrol-driven lawn mower with additional seating. But nowadays, and this is shortly after the Berlin Wall came down and Germany was reunited, there were Trabants laying around on the streets waiting for new owners. I believe they were just left behind by the people who retreated back to Russia once the Soviet Union collapsed and they lost control of East Germany.

The time that I spent in Berlin was one of the most amazing times of my life, and one in which I think I was the happiest. When I arrived in Berlin, it was shortly after the Wall had been torn down and there was a vibe in the air of the city that was addictive. I found myself squatting in East Berlin in an old factory that, in its hey-day, had been a primary manufacturing location for Gestapo uniforms. When I was there it was just an empty, run-down, abandoned building, which made it perfect for our needs. We painted the building in black and yellow chequers. Ironically, in Berlin at that time, you had to get a government licence to squat in a property. Just simply requesting a permit to squat somewhere because you wanted somewhere to sleep, or to build a home was not allowed. You needed a genuine reason. The licence was an official document, which spelled out what you were legally allowed to use the space for. These licences were not too difficult to get. In a stroke of absolute genius, we managed to get ourselves a government licence for holding rave parties in this old factory every Wednesday, Friday and Saturday night. It was what we had been doing all over England before I was forced into exile and now I could keep doing what I loved, legally! It was pretty amazing.

Around this time, many members of my old UK crew were also getting out and heading towards the European mainland - some of them with Berlin on their radar. There was already a travelling community already well established in Berlin called the Mutoid Waste. This was a good group of people who had formed into a crew in the mid 80s out of the Peace Convoy; they were the second generation of travellers after the New Age Travellers (hippies). This crew was well and truly a part of the punk generation, and they had largely begun leaving the British

It's Not About Me!

Isles after the Battle of the Beanfield, when many of them had been the victims of the police force's heavy handedness and seen their buses and coaches smashed up mindlessly by the British Bobby. This was around the same time as the Miners' strike, so the energy amongst certain constabularies was one of revenge violence. My crew and I were the next generation, the third generation travellers - the Techno Travellers. The Berlin crew knew about us and they knew that we brought with us a growing audience for our festivals, parties, shows, etc. and an impressive knowledge of and access to a range of drugs that weren't previously so easily available before our arrival. Mutoid Waste had an established piece of licensed land where they were hosting an awesome creative festival. Their push was to turn symbols of urban decay into sculpted futuristic creations.

When I was there, they had some old Panzer tanks face down (i.e. head first, upside down) in the ground with armoured vehicles as the cross stones and a couple of MIG fighter planes dotted around the place. They had created a modern Stonehenge out of war machines. War machines that were painted in the raver Day-Glo paints that made them psychedelic to look at day or night. The most spectacular thing about the Mutoid Waste crew's creation was the space that they had. This piece of land started at the old Checkpoint Charlie (the Communist side) and it just spread out across a no man's land of dead, abandoned earth.

The land had been poisoned long before to ensure that no shrubs, weeds, grass or life of any kind could grow or flourish here. The whole point was to ensure that people crossing the border had no shelter, so that they had nowhere to hide when the snipers were taking shots at those trying to leave the Eastern German regime. But even more remarkable than this, the ground beneath our dancing raver feet held more history than any of us really allowed ourselves to understand at the time. We were partying on the ground on which the Reichstag had previously stood. In 1933, the Reichstag was burnt down by the Nazis to frame the Communists in a political move to win more seats in government.

Not too long after we left this piece of historic ground and moved on with our adventures, the New Reichstag of United Germany was built - hopefully carrying some of our magical loved-up energy with it. One night I do remember vividly. It was a Sunday evening and we had a guest DJ - a certain Paul Van Dyk. From out of nowhere the helicopters blasted us with their searchlights and simultaneously the most high-tech riot police marched in. I remember they came in waves of twelve policemen. They marched in single line formation with six of each section carrying a different weapon - meaning there was two of every weapon in the brigade. We put up no resistance, as this was a completely new level of policing that we had come across before in England. These were the future weapons of riot policing that we now see being wheeled out for use during every global gathering of our Democratic leaders - the G8 summits, etc. We didn't push our luck and the water cannons weren't used.

I loved the East Berliners. They were all crazy with this newly found freedom they were experiencing. Remember, the Berlin Wall had only recently come down. The creativity I saw coming from those folks brimming with joy was spectacular. It really was the best time to be in East Berlin. There are so many stories that emerge out of the happy times I spent in Berlin that it's hard to know what to include. But one story that could never be left out was my experience with the Russian Army.... and if that's not a good story, then I don't know what is!

2. The Benz Box Truck and the Russian Army

We wanted to get back to Amsterdam that Saturday night for Bones's (a settled English traveller and major dealer friend of ours) Full Moon Boat Party - infamous around our scene for many things, notably the free Acid punch. To do this we decided to steal a nice looking Mercedes Benz Box Truck we'd spotted parked nearby in West Berlin, with the intention of running it into France via Holland for resale. The guy leading the mission was a Welshman called Nigel (though, honestly, Nigel didn't look very Welsh). It was a pretty miserable rainy Wednesday evening and there were four of us involved. We grabbed the truck and instantly headed east (entirely the wrong direction!), trying to find somewhere Nigel had previously discovered where we could hide the truck for a few hours to re-paint it and replace the number plates, before we'd be ready to move it westwards. He took us about four or five hours deep into East Germany, where, as dawn arrived we were surprised to find out Nigel's 'parking lot' was in fact a far corner of an abandoned Russian Army base.

A quick history lesson: The Soviet Union had recently begun disbanding and there was a full military withdrawal back to the newly defined Russian borders, including the evacuation of Russian troops stationed in the previously occupied territory of East Germany, now reunited with Germany as a whole once again

It's Not About Me!

(occupied since the end of World War Two), also known as 'Reunification'.

We were well hidden between hundreds of giant piles of army surplus gear. These piles were easily as high as a two-storey townhouse and each pile was dedicated to one specific item - so you had a pile of boots, a pile of shirts, a pile of gas masks, a pile of jerry cans, a pile of rubber truck tyres, etc. There was what seemed like miles of these incredible mounds of leftover army stock, which were literally dumped behind, rather than transported back eastwards as the Russians withdrew their armies from East Germany. It was shocking to see such waste.

When we cracked open the back doors of our fairly new (maybe 6 months old) Box Truck, we revealed a few hundred brand new office chairs stacked neatly inside. This haul would have been worth a small fortune, and if we had known where to flog them then perhaps we could have made some good easy money off this treasure trove. But as it was we didn't have any contacts and had no idea where to offload this stock, so the plan was to leave them there as another pile of abandoned surplus. It was my job to unload these chairs into a pile while the others painted the truck and changed the number plates rendering it unrecognisable to the authorities. Once I had finished my job, I went off for a walk to explore in sheer amazement the maze of disregarded stock laid out before me. I climbed up on one of the piles and all I could see for miles in any direction were more and more piles of stock similar in size to the one I was standing on, but with many different army surplus items. What a complete waste! I was totally overwhelmed by the sheer extent of it all. It didn't take me long to come to the conclusion that I could start my own collection of army gear and sell it to one of the army surplus stores in Holland when we got back home.

So I began 'hunting and gathering', collecting my own pile of choice items. I had collected boots, shirts, pullovers, jackets, gas masks, socks, tunics and more. I was standing there, on the top of a giant pile of army surplus, my arms full of Russian army clobber, when I saw something that made my jaw drop. Forty men marching in double file were heading towards me. This platoon was winding its way through these castles of clothes and I just stood there, frozen. I considered the reality of what was happening. I was there, somewhere I wasn't supposed to be, with a stolen Russian truck, stealing Russian Army clothes and Russian equipment from the very same Russian Army that was marching determinedly towards me right on their very own home base. Here I was stealing from that very Russian Army and I had my arms full of stolen Russian goods. Busted and caught RED handed. I couldn't help notice that each of these Russians was carrying a rifle and I froze, more out of fear than anything else as they relentlessly approached. But before I shat myself, literally (wouldn't you?), something very strange happened.

They approached me in two perfect lines, and not one of the soldiers caught my eye. They were transfixed on the man in front in perfect military formation, stomping though the piles; highly disciplined, all looking dead ahead. All of them except for the leading officer, he looked at me. He held my gaze but remained completely expressionless. It was creepy and terrifying. As they got closer to me I turned around and shouted out to the others to watch out, trying to warn them of the advancing soldiers. Then to my absolute amazement, the soldiers didn't stop when they got to me; they just kept marching past me towards the truck. Then they stopped, before they reached it. Why?

They turned at the last moment and went to the pile of chairs I had offloaded earlier. Together, like a robotic machine they systematically grabbed the chairs. They stacked the chairs and loaded themselves with as many as they could carry. They reformed their strict marching lines, and returned to wherever they had mysteriously come from. It was, and to this day still is, one of the strangest things that I have ever seen. Amazed, astounded and completely in shock, the four of us got a move on. We quickly finished the painting and made sure that we were gone before they returned for the rest of the chairs...and, perhaps us!

3. Technivals

I hooked back up with Spiral Tribe in Amsterdam and we began travelling together again. We started hosting squat parties in Amsterdam, Harlem, Leiden and Rotterdam and built a nice following of around a thousand regulars to our parties. We left Holland after a couple of months and headed south to Paris.

As our reputation grew, so did the amount of people coming to our raves. Every time we put on a party, ravers would come from all over Europe just to dance with us. It was simple really, we were playing the best beats and we had some great DJs playing very new and original music, so people came. But the quintessential draw that had people flocking to us from left, right and centre was the drugs. We had the best drugs anywhere. My life was all about drugs, so the parties I hosted were definitely no different - they were all about the drugs too.

Our Technivals (essentially festivals of Techno music and other electronic beats) became more and more popular as we explored different parts of Europe, travelling far and wide from Czechoslovakia through Austria, Germany, Holland, Belgium, France, Spain, Italy and for some of these Techno travellers much, much further. We usually siphoned diesel along the way and we nearly always drove under the influence of amphetamines. One member of our crew had a particularly special key that fitted the underground fuel tanks for most petrol stations. So, late at night, long after gas stations were closed, we would drive in and use this magic key to open the huge storage tanks of gasoline and just help ourselves to a buffet of free fuel. We must have taken many thousands of litres over the following months.

We had a core fleet of between six to twelve vehicles to carry our sound system and equipment around the place, although while we were on route to a new Technival the size of the convoy could grow by the dozens to over fifty vehicles — similar to how things were back in England, although with a much larger playing field. We called ourselves the 'Circus of Sound and Light'. In some ways this was certainly true. But the sound and light part was really just a way of suggesting some sort of legality to cover up for the amazing giant raves we were putting on all over Europe. These raves that were born during my time in the 'Circus' were a phenomenon and are still travelling through Europe today taking bass, bleeps and beats to ravers all across the continent.

We had dubbed them 'Technivals' and it really isn't surprising that these events became the epicentre of the European designer drug industry, in a similar vein to how things had played out in England in the early 90s. However, these events were slightly different to when my crew and I had put them on across the UK. This time we were taking a much more hands-on approach when it came to the flow and distribution of the drugs. We were trafficker, smuggler, purchaser, distributor, dealer and consumer all at the same time. In some cases, we even took on the role of manufacturer (more about that later).

This was quite an exceptional period in my life and I was having the most incredible time. I remember sitting on one of our buses, reading the Electric Kool-Aid Acid Test by Ken Kesey. Have you read it? I realised there and then that what we were doing was precisely what the book described, just thirty years later with a different soundtrack - Techno music, and different colours

- they used day-glow and UVs, where as we used black and chromes, with Flower Strobes and smoke machines. We were travelling around living in a daze or 'trip' where we just wanted to distribute drugs to the world believing we could turn the world onto a more utopian society through libertarian and anarchistic ideas and principles. We believed strongly in expanded consciousness, selfless love and ultimate hedonism, and we weren't afraid to show it.

We spread our gospel of Techno music, free love and amazing drugs from all over Western Europe, even bumping into the incredible George Clinton and Parliament Funk, somewhere in Belgium (suffice to say these guys were looking a little worse for wear those days), and then ended up in Paris for a good while. We loved Paris and the Parisians loved us. They were seriously 'cheesy' (cheesy quaver is rhyming slang for ravers, but also the term cheesy describes a popular middle-of-the-road style, i.e., not too extreme or hardcore) in their fashions and dancing styles. Right from the start we knew the French ravers 'got it' and our following grew very rapidly from 500 at the first party to more than 5,000 people at our 'Goodbye Paris Party' before we headed south for the winter. We certainly left a pretty good mark on the partygoers of the city because they all came back to play again when we returned in the spring of the next year. After Paris, we headed south on a crusade towards Spain (we even took a few of our new Parisian friends with us) to settle down somewhere warmer for winter.

4.   **Playa La Malvarrosa:** Where LSD broke the elastic band

We drove our convoy of vehicles out of Paris in December of 1992, seeking warmer pastures. Spain was the destination in our hearts and in our minds. We used amphetamines to keep us awake so that we didn't have to take a break from driving. Because of the constant high, it only took our convoy of seven vehicles five days to reach Barcelona, siphoning diesel along the way, which is a large job when you have so many vehicles. We were sending out small squads of us each night to fill up our petrol butts and collect enough for the next day's journey.

We settled in Barcelona for a short week, realising quickly that settling down was going to be harder than we had imagined. The police were constantly moving us on. The intensity of the corruption also became very clear; they kept insisting that we pay ridiculously fabricated fines. So, we escaped late one night and headed further south in search of perfection in Valencia. Valencia was wonderful and, as luck would have it, celebrating its Feria (festival) when we arrived. The Valencia Feria lasts a full week and has one of the most expensive fireworks displays in the world. We decided to take part in the many festivities that the city had to offer. We assembled our sound system on one of our flat-bed trucks and danced around our vehicles as if we were busking. We had our hats out asking for booze (vino tinto) or money for fuel to keep our generator running.

In Spain at this time, they had their own style and brand of house music called Bacalao, which blended current hits with a big drum and some elementary effects. The locals loved it, and turning them on to our hard Techno music wasn't easy. But they did like our drugs, especially our Acid.

Living in Spain was another experience altogether, and brought its own surprises and life-changing events for me. We were squatting on an abandoned part of the beach in Northern Valencia, which was (from memory) called Playa la Malvarrosa. We lived on this unused beach next to an industrial zone, where we lit fires, built a bar and started having parties, hoping to attract local ravers. It was here, on this deserted beach, next to Valencia's industrial zone that I experienced what it is like to do too much LSD! After so many years of partying and tripping on all types of hallucinogenics, I took one hit of LSD too many and my whole mind shifted. I don't know if you will be able to truly understand what it is that I am about to describe, so I'm going to give you an analogy to try to make it a little easier to get your head around. First, just try to imagine what my brain must have been going through by taking such large doses of hallucinogens and psychedelics on a very regular (virtually daily) basis for around seven years. Scattered doesn't even begin to describe it. To really understand where I was at you must bear in mind that I did things that still shock me today. I took 21 LSD blotters for my 21st birthday. I took 23 Ecstasy pills one evening because 23 was our cosmic number. There was a time when I went on an intense bender and I didn't sleep for sixteen days, of which my peak was on day nine!

So, imagine an elastic band each time you stretch it. It will expand between your fingers and then bounce back into shape when you let it go. Now imagine the elastic band is your brain. Every time you take a 'trip' it is like stretching the elastic band, your brain takes you to a whole different dimension of experience and then when you come down off the drug your brain bounces back into place, recovering after some sleep. Is this metaphor making sense? Keep stretching and pulling on that elastic band. Sooner or later the elastic band starts to get a bit slack; it goes saggy and it no longer bounces back so quickly to its original shape. In fact, the original band gets looser and looser over time. This is made even worse by the fact that you now have to stretch it even further to get it to expand to the same tautness that it did before.

This is the key to the problem. When you stretch the band (your brain) so far to try to get the same experience that you did the last time, you push it harder and harder and further and further, it's not hard to imagine why the band doesn't want to bounce back anymore. And, at this stage, you really start to lose your marbles. Your brain, so confused by what you are doing to it, begins to make you paranoid and your behaviour is sure to become increasingly erratic and out of control. At this time in my life, as much as I didn't want to admit it to myself, this drug wasn't working for me anymore. I had taken so much of it that I was immune to the effect; I had snapped the rubber band in my brain. I couldn't find a way out, because not using was never an option. But the whole idea of losing control was becoming less and less attractive. I am a drug user. That is part of who I am. I love to use drugs. But these particular drugs were making me so paranoid, so scared, I was so unsure of myself that I couldn't even see that it was the drugs that were the problem. Instead I blamed the way I felt, my fear and my paranoia on anyone and anything I could. This is very typical behaviour when someone is experiencing a paranoid psychosis. I thought that everyone was turning on me - judging me and despising me for being there. I felt unwelcome and like I was a burden. I began to believe people were plotting against me and that at any moment I could expect a severe beating. This is blatantly paranoia.

Ironically, the only way to beat your paranoia is to finally come to the conclusion that it is just paranoia, and not truth. Once this assessment is reached, then the healing may begin. But first of all I needed to understand and believe that the LSD was causing me to become paranoid and then make a decision to stop using it. However, drugs were the very essence of who I was. They were who I was, what I did and the basis of my connections with my crew and my friends. I couldn't possibly admit defeat. I had to find a solution, and LSD could no longer be my drug of choice; I had used it until I was all used up. The solution I found may not surprise you at all. I was fed up with losing control. I was done with drugs that sent me into places where I lacked the ability to control my experience. I needed something else. I needed a new type of drug sensation.

Now I needed drugs that made me feel like I had control. I turned my back on psychedelic drugs and opened my arms to drugs that made me feel in control. I found Cocaine!

I let go of being out of control. Cocaine gave me the ability to feel absolutely in control!

It was very easy to get caught up in it all, especially when you have already established yourself firmly in the centre of the action. It wasn't even that I couldn't find a way out of it all; it was more that I was not looking for one. The world outside this world of drugs and parties didn't exist to me. In Spain, I found myself partying with a guy who came to our raves, a guy whose day job was as a policeman. He would tell me that his job was his job and his own time was his own time as we smoked Cocaine together in a local bar. He was a nice enough guy, but that was the Spanish attitude towards Cocaine. LSD and Ecstasy were actually more expensive than Coke. And, although times were financially pretty tough for us back then, I got myself hooked on Cocaine - at least in a psychological way, if not physically...yet. I had had a taste, and I wasn't going back. I stayed there, with Cocaine firmly by my side for the next seven years.

5. C.C.C.C.C.Co-caine

Cocaine made me feel like I was in control. It made me feel like I had power, a purpose and a direction. It felt so good to finally be in command of not only myself but also my surroundings. And, I tell you what, if you have ever felt like you were out of control, the feeling of suddenly being in control is in itself intensely addictive. I felt so in control, and it was an amazing change from the six or seven years that had just passed, when I hadn't known which way was up or which way was down. I felt unbeatable. I felt like nothing could stop me. This feeling was perfect for me, and it became my best friend. Cocaine and I went everywhere together, I couldn't live a moment without it. I had to have it, all the time. I had to maintain that feeling of perfection. Therein started what I presume most of us can understand as the formative turning point towards my descent into the darker side of my drug using past. I had always been addicted to drugs. I had always loved them. I had always had so much fun on them. But

I had never felt like I needed them to survive...until now.

As we drove north in the mid spring back into France, I knew my life was changing. The parties we had begun hosting along the south coast of France that April and May set the scene for what was coming. Sex, drugs and Techno music were to be the menu for the near future. Just the way I like it.

Throughout this book I've openly admitted that it was all about drugs. But did I mention yet that it was also about the women? My entire life was about drugs and women. W.D.A. We Do Anything - Women, Drugs and Alcohol, but certainly not necessarily in that order. It was about living a liberated and irresponsible, carefree life with free drugs and free sex. There was very little time, however, for sex in Techno City, so I would often find myself going off from the main tribe and travelling with a small band of brothers on a mission to drink and womanise. I am not ashamed to admit that I found French women particularly enticing; they were indeed an addiction in themselves.

6. Montpellier Alcoholic

By the time I had arrived in Montpellier in France, it was sometime in late spring 1993, alcohol had become my constant companion. Although what I really wanted was Cocaine, I didn't yet have the means to support such a taste. Cheap alcohol was about all I could reach for at this time. Fortunately, I immediately fell in with the crowd of beggars and vagabonds who spent their days drinking and amusing themselves in the town's central plaza - Place Jean Jaures. I drank with them. I begged with them. I squatted in abandoned buildings with them. I found amusement with them. I learnt French with them. Absolutely the best way to learn a language is to get drunk with the locals and have no other choice than to figure it out as you go along. The booze takes away the fear of getting the words wrong, and you just push on through. Yet another skill: French linguist.

So I continued my alcoholism, becoming a full-blown wino for those wonderful spring months from late March all the way through the summer and beyond. Despite being filthy and permanently hungry, I loved the life of absolutely no responsibilities. The only thing I had to do every day was to beg for enough money to purchase the next bottle of very cheap, but drinkable French plonk.

It's Not About Me!

There is a certain camaraderie that grows from the street drinkers; we kept an eye out for each other, especially the females. But I was still a Techno traveller at heart and I knew that Techno music would pull me through this and into the next stage of my life. I would start hitchhiking across the South of France to get to the next party, where I would hook up with my tribe of friends and become hedonistic for a long weekend. Of course, I knew that it was at the parties the Coke would come out. But, strangely, at the end of the party on a Monday or Tuesday I would begin the adventure of returning to Montpellier by hook or crook. Why? I genuinely enjoyed being a street drunk in a warm Mediterranean wealthy city, that's why. It was while I was off gallivanting between the parties and my adopted city of Montpellier chasing tail that I made friends with various French ravers, from many different French towns and cities. I'd hit the jackpot and fallen in with some seriously cool French dudes with a pile of Cocaine and a very healthy attitude towards 'more'!

After my experiences in Spain that previous winter, I knew that I wanted Cocaine. Cocaine would give me access to beautiful girls and happier times. The best accompaniment to Cocaine would be to be a DJ myself. More importantly, that would get me laid. And being a DJ would also get me closer to people with Cocaine! As I have previously indicated, Cocaine was to be my 'new best friend'. Cocaine gave me the things I wanted and allowed me to feel the way I wanted - powerful, dominant, courageous, ambitious, handsome, attractive, sexy, wealthy; all the sorts of things I had never cared about while taking psychedelics, but now seemed so important to me. I was changing! From wino to Coke head was a long distance, but I made it in record time!

We had a party on a beach near Montpellier, and I started meeting people. Since I was the only person able to speak French, albeit badly, I translated deals and became the go between, which normally afforded me the luxury of tasting the goods alongside both parties.

When I was brokering deals, I would normally be able to take a cut for myself. I had Cocaine. Then I had girlfriends, and from that I came off the streets to start sleeping at these lovely French girls' apartments. Now I had somewhere to stay, a little money in my pocket and a steady stream of beautiful girls by my side. I began the next stage of my transformation - I began buying records and playing them! I became a DJ - simply by buying records, playing them out to people, learning the patterns on the tunes, and mixing them when the drums didn't crash. I immediately understood the make-up of the music and self-taught beat matching, cutting, blending and proper mixing, but it started very simply. DJ - another skill added to my portfolio.

By the end of the summer of 1993, I was a recognised DJ in the South of France (I must admit to having some musical talent here, and I took my job very seriously as a performer). After a full summer of partying, I landed in Toulouse - La Ville Rose, where I settled for the next four years. Here, women, drugs and Techno music were my gospel and I was welcomed into the scene as an accomplished DJ.

7. D.J.Nerate: Sex and Drugs and Techno Music

So, together with some of my new French mates it made sense to take my experience and see what we could do. We started the first French Sound System, which we called Les Nomads. We were the very first travelling French Sound System and I became the primary DJ, known as DJ Nerate (degenerate, get it?) along with a couple of other French mates – Benoir aka Ben Bon Beat and Willy aka Willyman. Sadly, this pioneering crew would only last for a few years before we disbanded in a haze of Heroin...but that is, of course, a story for later.

I became a DJ; the man in control of the sounds and the ravers. All eyes were focussed on me. I was the centre of attention, and I loved it.

I figured it couldn't be too hard, especially since I'd always loved music. I still do. I am rather obsessed with music - all types of music, and what music says about a culture or a group of people. I'm sure music is connected to the spirit and what you enjoy listening to is a true reflection of your personality. I feel so strongly about it, in fact, that to this day I will leave a room playing music that I don't want to be associated with or if it conflicts with my aural pleasure. I will find it hard to sit still if there's a piece of music on in the background that I either love or hate. In fact, if there's music on and I'm around people, I find it very hard to concentrate on any conversation or business. Nowadays, when I work alone from my office, I always have my iPod playing in the background - on shuffle, so I never know what's coming next, except that I'll love it.

I'd had a history with music since a child. My father was very musical and came from a musical family. He sang in the London Philharmonic Choir and played a

It's Not About Me!

few instruments. Indeed, my cousins are all musicians too - one is an orchestral conductor and moves around the whole British and International classical music scene. A couple of them are very talented musicians in a successful jazz band called Kairos 4Tet and they won a MOBO award in 2011. So I was encouraged to learn instruments, too. I played recorder (didn't we all?) as a child, before going on to learn the trumpet and trombone. I was taught piano to grade 5 and can still sit down and knock out the odd tune, or improvise with chord structures and harmonies. I taught myself rhythm guitar and even managed to busk my way around Europe in the summer of 1988 with a mate. We ended up spending most of our time drinking along the south coast resorts of France, but we did make it into parts of Italy and over to Belgrade (Beograd), the former Yugoslavian capital, where busking for money was pointless due to the universal poverty and insignificant value of the dinar, for which a few hundred thousand couldn't even buy a sandwich.

I loved music, sure, but that wasn't the reason I wanted to become a DJ initially. My primary motives were twofold. First, I was motivated by sex. Being a DJ, I thought, was sure to attract more beautiful women and, in hindsight, I was 100% correct in that theory. And second, being a DJ would allow me to consume and sell more drugs. Furthermore, I could participate in the consumption of other people's goodies, too. When I played at clubs I was given free booze, and when I played at raves I would be given Cocaine, Ecstasy (or other such narcotics) often as part payment for my services and often just to be polite and to encourage my complete participation. Not surprisingly, I preferred to play at the raves.

I was a DJ and I did all right. Actually, as DJs go, I was very good. I was passionate about the music and able to follow the crowd and play the right beats to keep the atmosphere pumpin' and jumpin'. Rather than just forcing a crowd of hopped-up ravers to listen to my particular niche, I gave them what they wanted to hear. I always played to the crowds' vibe, not trying to project my own. I would respect the previous DJ and follow on from their final tune with a crossover sound to bring the crowd into a new vibe. Please note, that although I never did take requests, I did seem to have a good ear in figuring out what to play next - except for the time I tried to play under the influence of Ketamine. There's only that one example of a set I played where I look back and am truly ashamed of my sounds. That evening at a party back in a London squat with the Bedlam and Jiba Sound Systems circa 1995 (I was on some sort of mission to bring some good stuff over from the mainland) I took some 'K' just prior to going on to play my set. I was unable to get a single mix in time. It was so un-calibrated! The beats mashed and crashed over one another. And this was my home turf. I knew I had performed ashamedly. I shocked myself into never playing under the influence of Ketamine again. In case you're unfamiliar with the effects of Ketamine, it gives you the sensation that you've just drunk two litres of whisky in one go, and then you spend the next three or four hours sobering up. Clearly, not a suitable drug for beat matching or performing in public.

Aside from playing with Les Nomads, I personally developed quite a reputation around Europe and, within a short time, I could attract a couple thousand people to some of the gigs I was playing. Every weekend when these hordes of people would show up to dance to my beats; I was convinced it was because of the music. Or perhaps that was just what I was telling myself. Many, many people would tell you it wasn't about the music at all. They would tell you that those thousands of people where showing up for the drugs, my drugs, because they weren't just good, they were the best. And there certainly is some truth in that. My drugs were sourced from the best. I never cut them up (except for one occasion, when I used a yellow pill to cut my Cocaine to try to maximise some sales – but everyone could tell and so I ended up doing all the Coke by myself, because no one else would touch it). They were always well dosed and clean, never under 70% of the stated size or strength. Mostly I sold 0.8 of a gram, which is generous enough when you're trying to support your own habit as well (buy five grams and sell five, but sell .8s and you get a free one for yourself).

Once again, I was in my element. I was the drug man. I was the music man. I was in charge. I was in control. I was the boss. I felt fucking fantastic!

8. More about Les Nomads

As I said earlier, in the summer of 1993, I formed the very first travelling French Sound System called Les Nomads. We were an odd bunch which included two guys from the underground jazz scene, someone from the bat cave scene (French gothic punks), an extreme metal punk called Gwar, a guy from the French black music scene (though he was white) called Willyman (pun fully intended), and an ambitious guy from the hip-hop scene (Marvin to his mates) and me, of course. We had great fun together. In fact, we had so much fun that we really needed a way to unwind and come down afterward. Heroin seemed to be the perfect remedy. Heroin began to do for me things that Cocaine couldn't. Cocaine brought me up and gave me power, but Heroin gave me the centeredness to be cool under any situation. Heroin allowed me to feel the way I'd always wanted to feel - very calm, cool and collected, and in charge! I was in charge of myself now. I controlled myself by getting high, energetic, wild and wonderful on Coke, then by maintaining my sanity and staying calm, cool and collected with the Heroin. It was a perfect concoction, and I loved it.

Mind you, the first time I snorted a line of Smack it made me throw up. Marvin (who had provided me with the Smack) decided that the vomit had nothing to do with the Smack but more to do with the mixture of booze and milk in some cereal that I had eaten to line my belly just before. I never mixed booze and milk again! However, I took Heroin virtually every day after my first go and I never threw up while using Smack again. Please don't take this as a reflection on the dangers of mixing milk and booze. Although that's not a great mix, it's delusional to think that was actually why I threw up. I threw up because my body was experiencing a new poison for the first time and it wanted to show me that this wasn't a great move towards better physical health. I never listened.

In my current professional capacity as an Addiction Consultant working with many, many people, I hear a lot of people talking about taking Cocaine and then becoming paranoid. But that simply isn't my experience. When you do enough Heroin, you're not paranoid at all; quite the opposite, in fact. You feel completely relaxed and yet absolutely in control of your own life and destiny. You're not. But you certainly feel like you are.

Now I am not going to suggest to anybody that they go out and experiment with Class A drugs. That would be very foolish. I am never going to suggest that if you're a Cocaine user who is identifying with becoming paranoid after using Cocaine, that you go and add Heroin into your mix. That would be madness. Do you hear me? It is not sane to treat a drug that is making you paranoid with another drug to stabilise yourself. Is it? No! Surely, if a drug is inducing paranoia, the best course of action is to stop doing the drug altogether. That would be the sane response. I hope we're clear on that. Because I was in no way clear about that back in the day. It seemed very obvious to me that I needed more Heroin in my life. It never occurred to me that I ought to stop using Cocaine. Durrr! But for those of you reading this book that have already experimented with the stuff, I wonder how many have tried Heroin to overcome their feelings of paranoia. Benzodiazepines also do the trick. I'm amazed when people say that paranoia was a side effect of these drugs. You see Heroin is the way I allowed the Cocaine to keep me focusing. It was how I ensured that I never had to deal with the debilitating paranoia that had haunted me when I had been using psychedelics. In my experience, Heroin kept me so centred that nothing could stop me and I remained feeling in control; totally in command and little else apart from safe, sound and comfortable. There is no reason for me to be paranoid when I am using Cocaine and Heroin. Heroin takes care of paranoia by replacing it with extreme self-comfort and a chilled-out demeanour.

Being calm was the perfect place for me to be...and paranoia was something I didn't need any more of, especially since the police really were following me!

Sounds like a nice place to be, right? Well, it almost killed me.

9. Criss-crossing Western Europe

Just as an aside, I figure I ought to spell out for you some of the things I was up to during this period, without going into too much detail (I don't want to incriminate myself too much). During the next couple of years I was busy designing myself a small but rather lucrative import-export business. I started immediately building my own routes through Europe. My cities and their routes were born organically through the connections and friends I made, crossing Europe through certain borders that I came to know and respect. Cold Vienna, exciting Berlin, colourful Amsterdam, dreary Rotterdam, grey Brussels, heading south via bleak Lyon and across to affluent Geneva, to go around the magnificent Swiss Alps and through to Northern Italy. Across along the Mediterranean coast and the glorious the South of France through Monaco, Nice, Cannes, Toulon and Marseille. Then on through Aix en Provence, Arles, Avignon, Ales, and Nimes. Going west following these beach cities and sunny seaside resorts, turning south at Montpellier going through Narbonne and Perpignan right into Spain to Barcelona and Valencia. Coming back north via Clermont-Ferrand, Paris and Belgium. Alternatively, I could travel to any one of these destinations in any order and trust that I was going along vaguely safe routes that would keep me from being too inconvenienced. These were all routes I became familiar with.

I travelled along my routes by thumb (hitchhiking), car (most likely stolen), coach (the cheapest but most likely to be hassled), train (the safest mode of transport), lorry (usually carrying sound equipment), or convoy (when we were travelling as a circus). There was a complex pattern that I had designed going through Europe's drug centres carrying drugs from left to right and up and down. I was absolutely in my element and having a lot of fun. I took the time to get to know my routes better and better and I always took pleasure in beating the system. I knew where searches would happen, when they would happen and exactly how to pass through safely with flying colours. Strip-searching became a normal part of my everyday life when I was crossing the frontier, so it was important I became a proficient at it. I don't think I need to go into all the details of this business, I'm sure you can fill in the blanks yourself, but suffice to say that it was a rather dirty job.

I ended up making friends (more often than not female friends, strangely enough) in every major city. And, with business being what it was, I brought the party with me, everywhere I went. Essentially, trafficking wasn't my top priority since I ended up organising and throwing some of the most incredible raves all across Europe, but it was a nice hobby on the side that kept me busy and motivated. I could now add tourist guide to my long list of skills.

10. Border crossings: caught with my pants down

I got arrested a number of times crossing European frontiers and I knew the precise route I needed to take to cross safely between Belgium and France. I knew exactly where they were going to pick me up, and I was fully prepared to be strip-searched. I had long ago mastered the art of creative fictionalising (bullshitting) my way through being strip-searched. Time and time again I got through despite being asked to squat down and bend over. You see, not bathing too often did have its silver lining after all. I'm pretty sure no officer in his right mind would want to get too close that that end of me. And they backed off pretty quickly when they did.

I got arrested about thirty times before I was even nineteen. Mostly because I was off my head and in places I shouldn't be. I used to take LSD and go into building sites and explore them in the middle of the night, I was arrested for political violence and being involved in the poll tax riots. I was involved in organising illegal free parties and festivals, and I was often getting arrested for that sort of stuff. I was fairly successful at not getting caught too often for any drug offences. I had gotten arrested for a small possession aged about twenty or so, when police broke into a squat I was in and found some Hash and Acid. It is fair to say that I was familiar with the police, and they were pretty familiar with the likes of me.

I ran the route from Holland through Belgium and into France often. It was due to this (and to the way that I looked I'm sure) that I was stopped and searched regularly. It was a given, so I soon got into the practice of being prepared for the inevitable strip search at the Belgium/France border. I would routinely be escorted off the bus or train I was on and, in the case of the bus, the driver would wait for me, but if it were a train, then it would go on without me. I would be asked a few questions about where I was going (normally I'd answer Spain in search of sunshine), where I had been (in Holland working in the tulip fields or some other seasonal agricultural work) and whether I had smoked any Marijuana while in Holland to which I would confess to having tried it and not liked it, preferring my long-time favourite drug of alcohol.

More often than not they would then put me in a cell and ask me to undress, while they search my bags for drug paraphernalia and then my clothes for any hidden pockets that I could have been smuggling drugs in. They would then ask me (when I was as naked as the day I was born) to squat and then cough. I'm not entirely sure that this is a great method to reveal a concealed stash of drugs, but it certainly works as a psychological test. Most newbie smugglers surely would reveal their stash just by the look on their faces. I would, of course, remain confident, since all my drugs would be in my gut, not up my bum!

They were in my gut because I swallowed my consignments, rather than 'plugged' them (going in the other end). I did this using bees wax, which after being melted in a small saucepan or other contraption (often a beer can with the lid sheared off), I would dip a cling film (plastic) wrapped small package of drugs. This would give it a water-tight seal that wouldn't cause any toxic damage to my internal organs as it went through my system. Each package was about the size of my thumb, and I would swallow up to forty of these at a time. It was a fairly decent sized package, but not really on a par with the big players. I was mostly carrying pills and powders, although in later years I would also bring paper LSD blotters through by the thousands hidden inside one or two vinyl record sleeves (I would carry hundreds at a time) since I was a travelling DJ.

It's Not About Me!

So, I was always the one who got through the border control net, mostly by being confident enough to look them in the eye and express my genuine innocence. I had mastered the art of creative fictionalising.

However, there was one time...

I was doing a run from Harlem in Holland down to the South of France with an English guy who had lived in Holland for about fifteen years. We would often use his squat as a safe house to score our consignments and smoke Crack and Heroin while we were in town. We had put together a plan to transport Cocaine and Heroin down there in his car. On this occasion, though, we had both plugged and swallowed our consignment. However, once we were through the border into France, he decided he wanted to taste some of his merchandise, and once he'd unplugged himself, we shared some Cocaine and he left over 50 grams in his side bag, despite my warnings of flying border control police, who could pull you over anywhere.

We were about a third of the way across France - well past Paris, towards Orleans, when we were pulled over at a tollbooth. Looking as strung out as we did, we were searched and they quickly found the small wrap of Cocaine we were sharing for personal use. They then directed us to their offices/cells where they took the car apart and discovered the stash of over 50 grams. He refused to own up to it, despite it being in his bag and I refused to admit the bag was mine, so we were both put in holding cells. I knew we both still had plenty of drugs inside us and that within the next 24 hours they would come out, whether we liked it or not.

I did my usual trick of being friendly and obviously unscarred by the fact that we were being held in cells, because I was clearly innocent and had nothing to hide. And they seemed to buy it. They believed me, but didn't release me. I was beginning to feel the effects of my Heroin habit withdrawal come on - sweats, nausea, and a desire to empty my bowels (Heroin constipates you, so being in withdrawal allows your body to flush itself uncontrollably). Ouch, I was holding it in, but didn't know for how much longer that would be possible. Sorry about this if you are eating your dinner.

I guess we were fortunate it was a Friday, as we were dragged before a judge at the end of the day, before the weekend kicked in and everyone went home or to the central prison. I was delighted when the judge gave me bail, since I had only been caught with a small amount - under half a gram that we were snorting from. My colleague, however, was remanded in custody. I was dropped off at the station (the car was impounded) where I took the first train heading south, and jumped into the toilets of the train, to make a full deposit. Phew, it was really rather uncomfortable, and I really needed to put some Heroin up my nose! After rinsing the packages, I continued my journey south with them in a side bag. I left it to fate, and fate treated me well.

A vaguely similar story happened to me as I was heading east towards a Technival in the Czech Republic. Having driven from Holland, through Germany and into Austria, we were held up at the Austrian/Czech Republic border and we needed to park overnight in this little border village.

The only problem was that I was going into Heroin withdrawal, and I didn't have the strength to hold the goods inside me – it was too painful and the load was too large. I ran to some truck stop toilets where I let my eggs go. But I was now faced with the problem of finding a way to conceal them before the next morning and the crossing of the border. I shoved everything into a bag I was carrying trying to come up with a solution, quickly.

I walked into the streets of this border village looking for some place with showers - maybe a small hotel. I came across a group of young adults hanging out at the village centre and I made friends quickly, which was surprising since I spoke little German or Czech. Somehow I managed to make a good friend very quickly who invited me back to his house, where I asked if I could take a shower. Safe in his bathroom, I took over an hour washing and plugging all my fallen items. He was knocking on the door asking if I was all right, and wanting me to hurry up, since his parents were not pleased with my presence. I left shortly after finishing my dirty work, making my excuses of being tired. We crossed the border safely the next morning.

There was another occasion when we were squatting in Vienna, Austria, and I was making a journey back towards Holland to re-supply, but I was carrying LSD (which I always seemed to have in large amounts) with me to barter and exchange or sell along the way. Unfortunately, our truck was stopped at the German/ Austrian border and I was arrested because I didn't have any identification. My false passport had run out, so I was travelling without any documents. They put me in a holding cell before sending me back to Vienna the next morning. There I was given consult with the Embassy who gave me a new passport in my real name. This was the first time I'd used my real name in over four years! The passport photo had me with a full beard and a very tatty brown pullover full of holes. It was minus 20 degrees outside, hence the beard.

Those winters were cold, especially living in vehicles. We would go out to railway depots to steal coal to keep our burners alight. That journey back home to the South of France took me five weeks as opposed to five days, but I was never really in a rush to get anywhere. I just wanted to get back to the sunny south.

As I began to gain access to larger amounts of money and increasingly larger amounts of drugs through my ever-expanding groups of contacts, I began shifting rather large amounts of Cocaine. And, since I had access to such large amounts of Cocaine, it made sense to consume as much as I could. It just made perfect sense. After all, the reason we consume Cocaine is because it makes us feel wonderful. So, I was feeling pretty wonderful most of the time. There came a point where Cocaine and Heroin became far more interesting to me than cannabinoids, amphetamines and psychedelics. However, Cocaine did require accompaniment from alcohol and Heroin. All the time!

My Heroin addiction crept up on me swiftly and overwhelmingly. Though I managed to maintain myself and still hold down relationships, inside I knew I was making a big mistake. On the outside I was having a great time. The courage that Heroin gave me to confront and deal with my day-to-day challenges and adventures was so powerful that I allowed myself to become dependent upon it without even challenging it. But inside I knew I was going down a one-way street. I kept myself together largely because for the first four years I was only snorting my brown Heroin. I thought smoking it was a waste, and I wasn't prepared to begin injecting it...yet.

Anyways, I knew that I was a junkie, even though I prefer to present myself to you as principally a Coke user.

11. From Heroin Chic to Caribbean Crackhead

My DJing career was a successful one and I travelled over much of France every weekend to play before many hundreds if not thousands of people. I built myself a great reputation and I had my 'new best friend' Césario manage me. I had met Césario one Sunday morning when I went into Toulouse city centre to buy a bespoke sandwich at a nice place he was working at. Me being high and chatty, we got on really well immediately. Césario is a very amicable and fun guy to be around, and we just instantly became great friends. He took me on as his act, so he could get away from his day job and do something exciting. And me, by allowing him to be my manager meant that I had a totally loyal French-speaking friend who would literally take care of all of the details, including many of my bookings and the transportation for us both to get there. He always partied as hard as I did, but would then peel off Sunday night and return to a relatively normal routine Monday through to Thursday. Césario loved to party and he loved the chicks, especially the ones that hung around the DJ booth as I was playing. We would never have any trouble with female company after I'd finished playing my set. Césario and I were inseparable during the weekends, and our ability to bring a party alive preceded us. We were in high demand. But let me say this, Césario was never an addict and he never did anything he didn't want to do, or lose his control. He partied as hard as me, but he was never an addict.

By 1997, both he and I knew I was potentially heading for some serious trouble with this addiction to Heroin that I had developed, so we figured we'd go out to the Caribbean for six months to clean me up off this Smack habit. It is definitely worth pointing out that since I was a DJ, going to the Caribbean was potentially a good move because I could take my records with me and earn us a living.

So, along with Césario and Lolette, my long-term girlfriend of four years, we went there and both Lolette and I did a cold turkey detox without any form of medical aid or medication. I clucked and I shivered and I shook, and for two weeks I drunk myself stupid on native rum to survive. Once I had finished my detox, I began feeling human again. Now for the first time in almost three years I was completely Heroin free. I made a new friend. This new friend was a certain substance that I already knew a little bit, but I was now going to become really best friends with. My 'new best friend' was Crack Cocaine! It's similar to Cocaine in some ways, but different in many, many more. Crack Cocaine is like the angry older brother of the younger beautiful sister. And Crack wants a ruck! But I had thought, "That's a good idea, it's not Heroin after all" and off I went. All of a sudden

It's Not About Me!

there I was merely days after kicking my debilitating Smack habit, smoking Crack with the Rastas, downtown on the front line and in the ghettos in the French Caribbean Island of Guadeloupe. This was the sort of place where the white folk didn't go. Furthermore, it was unheard of for the Europeans to touch Crack, only Cocaine powder. And yet, here I was, a white kid who just didn't seem to care about getting down and dirty with a Crack pipe and the locals. They thought that was pretty cool, and so did I. I would spend much of my daytimes on the beaches with other travellers, wheeling and dealing between everyone, so that I could go spend whatever money I made on my own personal hit of Crack.

Smoking Crack is a profound and intense effect. You feel like you've suddenly been given power by the Gods and this goes straight to your head, though you're not necessarily empowered to do anything, you feel like you've already accomplished everything the Gods have asked you, and not you're reaping to rewards. So you expect everyone to treat you in a certain manner of respect. It renders you seriously selfish and self-centred. Everything must be done by your schedule and on your terms. Anything else is not acceptable. Meanwhile, you keep smoking to maintain this feeling of royalty, because during the comedown and withdrawal you feel dreadful and unable to engage in anything. The withdrawal leaves you obsessing about only one thing - getting high again. So that's what I found myself doing; permanently chasing something just out of reach.

Meanwhile, alongside my entourage from France, we put on a load of awesome outside raves, in some spectacular locations. Someone brought over a load of Es from Europe and we made money selling them and playing records at various raves, bars, clubs and parties for the full season - six months. But somewhere along the way, a guy showed up who had Subutex. I had no need for them. But I had a desire. I loved how they made me feel. And with Subutex, no one could tell you were stoned. So, believe it or not, I got myself connected. It was 1996/1997 and Subutex was not well known outside of the junkie circles. Subutex is synthetic morphine, which you consume by letting it dissolve under your tongue. It didn't get you high, but it did give you a warm sense of comfort and, for a junkie like me, it was easy to become attached. So when I did return to France that April, despite having kicked the Smack, I still returned with an opiate habit.

12. France, with a broken heart

I delayed coming back to France from the Caribbean because I had some unique DJ opportunities, but Césario and Lolette with whom I was firmly in love, left just as planned, three weeks prior to me. It then transpired that once she had got home, she had picked up her Heroin habit immediately which was truly disappointing to me since we had gone to the Caribbean mainly to help her give up Heroin, after all, I could deal with it. Not only that, but she'd also hooked up with a DJ friend of mine who gave her that first fresh taste of Heroin the very day she returned. In fact, it turned out that he had picked her up from the airport and she was stoned before she even got home. Effectively, by the time I came home three weeks later, she had moved him into our house and I was firmly pushed out. I was devastated! Then to rub salt further into the wound, she had given him most of my contacts for DJ bookings and he now answered the phone calls at her house, which the promoters used to contact me (this was before the era when everybody had a mobile phone). I found myself struggling for work, homeless, loveless, with my ego firmly battered. Crushed! Angry! Bitter! Revengeful!

I hit the Smack. I hit the Smack hard. I hit the Smack very hard indeed. I swiftly developed myself a very large habit as it was the only way I felt I could cope with the pain and perceived humiliation that I was experiencing. I was so resentful, and my thinking was crazy and twisted. I couldn't get them out of my mind. I had some friends who came from the Tahitian Mafia (Tahiti is another French-speaking colony) living in Toulouse. They were supporters of my cause, mainly because of our Cocaine business-related friendship, but also due to their integrity around how a man should treat another man's woman, and they rallied around me. They offered their assistance with whatever consequences I felt should be dealt to either of the deceitful pair. My decision was a 'middle of the night' visit to their residence, where they would castrate him and remove one of his hands, so that he could neither please my woman, nor play to my crowds. My revenge would be absolute. Now I've not shared this too often before, but as the hit was under way and they were driving out towards her house, they were stopped by chance at a peage (a French toll booth, all along their auto routes/motorways/highways - I feel like I'm writing this for various different dialects) by the flying customs (Les Douanes in French), who insisted on searching their car. They were all arrested when the weapons were found. My intended victim and my ex-partner never knew just how close they had been to a terrifying ordeal that would have changed their (especially his) lives forever. I knew that their escape must be a sign from karma, and so, despite feeling so much pain, I knew I needed to 'let go' and move on. But I couldn't. I was still totally obsessed with her. She had broken my heart. I would phone her, just to hear her answer the phone. If he answered, I'd put the phone down. If she answered, then I would listen until she put the phone down. I was really screwed up. But, fortunately, Smack brought me the oblivion I needed. Especially once I started injecting it, which I began doing with more and more frequency.

13. Scrumping

It was late spring 1998, and we were living in Toulouse - La Ville Rose. I had held down my Heroin habit for over four years already, but we were always looking for next enterprising idea.

In England, traditionally young boys (and girls) would go to farms and fields and steal some crops to take home to their family to feed them.

Scrumping generally refers to stealing apples and pears and other low-hanging fruit. We figured we'd try our hand at scrumping. We thought we could go to Normandy where the pharmaceutical companies grow poppies for opiate-based medicines such as codeine and morphine.

This was a six-man job (well, five men and one woman). We took two Transit vans out of Toulouse one morning, arriving in Normandy about eight hours later. We sussed out our target and, under the cover of darkness, we filled both of those Transit vans full of bin liners stuffed with fresh poppy heads. These vans were totally stuffed full to the brim with our illegal goods. It was simply a smash and grab job. If we had ever been pulled over with our stash in the van, there would have been no denying the evidence. So, we took our chances and headed the eight hours back south, homeward bound with our treasure.

Back in the safety of our site (usually squatted land), we took the poppy heads and begun to mix them with acetate to make a very low grade of opium, known in French/Arabic as 'Rashasha'. We made an impressive 13 kilos of the stuff. We tried to sell it but it really wasn't a popular buy in our area so we kept most of it for personal use. It was, as we discovered, extremely effective at getting us and anyone who came near us, very, very stoned. One of the by-products of the Rashasha manufacturing process was Poppy Tea using all the discarded poppy heads, which was a very large pile indeed, considering we had filled up two Transits vans full. So, we had ourselves Poppy Tea as our primary beverage for the next few months. It had an unusual and acquired taste that needed some getting used to, but I grew to love it, and I'm not usually a tea drinker.

On the first day, a single mug of Poppy Tea would leave you on the floor stoned and spinning out for eight hours or so. A single mug! Over the next three months - the time it took the six of us to work our way through the entire 13 kilos of Rashasha - I continued to consume cups and cups of that Poppy Tea. I had certainly acquired a taste for it and had developed an intense love affair with the stuff. It was the second best opiate-based drug I had ever gotten my hands on. Unfortunately, over time, my body developed a tolerance to it. By the end of the first week I was drinking three cups a day. By the end of the first month, I was drinking six or seven cups a day. By the end of three months, and towards the end of our stashed supply, I was drinking the poppy-head tea all day long and remaining comfortably happy, but not stoned. That was fine by me, but there came a point when there was simply no more tea left to drink. Now I needed to search out Heroin to replace my opiate addiction and I needed a lot of it to keep me happy. I needed a minimum of three grams to keep me from being sick in the mornings. I had taken my body to a whole new level of dependence. I tried to recover from this dependency, but I was never able to until I hit total sobriety. From here on in I would always be anxiously in search of my next good hit. I would be carrying with me a certain level of junkie sickness as my body physically craved a similar level of intoxication. It was downhill from here on in.

14. Needlework

I had been sporadically using Cocaine intravenously from the age of twenty-one, though I resisted consuming Heroin and other drugs regularly in this manner for a few more years yet. By the time I was twenty-four I was using the needle to get my hit on a daily basis. By the age of twenty-six I realised my body was shutting down and my physical health was deteriorating rapidly. At that point, I started looking for a way out. I was beginning to feel dreadful too much of the time, and no one really enjoys feeling dreadful. So I began my slow progress towards searching for an escape from this ever-increasing circle of destruction. When I was injecting myself, the intensity of the pleasure was limited to never more than forty minutes, and often much less. The consequences that came as a result of my addiction and drug habits were profound. Every morning, upon awakening I felt sick. I felt very poorly indeed. Whenever I couldn't find my drugs of choice - powdered Cocaine and brown Heroin (though I preferred white Heroin if I could ever get it) I would substitute it or rather fix it with various alternative drug cocktails, such as Subutex (synthetic morphine) or Methadone or codeine tablets from the doctor, the chemist or the street. I even became addicted to Nurofen Plus, buying from different chemists my habit was one box of 72 pills per day! I would always try to have a decent-sized stash of these alternatives, which I could use just in case. I was alcoholic, too, so I was constantly trying to pour enough alcohol in my system to keep me sane. Just getting out of bed every day, getting enough substances into my body to make me feel human, and putting a smile on my face was all becoming too hard. I didn't know how to handle it. I was losing it.

I was killing myself and I knew it. I started messing around with needles because they were exciting. Injecting Cocaine, I discovered, was an incredibly intense high. Injecting Cocaine did for me what nothing else had ever done for me before. But, naturally, to stay in control I had to balance it out with the appropriate amount of Heroin. I had a serious problem with Heroin, and I knew it. I needed a gram of the brown powder just to get out of bed and function. I couldn't get on with my day without it. I was addicted. The funny thing was, I thought I didn't have a problem with injecting Cocaine, I loved it... ...there was nothing wrong with that as far as I was concerned. But, my God, did I feel shitty once I woke up from my party.

I guess I was one of the more fortunate ones (or less fortunate depending upon how you look at it), since I had a reputation as a hard partying DJ with quality drugs, selling them to raise funds to keep my habit alive was fairly straightforward. I'd hit the streets of Toulouse with 10 grams of Smack in my left pocket and 10 grams of Coke in my right-hand pocket and I would sell it as I went along through my day, returning back to my pad to pick up more when it was required. I was using drugs anywhere, without shame or discretion. On the pavement, inside bars, at anyone's house, in any way. I didn't care. By the afternoons, I would be found in various bars drinking L'apero (early evening drinks), mostly Pastis - a favourite French drink made from aniseed and mixed with water. Please note, this is in no way part of the Pernod family. This was a 40 to 50% proof alcohol and the trick was to add as little water as you could tolerate. Certainly, the way I drank it was pretty hardcore. You would normally see me drinking it while DJing out of a plastic 2-litre bottle that I'd mixed myself. It was a staple part of the after-party diet. I am definitely guilty of drunk driving with it. In fact, I operated completely under the influence of Pastis, Heroin and Cocaine. Pastis was virtually the only liquid I consumed, aside from beer to accompany the cigarettes I'd be smoking when out and about. I never let go of my alcoholic tendencies right up to the end. The very end!

I suppose it would be appropriate to mention my first overdose at this point in the story. I was only using Cocaine in my spoons at the time, so when I put the spike into my arm it was just pure Charlie going into my bloodstream. I was still sniffing the Heroin for the moment. Having my own source of good quality Cocaine, meant that I had a pretty regular standard of purity. But I was out DJing at a Technival somewhere in the Pyrenees Mountains near Toulouse, when I met an old acquaintance of mine who was also dealing Coke. Believing my product to be superior to his, I did a straight swap of one gram for one gram really just to turn him on to my stuff. The idea in my mind was that he'd realise how much better my gear was than his and he'd start scoring off me in the future. How wrong and just how arrogant was I? I put his gram away for safe keeping until later, or for when I ran out of my own.

I played a couple of sets that weekend and headed back to a safe house that Sunday evening. I had been staying with another DJ friend and it was with him that I was doing most of my jacking up. I remembered I had this 'other' Coke to try out, so we split it between us. When I injected Cocaine, I always found the perfect amount was half a gram at a time - in a single hit. Half a gram straight into a vein took me to a place instantly overwhelmingly wonderful. Nothing mattered and nothing could stop me when I was high on that dose. This particular dose had always had the same effect on me. I felt on top of the world and for a brief moment I would feel completely connected to whomever I was using it with. It was a spiritual feeling of oneness and it sent a whistling sound through my ears as if all the bass had been turned down and I could only hear the secret whisperings of the treble and midrange. I felt love and I believed I flowed outwards with love too when I was in that place. It would last between 15 and 30 minutes before I began to come down enough to think about doing it all over again. Even writing it now, I'm feeling those sensations all over again. Cocaine calls to me. It is a simply wonderful disaster waiting to happen.

It's Not About Me!

My doses were always half a gram at a time, but this particular dose was a half gram that proved itself to be a lethal half gram size!

So, on this particular evening, at my buddy's flat, we hit up with this other Cocaine. I felt myself getting higher and higher having a major rush of my senses and feeling. Wow, this was a big one! I was going up and up, well past the place I'd normally go. Oh, no! This is 'on top'. Whooosh.

It turned out his Coke was actually a much higher quality than my own, which I was only to realise well after the hit. As the drug mixed with my blood and began rushing through my body I felt myself getting higher and higher and higher and higher. I knew this was a big one. Everything audibly went into top notes and the air began singing to me like a kettle boiling. I was instantly drenched through with sweat and I remember grinning and moaning with pleasure as I went so high and passed out.

When I came to, first of all I had no idea what had just happened. I came around to find my mate stood over me and my face throbbing with pain. I knew something had gone wrong. I was drenched in sweat and my ribs were badly bruised. I had a feeling of terror; I experienced this feeling of not knowing what had happened and not being sure why my brain seemed so slow to react. He had been punching me in the head and slapping me trying to revive me. He said I was out for over ten minutes. Out unconscious and he was genuinely fearful for my life. I couldn't believe it.

Here I was with my brain going through the reload process, which is similar to after you've fainted or been knocked out; it's like your brain is restarting as you gather your thoughts. It's definitely a scary place to be. It was as though my brain was being re-booted like a computer; everything turns itself back on, but it's not running on all cylinders yet. It takes a few minutes before you truly know what just happened, although you never truly know.

But he had done it; he had managed to keep me alive long enough for me to come back from this overdose. It shocked me right through, but the hardest, most shameful part was trying to justify to people why I had two black eyes for the next week or so, without letting them believe you've been beaten up or anything.

You see the thing about overdosing is that you don't know you're about to overdose. You just go over. You don't have time to make sure your affairs are in order, or to check that you've said what you want to say to whomever you deem important enough to say good-bye to. You simply go!

There are far too many people in coffins who never knew they were going into one. Overdosing is a one-way street that you never know you're about to turn down. You just never wake up from the rush. Strangely enough this was a loss of control that I enjoyed. And the first thing I wanted to do after coming to, despite the pain, the confusion and the muddled mind......was to have another hit, immediately. That, ladies and gentlemen is referred to as "Insane in my membrane"!

Did I learn my lesson? No, not exactly, but from this point on I did begin wearing long sleeves to start covering up the bruises that were appearing on my arms.

15. Washing up and Serving up

I built ties and made friends based upon my newfound situation, and this meant I also needed new suppliers and customers for drugs, especially Heroin, and the ever-expensive Cocaine, which I was consuming without impunity. I began washing my Cocaine to make 'freebase' aka Crack so I could smoke and get a bigger hit. This involved larger and larger amounts of Cocaine, so I could make enough to smoke sufficiently to make me feel like I'd hit the spot. With time, this would develop to such an extent that I would only hit that spot after four days of smoking.

I teamed up with a crew of guys who were importing Coke from Spain and Heroin from Holland. We distributed large amounts and were able to supply more than we could possibly consume. So when you've got more Coke and Heroin than you need, you feel obliged to consume as much as you can. I was washing Coke into 'freebase' for personal use initially in one-ounce ladles, and later five-ounce ladles, before finally graduating to ten-ounce ladles. It became my constant companion. I would come to a client's house to sell them Cocaine before heading into their kitchen to make my own rock and smoke it in their place. The saddest part came later. Once I had run out of my own supply of Coke, and before I could pick any more up, I would find myself desperate for a hit. I would then retrace my steps and return to the homes of the clients I'd previously visited to go through their used kitchen utilities and pipes which may have been used, scraping out any resin or tiny pieces of Cocaine or rock that I could find and attempted to re-smoke any dregs.

This was one of my lower points, since it shows me just how completely obsessed I had become with the drug, putting aside all personal relationships and social etiquettes, just to attempt (and normally fail) to achieve some sort of peace and comfort by smoking whatever discharge was left over in the trash.

These were the times I began to humiliate myself and I saw myself over a period of time become the person I never wanted to be. I started treating people badly, rudely and insincerely. Manipulation and deceit were the principles I began to live my life by. I began breaking all of my own taboos regarding the way I treated people. I stole from my friends and began ripping people off with more and more frequency. I did dodgy deals where I never delivered the goods, despite receiving the money, and I broke into various people's houses to take what I wanted. I took hostages as I would hold drug parties at people's houses despite their protestations of work the next day and I became less and less welcome. The way I treated people and the way I would take over someone's next few days were leaving me with fewer and fewer friends, and even fewer people that I could depend upon for support.

Someone, a friend of mine called Nico, who hadn't seen me for a couple of years had (dangerously) smuggled some white Heroin back from Thailand by himself in order to make his own fortune. There was just under 250 grams - a quarter of a kilo. Certainly there is a fair amount of money to be made with 250 grams of white Heroin, which is traditionally much more expensive and better quality than brown Heroin. He could easily be clearing £10,000 with an outlay of perhaps £250 for the actual gear over in Thailand. Unfortunately, he trusted me with the bulk of his gear, and he foolishly asked me to sell it for him. I ended up using most of it myself and keeping the majority of the money from any sales. I would tell him simple lies about where the sales were coming from, and bamboozled him with excuses as to why there was never any money materialising. Sadly, for him he had caught me at a time in my using career when I wasn't treating my friends very well and he became another victim to my addiction.

One Sunday morning, after a party the night before at someone's house for an after party from a Rave that had begun on Friday night, I was being pestered for some Cocaine. It wasn't widely known that I was a huge Heroin user. My DJ persona left most people believing I was using a lot of Cocaine, but it never really occurred to people that I used Smack also – especially when it game me such a rush of energy. Strangely perhaps, I got high on Heroin, not stoned. Because I was always wired and the Heroin didn't make me slow down, I just became more and more confident. This gave people the belief that I was taking Coke all the time, when in fact, I was using Heroin all the time, especially whenever I was out in public. In fact, Cocaine really became a private experience for me, something I did by myself, and not in public, particularly since nowadays I was injecting it. Anyhow, at this particular after party, the folks were convinced I had Coke and they became insistent that I share it. After about 45 minutes of my denial, I said they could share with me what I had, but that it wasn't Coke. They didn't believe me, especially after they saw me pour the white powder on to a mirror and tell them to help themselves. They were so greedy they cut themselves very long and large lines. I even asked them to cut one for me the same size and I insisted I take the first one (just to show them what I was capable of doing) and then I let them snort their own lines. Every single one of them (there were seven people there at the time) snorted their line eagerly, looked at each other with a puzzled look since they didn't recognise the taste of the line (snorting powders still allows you to taste the powder, but through some different receptors to your mouth or tongue) and then they hit the deck. They were all vomiting and severely gouching (nodding off). I needed to make sure no one overdosed, but I did laugh to myself watching them all completely out of it.

It's Not About Me!

Part 3.
ADDICTION
– the dying years

"Being the person I never wanted to be"

1. Death of a DJ

I didn't know much about denial. Now, looking back, I know that I had seen it a lot, in my friends and in the people around me. But I don't remember being in denial myself. Perhaps that is the whole paradox of denial, the person in denial doesn't know. I don't remember my own denial. However, I do remember that I knew I was an addict long before I was willing or ready to stop using completely. I just couldn't consider not using. That wasn't an option. The only option I would consider is using slightly differently, or altering my drugs slightly. Maybe I could use a new spot to inject into, or a new pipe to smoke through. I knew I was addicted. I even knew it was a problem. But it was a problem I was prepared to live with; my version of pain management. I knew there was something different in the way I behaved around drugs and alcohol. I knew that I had both a need and an overwhelming desire for them. I had an inability to say "No" to drugs, a gift that most of my mates, ravers and clients did seem to employ. Most people, including many of the people I was selling Heroin and Cocaine to simply had the ability and desire to choose when to use and when to remain straight. I never had this ability. I always used when offered drugs. In fact, I would take whatever drugs were in front of me without really considering what they were or to whom they belonged. I was reckless and chaotic. Often I would be up for days on end while the civilised world went about its business. I cared not which day of the week it was. I only cared about being high. And much of the time, I didn't care too much about what the source of my high was, so long as I reached oblivion and painlessness.

I knew I wasn't like other people in my behaviours and my patterns. I was far more extreme in my using. The lengths I went to just to ensure I would continue to be high or drunk were extraordinary, and just not normal. Long before I was willing to stop and long before I even attempted to stop, I knew I was an addict. I embraced it. I had no problem with being an addict as long as I had my gear. I had no problem being an addict so long as I could get my hands on everything I needed and it was all running smoothly. I had no problem being an addict so long as I could maintain my source of drugs and my multiple sources of income with which to keep purchasing them. As long as I had what I needed in my arm, up my nose or in my mouth to keep me feeling the way I needed to feel, I had no issue with the addiction itself. No issue at all. I don't know about denial, but I certainly didn't see it in myself.

As in many of the cases I deal with these days, I was the last person to know I had a serious problem, because despite the fact I knew I was an addict, for a long time I believed I had it under control. I still believe I successfully maintained my Heroin addiction, right up until the last year or so. For many years as a functioning addict I was a successful DJ, I was successful at generating money through smuggling and trafficking, I had successful friends and even a semi-long-term girlfriend, who was drop dead gorgeous - a complete eye turner. I achieved what I had wanted to achieve; I had arrived! I had become what I wanted to become - the successful DJ with an unlimited drug supply and the ability to consume as much as I wanted. Topped off with a beautiful woman by my side, supported by plenty of lovers and one night stands in the background whenever I could get away with them (without being caught by the girlfriend). It was the other people who knew me a little longer who saw the changes in me and noticed I had a problem. The changes were subtle. I became less friendly, less happy, less smiley, far more intense, with a frown perpetually plastered across my face. With Heroin, I would see something that was funny but would find it impossible to laugh. My emotions were flat. Despite my cognitive senses knowing that a situation was happy or sad or funny or painful, I just couldn't feel it. Heroin suppressed my feelings sufficiently, so that I cared for no one except myself and for nothing outside of my own selfish grasp.

When you're using Heroin, you understand a situation and you can comprehend what's going on but you don't feel it anymore. I would be having what could be described as the greatest time of my life, yet I wouldn't feel it. I would feel quite numb, so I would go through these events and experiences over days, months, years, and not really achieve anything. I noticed I started changing my drug using patterns so I would use much more often by myself. I began to prefer my own company and I became self-centred and self-sociable. I began missing gigs I was booked for, or I would disappear shortly after playing to be by myself with my drugs. People saw that I was no longer the happy-go-lucky person I was before. I was no longer the party animal and the centre of attention. The smile was literally wiped off my face. I became the most anti-social person at the party and, once my drugs were sold or my deals were made, or once I'd played my set I would go off to use drugs by myself, often for days on end. I would probably still be awake mid week sometime.

Due to my irregular behaviour and my anti-social attitudes towards other people, the DJing work dried up and I effectively ruined my own career. I sabotaged the chances life was offering me. Instead of being able to hold down my real passion and live my life through music, I had opted for the other life following the drug highs and lows, and I was struggling to keep that together now.

So, when I started using needles, it became a much more personal event. Smoking Crack became smaller groups rather than larger groups. In order to keep generating money, I became more of a shark. I started ripping people off and I started becoming the kind of person I didn't want to become. I started doing things I didn't want to do. I was doing all the things I'd seen people doing when I was just starting out in my drug-using career and said to myself "I'm not going to do that." But, I still could not imagine my life without drugs and alcohol.

2. Run away!! Run away!!

Living in Toulouse in 1998 with a tasty Crack habit to supplement my Heroin habit was one thing, but once I began messing around with my newfound needle fixation, injecting Cocaine seemed to be the only antidote for my ever-decreasing life. It still made me feel absolutely wonderful - at least for 15 or 20 minutes, but karma was no longer on my side. Things were going to change. They were bound to change. Whereas previously I had been an inherently good person who messed around with drugs and things, now I had become and inherently bad person for whom everything revolved around taking and finding and supplying and consuming drugs. It's no surprise that my standard and quality of life was deteriorating with this sort of karma being thrown up around me.

I crashed around from house to house, party to party, abusing my welcome. I even dug out a space for me and my girlfriend (of the moment) in someone's garage during the 1998 World Cup in France. I remember celebrating on the streets of Toulouse with loads of English fans after they won a match, and selling them Charlie and showing them to some good clubs where I could keep an eye on them and sell them more as and when they required it. I also remember banging up Coke throughout that tournament and when France finally won, celebrating alongside them with a large speedball - one of the first times I started mixing Heroin and Cocaine and injecting them together.

Another place of residence I often enjoyed was a walk-in wardrobe in a friend's small flat, which I shared with her and her daughter, often sleeping in her daughter's bed after she'd gone to school, and getting up as she came home that afternoon. It was while I was dossing here that I had a delivery to make back in the UK. But I still had a bag of Cocaine to consume - about 40 grams. I had a boat booked from San Sebastian in Northern Spain - about a four-hour drive away - to take me back over to Portsmouth, but for four solid days I kept cancelling the boat ticket and would get it put off for 24 hours, promising myself I'd get the next one. I was, however, absolutely powerless and unable to stop injecting the Cocaine, until it was all gone! This is one of the more profound and extreme examples that I recall when I think about my powerlessness; my absolute inability to do what I was tasked to do, because of an overwhelming power that controlled me so much that I simply couldn't stop injecting all that Coke until it was finished. I didn't sleep. I just kept on going through the bag of Charlie until it was done. By then I was far too out of it to drive to the ferry and fortunately I had the foresight to know this. I just had to crash out. I slept for the next 24 hours before scoring enough Heroin to get me started again and headed off on my return trip back to the UK on a quick mission to transport something over there - I think it was Spanish Ecstasy tablets.

Cocaine and Heroin seemed to be the best of partners and they became my love affair for seven years. I had experimented with all the different methods of consuming both the drugs. I was an intravenous drug user. I used to love injecting Cocaine. Injecting half a gram was my number one hit. It was always half a gram. But, strangely, I enjoyed sniffing Heroin, which is really weird because

ADDICTION – the dying years

most people will tell you to inject Heroin and snort Cocaine. I had it the other way around and maybe that is why I found Heroin so useful. Heroin kept me going. I might be completely delusional here, and I probably am, but I don't believe too many people actually knew. I don't think many people truly knew I was a Smack addict. I don't think many people figured that I was speed-balling my way through life and that I was using Heroin and Cocaine together quite so much or so regularly. I think I held it together pretty well, considering. Even when I was sweating through my clothes, people just thought I was using Coke. When I was twitching they thought it was because I had had too much caffeine. When I was nodding off to sleep it was because I was genuinely tired, I had been working far too hard. But for those next seven years I chose to be a man who kept many secrets closely concealed, allowing only a limited number of very trusted friends to really see what I had become.

So I was in a small gang from Toulouse, selling fairly large amounts of Cocaine, Heroin and other bits 'n pieces around South-West France, and the police knew what we were up to; even who many of us were. We were a team of twelve dealers and I we knew we were under surveillance.

The police were keeping an eye on us and they knew that we were responsible for a fair amount of Cocaine and Heroin trafficking and distributing going on around Southwest France and Northern Spain at the time. I watched from behind a Cocaine haze as the other eleven got picked up. They were all arrested and some of them began squealing (informing to the police on the others). Most of them got a few years prison time but some of them could still be inside today some 13 years later. We were some serious players. I knew that my time was coming and the reports were coming back to me as to who had informed on me. It was another needle-using junkie buddy of mine. I was dismayed at his lack of courage to front up the police and keep his mouth shut. But he squealed and he squealed loudly about me - Le Salle Putain D'Anglais (the dirty English bastard). I knew it was coming on top for me, but no one ever really knew where I dossed. I had no fixed address and neither did my latest girlfriend, a sweet-hearted, Cocaine-loving, drop-dead gorgeous Go-Go dancer called Leticia. We were currently hiding out at her adopted Mother's apartment in a respectable neighbourhood, with her husband who was about thirty years older than her. I never quite knew the family dynamics but I knew I was safe and unlikely to be located.

So I knew they were looking for me, but they never knew where to find me, particularly since I always just floated from one place to another, rarely staying for too long, unless I began drinking in a bar, in which case I'd likely spend the rest of the evening there, before heading back to the safety of my girlfriend's place with her adopted family. I don't think she was actually adopted, but I think she felt so safe with this family that she adopted them, and they had no kids of their own and thus had given her a room and some space of her own.

I watched them all get picked up and start grassing one another up to save their own skin. I knew it was 'on top' and I knew that my time in Toulouse was just about up. I'd outspent my welcome. I needed to leave. It was time to leave.

November 1998, in Toulouse, Southwest France, and it was my birthday. So we were planning a large Rave to celebrate. We had sold 3,000 tickets, so there were plenty of guests coming to my party. I was the headline act, and between my Manager Césario organising the whole event, and Letitia my girlfriend taking care of the Go-Go dancers and fashion show, we had a massive event to pull off. Sadly, that night I never showed up. I had visited the site while everyone was setting it up, but left around 7.30 pm to go and get showered. I was never to return. I knew I was going to get picked up that night. I never turned up to my own birthday party because I knew the police were coming to arrest me. The heat was too much. We could feel them. We could sense them. We knew they'd be part of the crowd that evening. I later had it confirmed to me that there were indeed around twenty under-cover cops who came to grab me that night.

Finally, the police were catching up with me and I knew I wasn't ready to do time. The night of my birthday party, I was smuggled into Spain by some close friends, where I began a cold turkey withdrawal in the Spanish Pyrenees. Getting out of France had been the easy part. It was getting out of Europe and back to the UK that was tricky. When I arrived in Spain it was my birthday, at the end of 1998. I was now even more wanted in France, than I had ever been in Britain. It was definitely time to go home.

When we arrived in Spain, I lay low at a friend's place in the beautiful mountains that are the Pyrenees, while he was working during the pre-ski season, building chalets. When I told him of my dilemma he immediately agreed to take me in as we had been friends for quite a while by that stage and we had previously watched each other's back. It turned out there were a few other fugitives hiding in that village including a guy from Essex who had been caught up with the gangster Carlton Leach and had allegedly been somehow involved in the triple 'Range Rover murders' in Rettendon in 1995 which had been well publicised even over in France. I never knew who he was exactly, or his involvement in the actual crime, but I got the strong impression he was concerned he'd be killed if he returned to England, so who knows what he'd been up to?

Anyhow, as I said, I lay low a few weeks and did my own detox there in the cold mountains with just Pastis to take the edge off. Before long I was chomping at the bit ready to go party again. I set myself up with a few weeks' worth of DJ gigs in Spain around Barcelona, and headed down there for some fun. My girlfriend Leticia joined me down there and, strangely, out of a place of loneliness and dependency I proposed marriage to her. She accepted.

My partying was still wild and the weekends were very long affairs, which involved travelling all over the place between after-party and after-party. One end of weekend on a Tuesday, I ended up in Perpignan, just over the border back in France. I must have been particularly hammered to have agreed to go back into France, but as is often the case when you're high and in party mode, you simply go where the party takes you. So, once in France, I figured I'd take the chance and quickly visit Toulouse again, checking in on one of my Cocaine-dealing friends called Sam (not likely to be his real name). We went off to party again and subsequently rebuilt my Heroin habit. Sam was a French Arab whose family came from Tunisia, and he had great integrity. He never let me down; if he said he was going to do something, he did it. Similarly, he would let me know the truth if I was being foolish. Sam offered to help me with my plans to get home.

So, with Leticia and Sam, I went back into Northern Spain, crossing somewhere through the Pyrenees, and headed towards another party. I hooked up with some of my DJ friends and one of them had to cancel a forthcoming gig he had booked for the next weekend in London. He offered to give me his slot. So, armed with this motivation to get back into London (I was still being hunted in France), and with a large number of records (my only prized possessions), I took Leticia and Sam with me to San Sebastian the Northwest Spanish port. From there, we drove Sam's car on to the boat where they didn't look too closely at my passport, since I was an English guy going home. The scrutiny was more on the French passports coming from Spain. Sam financed the trip for us and, arriving back in London, I showed him around the city before he headed back to France. Leticia stayed, and that was the beginning of a new and terrifying chapter of the dying days of addiction.

Now I was back in London with a nasty Heroin habit and Cocaine obsession, a very cute French chick to support, a few boxes of records, and little way of earning any money or being able to support her love of Cocaine and my desperate need for Smack.

I had arrived back in England after a six-year self-imposed exile. It was early 1999 and I had returned home with a serious drug habit. I had no money, I had no connections and I didn't know whom I could trust or where I could stay. I was back in my homeland and I was sick to the bone. It was one of the loneliest periods of my life. My life was in shatters. I didn't come close to resembling the proud and accomplished Ian of a few years ago. My life had taken a turn for the worst; but there were bad times still to come!

3. Family ties

Having left my parents' house aged sixteen at the earliest moment I felt I could run, I carried this attitude of arrogance about me. I carried a rather juvenile "I'll show them" type of mentality. I made sure that they knew as little as possible about what I was up to, what challenges I was facing and the drugs I was using. Often they had no idea where in the world I was. I wanted to shield them from the truth about me as well as protect my lifestyle and allow it to continue unchallenged by figures of authority or potential influence. I knew that I was heading to places, both on earth and in my mind, they would never comprehend. The concept of living my life out of society and wandering around Europe having fun was far too removed from their middle-class western ideals of what life should be. They never would have understood. I had turned my back on society and its principles and I had run with theories of Libertarianism and other idealistic ways of life - anarchy and individual freedom from the oppression of authorities that may try to stop us from enjoying ourselves at the expense of society and mainstream lifestyles. I was living such an outrageous alternative lifestyle, that even hippies would throw caution my way.

So, I caught up with my parents only once or twice every year or two. Certainly during the early 90s they heard very little from me, although towards the end of the 90s, when Lolette and I were involved in a vehicle accident in Toulouse and both of us were hospitalised, my parents did come over to visit us. We had been travelling back from a Technival in North-West France, driving a medium-sized Mercedes truck full of people and sound equipment all the way back to

Toulouse - a nine-hour trip in one journey! A mammoth task, complicated further by the owner of the truck insisting that he was the only one allowed to drive and even more so by his Heroin habit. Inevitably, he gouched out before we made it home - although we were actually on the outskirts of Toulouse when he gouched out - and the truck veered across the road and into a petrol station sign (fortunately not into the pumps, for that would have been absolutely fatal). Of the dozen of us in the vehicle, I hit the back of my neck on the crossbar of a generator with a fairly large and heavy 500w speaker on my face pushing my neck back. To this day, I have damage to my neck and upper back from that accident. But ultimately, we were all bloody lucky - very lucky indeed. God was watching over us that day. My parents were always supportive and never turned their backs on me despite my rudeness towards them. They stood by me and bailed me out from time to time, when they saw me or heard from me and I chose to manipulate some money from them, which, certainly in later years, I began to do more and more.

I knew that my lifestyle was taking me further away from reality and what society called reasonable behaviour, but I was so caught up in it all, that it became my reality. I was living the way I believed was right, although retrospectively, I was causing more and more harm to myself and other people.

After returning to London late in 1998, I began to have contact with my parents and, more importantly, my little sister again. In fact, for a short while, Leticia and I lived at my parents' home, while we tried to get ourselves together enough cash to rent somewhere else. I remember my mother and Leticia really didn't take to each other. Leticia was certainly an abrasive character. If I'm honest, she was more a trophy girlfriend/fiancé to me. She was so very beautiful (previously she'd been a very sought after dancer), that when I seduced her I wanted to keep her just to show everyone I could be with such a head-turner. Unfortunately, she struggled with her own demons and we would frequently fight as we both fought for control of our own conflicting destinies. I guess my mother could see her manipulation and may have blamed her for some of the choices I was making. One thing I knew though, Leticia loved Cocaine and seemed to attract it easily. I loved Cocaine and I loved Heroin and I thought I loved Leticia, but I suspect I really just loved the image of a woman like Leticia. Not surprisingly, perhaps, our relationship didn't last forever, but while it did, it was certainly never without drama for too long.

4. A very grey looking London

Now I found myself back in London, but without any of the support I was used to in the sunny South of France and the Costa Bravo in Spain. I had nobody to purchase drugs from. I had nobody to sell drugs to. I had limited experience of my scene and my culture and how it had evolved during the previous six years. I tried hanging out with some of my old mates, but that just felt so uncomfortable. There was so much water under the bridge, and such different experiences of the 1990s that we were unable to find a middle ground on which to connect. I tried assimilating back into the culture of ravers and crusties that I'd left behind, but even they felt removed from my world; at least that's how I felt. They were often the folks who'd not been able to find the courage, or enough reason to take their cultural movement to the next level and start travelling. Not that I judged them for this. It's simply that I was in a position and foolhardy enough to go for it and some of my old crew were held back by restrictions, mostly family and children, but often drug habits before their time, or some other responsibilities that tied them back home. Now I was back on their territory and I felt lost, like a fish out of water. I was lost in a city and culture that I knew so well, but yet not at all.

So, I was home and I was lonely. My relationship with Leticia was deteriorating rather rapidly, as we fought more and more often. Really, what I wanted was Heroin and oblivion, but what she sought was companionship and Cocaine. She had her own battles with mental illness, but we were devoted to one another, even if it was a misguided sense of loyalty on my part. We were worlds apart, joined by a few shared experiences. But she couldn't control herself or her temper. She would punch and kick me, or pull a knife out and threaten to cut herself or cut me. She would go into screaming sessions for little or no apparent reason.

We were living together in a very tense atmosphere. On one occasion, I was so appalled by her attitude that I took her hand and used it to punch my own face, refusing to actually hit her or cause any physical harm to her. I've never been a person that hits women. But on this occasion I was using her hand to punch my face and we heard her finger snap as it broke on my cheekbone. Filled with remorse and apologies, I took her straight to A&E to get it fixed up. Our relationship was so up and down, but we always finished off any big argument back in bed together, fulfilling our fantasies on one another. It was a dark relationship that reflected this dark time in my life. Did I love her? Yes, I believe I did.

Eventually, we were able to call it a day and she returned to France after about a year of some intense fighting, often violent and plenty of 'make-up' sex.

We're still in contact with one another and we encourage each other with our mutual paths. I've since made my peace with her, and I'm strangely still slightly protective of her.

But it was at this point, after her return to France, that my Heroin habit and lust for Crack Cocaine really flared up. Finally, I was able to do what I wanted and be whom I wanted once again. Disappointingly, all I wanted right then was to get stoned - very stoned. I wanted to get very stoned indeed. And, to get rather high in between.

5. Seeking the Dalai Lama

I was running around chasing the highs and lows, and generally staying out of trouble despite being in the middle of it and, at one point in the Autumn of 1999, not long after Leticia had left, my mate Adam and I went on a drug run to India to do some exploring, some soul searching and potentially get clean...again.

Adam and I had knocked around together since the very early 90s when we had met in the New Cross squatting circles and were part of the New Cross Posse together, living together and pulling tricks together. We were known as two likely lads who would head off on missions that would last days, even weeks, taking us all over England and later on occasion into Europe, to procure something or other and generally have a good adventure during the process, whether or not we were successful. He'd stayed largely but not uniquely in England, and I'd headed off to Europe, but we'd hooked up together whenever I was in London and whenever he was on the French side of the Channel. Now I was back to scraping a living again with Adam alongside me. We were almost inseparable, and one day, as we were knocking around in West London trying to support our mutual drug habits (there's strength in numbers) we had the wonderful idea that India would make a great destination to clean ourselves up and bring some business back into London. And so, we headed to Delhi in early September, with a vague ambition to detox from Heroin and bring some other drugs back into the country.

It's Not About Me!

The first surprise I had was our ability to score Heroin and have needles in our arms within 45 minutes of touching down, including the process of going through customs and heading to the Paharganj district - the street market zone filled with very cheap rooms and plenty of International hippie travellers. But the biggest surprise was that we'd been sold white Heroin by one of the Chiefs of Police, and even been supplied needles in his friend's shop where we had met him. Not quite the detox we had planned back in England. The Heroin was of such great quality and it cost such a pittance, there was little chance I would actually get clean here. It was a Smack Head's paradise.

We soon settled into this life and stayed a few weeks in white-Smack bliss, taking in the culture and people. I had a great time wheeling and dealing around there. I soon made friends with some local brothers who owned a small shop selling rugs and carpets, with a side business in cheap Heroin for tourists. Once again, I had landed in foreign lands and found myself on very close terms with a major dealer. They allowed Adam and me to sleep in their shop surrounded by luxurious cushions and drapes, in exchange for our loyalty and ability to further distribute their Heroin. It was really fairly comfortable actually.

I became a vender of Heroin on the streets of Delhi, although my clients were obviously not native Indians, but British, Western Europeans, Australasians, South African, some Americans and other Western tourists seeking La Poudre Blanc (white powder) in exotic India. I soon became a go-to guy for many of the regular users on the street, and I felt safe because of the relationship I had with these brothers, who were clearly well connected.

After about eight weeks, we became restless, and recalling our original ambitions we knew we had a vague itinerary we wanted to follow; the procurement of India's and the World's finest Hashish, but only after we'd been north into the beautiful mountains to chill out and potentially find a place we felt comfortable enough to cluck out our Heroin detox at.

We set our compass for Dhār masala, in the Himalayas, hoping to hang out with - or so we believed - the Dalai Lama. Up in these mountains the Dalai Lama has his permanent residence, and has been returning back to Dhār masala from his global tours ever since he was first exiled from his home country of Tibet in 1959. We thought we would pay him a visit. You know, just drop by and see what he's up to. In retrospect, it's not really surprising that he didn't give a couple of junkies an audience, but at the time we believed he would welcome us into his home.

ADDICTION – *the dying years*

We arrived in the mountains and found a small hotel. This 'hotel' was actually just four similar sized, simple and undecorated rooms with a single corrugated iron roof and single glassless windows with a small drape as a curtain, to plot up in. At least each room had its own shower (hose) and toilet combo, though none of them were enclosed. They were very much part of the room. It was my 28th birthday, 9th November 1999 and after the 11-hour coach journey northward out of Delhi into the mountains, we decided we each ought to have ourselves a hit of Heroin in celebration. I don't know why I overdosed that evening. The hit wasn't any bigger or smaller than usual. There wasn't anything different in my preparation. I just felt myself coming up on the Smack (so titled because it comes up on you so fast that it feels like someone's Smacked you right into a new consciousness) and I knew I was in trouble.

As the wave of euphoria exploded throughout my body, my blood swept through me, bringing me higher and higher until my body went into shock and began sweating profusely. I knew I was in trouble as I felt myself heading into unconsciousness. I wobbled over towards the shower as I felt myself coming up so strongly and turned on the tap (there was only cold water here) to douse myself and try to cool myself down. I collapsed in the shower. Adam, in the room next door had heard the thump when I fell and rushed in - there were no locks in this place - just as I was gurgling on the water collecting around my head. I would have drowned if he hadn't been there. He swung me over into the recovery position and began the process of trying to wake me up and get me moving again. Strangely, it was the vomiting out of the water that I remember saving me from the unconscious vortex that was waiting for me. I was once again very fortunate. I may have never seen my 29th year. Although that was by no means a wake-up call for me, it was to be my final birthday Smack fix. As you may have guessed, tomorrow was another day. For the time being, I wasn't ready to stop. In the morning I just wanted another hit. Complete insanity!

We ran out of Heroin after ten days and in the mountains we could only score Hashish. It was very good Hashish mind you. Some of the very best Hashish in the world to be precise. All Indian Hash is of outstanding quality. Nothing like the standard Soap Bar style Moroccan Hash you largely get in the UK and across Europe. It was brought up from the Malawi valleys, and distributed around India and the rest of the world. So we had access to the very best Hashish, but it was not Heroin. We figured that since Heroin largely came from Afghanistan, we should at least head in that direction, in order to secure the better quality and bigger quantities for our money. Looking on a map, it appeared quite obvious to us that we should be heading to Kashmir. Kashmir stood on the disputed region between India and Pakistan, and the area was still officially declared a war zone. Kashmir was the sort of place you could tell used to be a well-developed and exclusive retreat for the wealthy, maybe thirty or forty years ago. But it had been left unattended, underdeveloped and neglected for so long, that everything was becoming threadbare and rundown. Regardless of this, however, Kashmir was beautiful. It is located in the Western Himalayas around an enormous and still lake, with a perfect view of the magnificent mountains.

But it's SNAFU, which meant that electrical power was frequently being cut off and bombs could be heard on a daily basis. Even the UN presence had moved on a long time before and just left the Indian and Pakistani forces to fight it out for themselves. We stayed on a houseboat, where a family would rent the whole boat as an apartment for their vacation. But alas, the cold winter months were approaching and I doubted many families were still vacationing up here in this war zone.

Since we were withdrawing very heavily when we arrived, our priority was to score some Heroin right away, but we soon found this very difficult. It wasn't that we couldn't find any. It was that we couldn't buy any.

We were always sold fake products, such as soap powder and other white household powders. These people were very desperate for our money and had little sympathy for our plight. We were sold phoney package after phoney package and eventually we realised we were not going to score. We had also begun to spend the money we'd put aside to buy our drugs for importation back into the UK. We lasted in Kashmir a short week before heading back towards Delhi, very junkie sick and drinking Indian spirits from the bottle to keep us distracted from the rather discomforting withdrawals we were both undergoing. We needed to get back to Delhi as rapidly as possible where we knew we could buy Heroin that was genuine - so much for our detox. I guess neither of us was strong enough at that point, especially when we knew we could score if we made the effort to take the action to go and get it.

Via a series of different transits, I went back towards my friends at the shop we had dossed at when we first arrived. During the first leg of the journey, Adam got severely drunk, antagonistic and obnoxious as hell to everyone who crossed our paths as we came down the mountains in an overloaded Land Rover, and I somehow got lost from him when we stopped off to change vehicles in

Gurdaspur. I don't blame him though; getting drunk was a wise thing to do with the limited resources available and us feeling so dreadful in full withdrawal, and I would have been a grouchy nightmare with all my bitching and moaning. I didn't see Adam again for over two weeks!

Back in Delhi, scoring was easy. I waited for Adam to find me, and when he did, he turned up with a few hundred grams of Charas from the Malawi Valley. Charas refers to the method of the Hashish's fabrication, in this case hand-rolled Hashish; so, it's some of the very finest Hashish in the world, made by hand.

By this stage, it was time to get ready to go home, in time for the New Year. It would be a perfect time to be selling our wares. A cheap and easy way to top up our income back home would be by importing Ketamine. Buying Ketamine was simple in Delhi. It's sold at any chemist. I don't know why or what for, and I didn't care, I just wanted to stock up. In England, vets use Ketamine to anaesthetise animals, but in India, who knows what it's used for. It's an anaesthetic and it comes in a clear liquid, with no odour whatsoever. We poured it into a couple of two-litre empty bottles of Evian and carried it home disguised as water. Due to its lack of smell, colour and, to a degree, inability to have much effect if drunk in small amounts, disguising it as water was perfect. This was back in the days when you could carry liquids on flights. We also managed to build such a relationship with the Indian shop owners that they trusted me with 150 grams of Heroin on credit too. That was rather foolish of them for, as soon as we got it, we were gone and, of course, never returned to Delhi again.

6. Trying to get clean

I then entered the period of my life where I tried various methods to get clean, failing to realise what precisely becoming clean meant. All I ever really seemed to achieve, though I'd never have admitted it back then, was a switch in substance addictions, none of which were particularly helpful, healthy or leaving me feeling happy. In fact, I was feeling miserable more and more of the time. I began to grow another permanent frown on my face. I was turning unrecognisable. I was no longer the person I used to be. And I didn't like it!

I had various strategies for detoxing and getting myself off Heroin. The most successful one I tried was to inject liquid Ketamine for a week instead. I would draw the liquid directly into a syringe from its transparent container and put it straight into a vein. This meant I would anaesthetise myself immediately and completely, thus rendering me unable to feel the withdrawal symptoms from Heroin. Then, if I had anyone visiting me, or if people came over to buy drugs I would add MDMA (Ecstasy) into the mix, so I would not only feel nothing, but I would love everybody as well. It made me more pleasant to be around. I was particularly fond of this method. I said that this was the most successful strategy I tried. It was not actually successful. Not at all! At the end of a five-day stretch of self-medication, I would come out feeling largely better than before; not great, but not awful either. So then, a little voice in my head would tell me that I was better; that I had kicked the habit, broken my addiction, and that I would be fine. My system was cleaned out and I could now return to getting high without the consequences of a Heroin habit. Perfect, just as long as I didn't use Heroin. After all, that was my only real problem, right?

I would convince myself I was cured of my addictions, so I would promptly attempt to socialise and be the nice, funny, centre of attention guy heading out that night, and stumble upon some Cocaine. I would hit the Coke with relish, knowing that I wasn't using Smack, so I'd be all right. It was at this point that it would start all over again. I don't know about anyone else, but I never did Crack without Smack and, true to form, just as soon as I started using Cocaine I would need Heroin again, regardless of the consequences. I would set out just to use Cocaine, but at some point during that trip my mind would distract me from my goals and start chatting away to me about the benefits of adding Heroin to the mix, just this time...and then, I'd find myself under some sort of invisible instruction to go and do precisely the thing I never wanted to be doing. It was like I was hypnotised. I couldn't fight it.

Lady H was my lover, and she always helped me feel great. I would persuade myself that the only times I didn't feel great was when I turned my back on her, so I ought to just make more of an effort to ensure I always had her in my life. Cocaine made my head talk all types of rubbish, but the bigger load of bullshit I told myself was that this time things would work out fine. I was turning insane, believing that Heroin was saving me, and then feeling sorry for myself when it ran out. I was nuts believing that Cocaine was what I needed in order to be Ian, and then going crazy in my mind if I didn't have Heroin to keep me cool. Sadly, there was never any control. I was never able to safely use Cocaine without wanting more, just like I was never able to use Heroin without needing more.

ADDICTION – *the dying years*

I was out of control! As soon as I put Heroin in my system, my body would instantly begin craving Cocaine, more and more and more as the cycle continued. It went on like that for seven years.

Before I came back into the UK, while living in Southern France, with all my daily dealings and a fairly successful chain of customers, I had comfortably held down a habit of both Cocaine and Heroin. I would walk around with 10 grams in each pocket; 10 white, 10 brown. But I came back into the UK with no sources to score, no people to sell to, no people to play records for and no way to earn any sort of money. I had nothing going for me anymore apart from an old culture of friends I had left behind six years before who simply weren't in the same place as I was. Suddenly, at the end of 1999, my whole world started crashing in on me as I realised I had an enormous love affair with Cocaine and Heroin, and that I had no way of supporting that love affair. It was a feeling of sheer desperation. I started doing more of the things that I really didn't want to be doing, I started turning into a person who scared me. I started stealing from people who gave me any opportunity. I tried to limit my thieving to only those occasions when I believed the victim wouldn't know it was me who had done it. But that really didn't work out the way I had planned either. I started lying my way both in and out of situations, and since I had already successfully mastered the art of creative fictionalising, now I would use it again to get my needs met. Now, instead of using it to keep me out of trouble, I was using it to get what I wanted. I began finding ways of manipulating anyone who came into my life, making sure that I got everything I could out of them. Everyone was a pawn in my game and everyone served a purpose. I no longer respected personal relationships. It was always about what that person could do for me, what they could get me, what they could give me that would make them worthwhile. I was selfish and self-centred to the very core of my being. Any woman who walked into my life at that point was treated unfairly, was treated badly. She'd be taken for whatever she had in her purse, or whatever I felt I could get from her, including living expenses, food, accommodation or whatever else she had to offer. Sometimes I had sexual liaisons, but these were never romantic, loving or caring. They were simply handled as getting my needs met, and they were often, though not exclusively, with other junkie women, who had their own agendas.

7. Dying days

I knew I needed to make some changes but, in the last six months of my active using, I really knew I had become someone I didn't want to be. I was doing stuff I didn't like. I disliked the way I was treating people. I didn't like the person I'd become and I realised that this wasn't the life I wanted to be living. It had been fun along the way, but I wasn't having fun anymore and I wanted out. It took me a long time to process this idea both internally and externally before I was able to accept that at a gut level my old life was truly over, and I found the courage to start again. It took a very long time to surrender to my addiction. I knew the life I was living wasn't the one I wanted to live but it still took a great deal for me to actually make the changes necessary that transformed my world.

At age twenty-six, I was in Europe and I was dying. Physically, my body was deteriorating rapidly. I'd experienced my first overdose and, although it scared me, my love affair with Cocaine was so powerful that I wasn't prepared to stop injecting it just because of a near-death experience. I had a needle in my arm the very same day I had that first OD. When I overdosed three years later in India, I was hardly put off at all. In many ways it just reinforced my thinking that this stuff was much better and I must, therefore, be having an even better time. I was really getting more and more twisted emotionally, physically and intellectually.

When I got myself smuggled back to the UK early February 1998, I was twenty-seven and I was very ill. I started looking for some help but I didn't know what sort of help I wanted. I didn't really want to give up injecting Cocaine; I didn't really want to give up smoking Crack, in fact, I didn't really want to give up doing anything. I just wanted some help, maybe some money, a place to live would be nice.

And once Leticia had left in the spring of 1999, and after I'd returned from my gallivant around India, I really did enter into the darkest days of my life. The new Millennium was not bringing about much reason to celebrate, once the New Year's Eve party was over. Incidentally, on New Year's Eve, I found myself on the north bank of the Thames, opposite the London Eye, with a few friends. At two minutes to midnight I simply stuck my rolled up tube ticket and using it as a straw, I plunged it into my bag of five or so grams of Cocaine powder and took a massive sniff. I continued to do this all the way as we walked back to Maida Vale. It took us about three hours, but I don't say this to show off. I say this because what shocked me the most retrospectively was that I didn't share any of my Coke. I did it all by myself and was hiding it from the others, as best as I could by crouching down to mimic doing my shoelaces up, or pretending to take a pee. I was greedy, self-centred and thinking only of my needs and myself. I hated myself for this, but I simply wasn't prepared to share.

From then on, the year 2000 saw me scrounging around doing petty crime. My only source of grocery shopping was a 24-hour petrol station, as I couldn't frequent the streets too much during daylight hours anymore; I was too scared. Paranoid that something could happen to me. Someone could get me - the police, other junkies, dealers, people I owed money to, street gangs, anyone. I was even terrified of having to engage in a conversation with the general public. I'm not sure what I was scared of, but looking back I suspect I was scared of being found out that I was just little ole insignificant me. I wasn't who I wanted to be and I wasn't who I wanted you to think I was. Therefore, I didn't want to get found out. I felt like a fraud trapped in my own body, only able to communicate fearlessly when stoned. I went to the local GP Surgery and told the doctor, "Look I just need a little help. Can you give me a little something? Some codeine or some Subutex or some dia-morphine...Smack?" I guess secretly I was always hoping I'd get the dia-morphine prescription, though it never came.

The doctor sent me to the nurse and she was really sympathetic. In fact, she was really kind and she gave me clean syringes, which were certainly helpful. They gave me an air of legitimacy about my using and encouraged me to bang up more regularly, with cleaner works. She really appeared to care, but we both knew that she really couldn't do a thing. I did try to help myself by obtaining a few DF118 prescriptions, which are prescriptions for a drug that contains a high dose of codeine.

Clearly, this wasn't addressing my Cocaine and Crack addiction or my needle fixation, or my opiate habit for that matter. And it doesn't even begin to consider my daily alcoholic drinking. On a good morning I'd wake up to a 75 cl bottle of Baileys for breakfast. On a bad day I'd try to scrounge enough money for a tin of strong lager.

Did I mention I was still, and had been an alcoholic for the past nine years solid? At the time, my alcohol dependency seemed so insignificant, but I always needed a drink in my hand. I was like someone who needed to smoke a cigarette every 15 to 20 minutes. I needed a drink every 15 to 30 minutes. Always!

It's Not About Me!

But at the Doctor's clinic, the kind nurse felt like they were helping me and it was only a matter of time before the GP referred me to the Methadone clinic. I was delighted! The Methadone clinic allowed me to never feel junkie sick again. Even though I despised being on 'government' drugs, and feeling controlled by the State, it did give me access to more money that I was no longer spending on Heroin and therefore allowed my Crack use to go up and up and up. Despite what the government statistics may lead you to believe, Methadone maintenance is not reducing crime. Not being junkie sick allowed me to commit even more crime in order to afford an increasingly dominant Crack habit. Being high on Crack in turn allowed me brazenly to rob and steal even more to purchase the Crack, especially now that my Smack fix was being provided to me free of charge by the government. A Methadone clinic is not a solution. A Methadone clinic is a system used to disguise the government's inability to want to engage with the junkie problem, as society sees it. It is actually a monumental failure. Asking any drug addict what they want? Well, please don't be surprised when they say they want free drugs. It's madness in the face of the drug policy. It effectively legalises the whole stigma of a previously considered illegal pastime. Not that I cared at the time. I was getting loaded for free and it was making my life of crime and grime much easier. Thank you!

The reason why Methadone is considered successful is the flip side of just why it's also the stupidest thing. It makes you feel better, when you're withdrawing from opiate addiction. It takes away the aches and pains. It restores you to a state where things become manageable again. You're no longer incapable of functioning. However, when I was on Methadone I was more of a criminal than I ever was without it, because I never had to feel junkie sick. On a comedown, I'd just go down to the clinic and get a fix. Then full of life again I'd be back out on the street committing crimes to get the cash to support my other love, Crack. It never served to reduce my crime and placate me. It simply served to empower me to go chase an even more expensive habit.

That's the reality of Methadone. I was out there getting into no end of mischief because I didn't feel sick anymore. I was very comfortable and was finding lots of new ways to support my ever-worsening Crack habit. The amount of Crack I was using at this stage was making me crazier and crazier. I was getting more and more out of control. I would take crazy risks and break into places and do stupid things that were not only illegal but also very dangerous. I crossed boundaries that, without Crack, I never would have crossed. Before Crack I had only ever committed crimes against institutions and large faceless organisations, but now, anyone, anywhere seemed to be fair game to me and my selfish desires.

Those of you who have been on a Methadone programme don't need me to tell you how dirty the drug is. Methadone is a government-issued drug that comes with no health warning at all. It is handed out for free by the government and it's just rotten, legal Heroin that comes for free as long as you get off your ass and go to the clinic every day to be a statistic, give them your daily signature of compliance and pick up your dose. It won't get you well, how can it? But, I knew that and I didn't care.

The clinic I attended stabilised me after a few weeks on 50 milligrams of Methadone and then they told me they were going to take me off a milligram a week for the next year. That means, if you do the maths, that they were proposing to detox me over one year! That's crazy. That is simply nuts. If I ask for a detox it's because I want to get off drugs, not get stuck on them for a year coming off them slowly. After a few months, I realised that the Methadone was causing far more trouble to my internal organs than Heroin ever seemed to. My liver felt like it was suffocating and my stomach churned with a sensation of something toxic eating it away. Well it is still an actual poison, so I shouldn't be too surprised really. Since I did not think that was a suitable solution I went back on the Smack. It was the easier, softer option for me!

As you can imagine, at that point in my life I weighed about 40% of what I do today. I was around 8 ½ stones, or rather about 120 pounds - seriously underweight for a 28-year old male of 5'11'. I was pretty grey, I didn't have much hair, not because I was a skinhead, just because I just didn't have much hair through stunted growth and I looked very sullen and unhealthy. My body was decaying right before my eyes. I don't know about anyone else who does Heroin and Cocaine but sex certainly wasn't on my agenda anymore. I kind of knew that the things I loved and the things I wanted at the beginning of all of this had been left behind somewhere; I had travelled to a very different place. All my ideals about the Libertarian Socialist Division, free love, free sex, hippie, punk, raving, let's change the world through better chemistry, were gone. I had lost them all somewhere, they had just disappeared, and this new, raggedy me had taken over. This dying body of a man with nowhere to go and with narcotics as his only friend was taking a turn for the worse. I was living on a daily basis just trying to do what I needed to do to get the next hit.

In the later years of my addiction, food wasn't really a priority to me anymore.

It's Not About Me!

During this time, if I managed to eat once a day that was more than sufficient, at least that was what I told myself. I wouldn't eat a big meal I would just eat whatever I came across in my day. Normally crisps, chocolate and fast food. I needed all of my money for drinking and drugs, and I didn't see any point in wasting it on anything else. Hygiene was not important to me; I would quite easily go through a few weeks without getting undressed or changing my underwear. More often than not I was living in squats and seriously suffering the harsh effects of the cold London Winters, so I was adamant not to lose heat for a silly reason like washing. By the end of the season, my clothes were quite literally a part of my body, a creature in their own right. I was a homeless statistic for thirteen years. I refused to sleep on the street, particularly when there were perfectly good buildings just standing there, empty...it seemed like such a waste. So, I would break into them, alone or with friends, and they would become home until we were driven away or we decided to move on for whatever reason. Up until 2001, I had spent the entirety of my adult life as a squatter, either using empty buildings, or other people's generosity.

My days would begin sometime midmorning when I finally reached a conscious state, coming out of whatever party the night before had held. My first priority was to find my fix, immediately. Straight away I would start the hunt to find whatever drugs or alcohol were left over from the night before and get them into my body as quickly as humanly possible. I would make cigarettes out of rolled up cigarette butts, if nothing else I was certainly good at recycling. I would generally head over to a Crack house via the off licence and start my day there, because that's where I was most likely to get lucky from someone else's generosity, or begin my first few trades of the day. The local action all revolved around the local Crack houses and shooting galleries. There would always be people coming in and out, and the opportunity to share someone's hit was often an option if I didn't have any of my own. In the good times, we shared so that in the bad times people would share with us.

I never had any employment, I never had any education, I didn't have any time schedule, I didn't even wear a watch until after I had got clean and found my first job, having some sort of dramatic story as to why time was irrelevant in the grand scheme of the cosmos, and since we were all a part of the universe, time had no laws for which I ought to abide, or some rubbish like that. I never had any responsibilities. I never had a bank account. I didn't live in society, I lived outside of society, and I wasn't part of the mainstream world at all. I was an outlaw!

I had tried to get help from various places. I knew I was in trouble and I wanted help, I was addicted. I had tried talking to GPs, nurses and community drug and alcohol teams. I had given the Methadone method a shot (no pun intended). But none of these 'solutions' actually addressed the problem at its core. The problem was that I defined myself by drugs. My whole culture and life was dedicated to using and scoring drugs. I was a drug addict and I didn't know who I was without drugs. In all of the state-sponsored places I was looking for help (NHS, Methadone clinics, etc.), their solution was to give me more drugs in an effort to disguise the drugs I was already on. There were no actual efforts to assist me with a detox or full withdrawal, unless it took four seasons, and I simply didn't have the patience or the luxury of good health to test that amount of time. What they didn't understand was that it didn't matter what the drugs were; I was addicted to putting substances in my body; mine, theirs, legal, illegal, it really didn't matter. The worst thing you can do to a true drug addict is to give them more drugs as a solution. It makes no sense. This all seems very clear to me now but, at the time, I wasn't really as clear minded as I am these days. What I really needed was help. I needed help to change my way of thinking, my way of processing information and my way of seeing not only my life, but also myself as a part of that life. I needed help to change my attitude towards drugs, so that I could see that I was actually inspired by so many other things that had nothing to do with the drugs. I knew that the drugs were killing me. I knew that if I didn't stop I would die. But I couldn't get the help I needed to get out of this cycle of addiction.

From the ages of twenty-six through twenty-nine, I was aware that my body was dying. That knowledge was so profoundly sad that I would try to quit. I would take my last hit and tell myself I would never do it again. But, as I came out of it, I was still so haunted by the idea that I was dying, that I would need another hit just to ease the pain and suffering of the knowledge that I was dying. I became so overwhelmed and distraught by the emotional turmoil that came with the knowledge that essentially I was killing myself and the only successful method I knew of to overcome those feelings of despair was to do exactly the thing that was killing me in the first place. That's truly insane thinking! And so the cycle continued. However, this time, there was no laughter, there was no dancing, there was no fun. I was killing myself with drugs and sadness.

I was twenty-nine years old when I finally realised that it was the drugs that were killing me. I knew that my body was shutting down, I could feel it, and I could see it. I was dying. I knew I was becoming unhealthier by the day. I had holes down my arms, and my legs were pincushions of scars and scabs. They were so bad that some days it hurt just to stand or walk. I knew that all of this pain, this ugliness, and this horror was because of the drugs. I knew it was because of the needles. But addiction twists your mind and turns your brain around in circles. I was convinced that I was so sick because of the crappy quality of the Heroin I was scoring. I was sure that if I could get my hands on better Smack and get the needle in the vein during the first attempt that I would be okay. That I would get better. I just kept thinking about the fact that I kept missing the vein, I was convinced that this was the reason I was collapsing all the time, it was just that the Heroin wasn't strong enough.

To exacerbate things, my need to support my Crack habit had me hurting the people I genuinely cared about. I am not proud of the things I did during this time in my life just to get a fix of my drug of choice. I wasn't proud of it back then, either. Accompanying these actions was a great feeling of shame that washed through me, rendering my self-esteem and personal perspective rather low and careless. I was so guilty about who I had become I started to hate myself more and more every day. But this didn't stop me from continuing the behaviour. The only way I knew how to feel better, to cure myself from the shame and the guilt was to get high, and I couldn't get high without cash so it would start all over again. I was in this messy circle again where the only escape was to get more drugs even though I knew it was the source of the problem.

8. "Dear God..."

I was in this never-ending cycle. Whether the drugs were prescription, from the street or from a bottle, there was never any break. There was never any long-term or even short-term period where I got my head straight, or took a day off. Aside from one day hitchhiking from Amsterdam to Italy with a consignment of LSD safely stashed, when I actually went for a full 24 hours without even a beer or a spliff (though not by choice) there had not been a single day substance free. I got to a point where I simply knew and understood that I was sick and tired of being sick and tired.

Finally, I arrived at a point in my life where I decided once and for all that I would do whatever it took to halt the direction my life was genuinely heading -

an early death. I simply couldn't tolerate being me anymore. The person I had become didn't resemble the person I wanted to be or aspired to be. I had changed. I had changed so substantially that I couldn't stand myself; the way I treated people; the way I treated my friends and loved ones; the way I behaved; the things I was doing; the activities I was now engaging in: I just couldn't stand myself. I didn't want to live my life as this wretched, unscrupulous human being. I was done!

This was now about a year after I'd returned to England from India, my life had deteriorated fairly rapidly. It was early December in the year 2000, and I was injecting Cocaine, sitting naked (I always preferred to be naked when injecting Coke - it made you sweat so much that any clothing became drenched) in a very small room painted canary yellow. After spending three miserable years of trying not to be sick and trying to find different ways of not feeling so dreadful, I had gotten to a point where I surrendered, put my hands up and said towards the sky, "I'm done."

I have this image of myself from that era in my mind, and actually somewhere there is a Polaroid photo of me. I don't know who took it but it is of me right possibly just a few days before I changed my life, in this yellow room, naked and I was on the edge of death. In that moment, I am naked and I am looking for a vein and, at some point, I have had a hit and I put pen to paper. Between obsessively rearranging all the furniture and putting up all of the posters and putting everything back into lines and rearranging the whole place and then having another hit and rearranging it again; sometime between all that I wrote a letter and, for some reason, I addressed this letter "Dear God."

So there I was, stark naked, writing a letter. I was broken and I knew that I couldn't keep going on like this. I knew I was dying. In that letter, I set about asking for help. I do not know why, seeing as I had never used the word before, certainly never in that context, I wrote that letter and begun with the words "Dear God." All of a sudden my heart and soul opened out onto the page as I wrote this letter to a God that I had never spoken to before, a God I didn't even consider to be real, a God I had never previously considered or even wished to acknowledge, and I asked this God for help. And strangely enough, within a couple of weeks of writing this letter, I found myself being introduced to the very people who were not only on their own path to recovery, but able to signpost me in the right direction to save my own life...finally.

I don't know why I wrote a letter to God. I had never written a letter to God before, I had never acknowledged God before, I had never had any relationship with God before, and I had no concept of God. I don't know why, but for some reason I wrote a letter to God and in this letter I basically told God that if God could help me feel better, and help me stop injecting, and help me with these problems, and help me not feel so miserable so much of the time, I would go straight, get a job and I would turn my life around.

I believed I was done and I would do anything. I would do anything to stop feeling like this. Even change my life absolutely. I would go to any lengths to stop feeling so dreadful. I was done! It was just that defining moment when I promised God, that if God could get me out of here, everything would be all right and I would be a good person.

Then I had another hit.

You won't be surprised to know that I had another hit and then another hit and then another and that letter was forgotten.

But the seed had been planted. Magic was about to occur - a true miracle. My life was now set on a different course despite myself. Divine intervention or personal intention, who knows? But life would never be the same again!

I still have that letter tucked away safely in a box somewhere in my garage. This is a letter that can permanently remind me how bad it had gotten. A letter to remind me of the first time I actually reached out for help. A letter I wrote when I had no idea what spirituality was but I knew that I needed it. I yearned for it. I needed someone or something to help me. So I wrote a letter to God. A God that I didn't even really believe in. A God I had no personal relationship with, but I didn't know anyone else to ask. So the letter began "Dear God." And it seemed to do the trick - magic happened!

9. Insanity

In the tail end of the year 2000, I was living in this house in West London that resembled a squat, and since I was no longer paying any rent, technically it was. And there was this girl (there was always 'this' girl) who was scoring skunkweed off me at the time. We were getting skunk by the golf bag delivered and selling it was one of the ways I was earning a little bit of money. So this girl came over one day to score some skunk and she noticed my collection of Methadone bottles. Although she seemed surprised that I was into Smack (I must have been doing a good job of covering it up) she told me she knew where I could get some help, if I was serious. My first thought was, "Fantastic, I really need some help; especially if you're the administrator of such help, my dear." (I had a rather large crush on her). Next, she told me that she knew a group of people who had been using drugs the way I had been using them, but who had then stopped and had managed to stay stopped! I barely could believe what I was hearing. I had never heard of Smack users who had stopped using and stayed stopped. I always believed we were simply between hits for the rest of our lives. She told me that she used to go to these group meetings, and that it had helped her. Even though she didn't attend the meetings anymore (hence why she was buying drugs off me), she told me that she thought they might do me some good.

This was the first potentially positive prospect towards my chronic addiction I had heard in a long time. Here was someone, standing in my own place of residence, showing me the old track mark scars on her arm telling me there was help out there. She was nice, she was my kind of person, and she was telling me there was a solution! I liked what she was saying. I liked this idea of a solution, but honestly, I didn't really have the ambition necessary to stop. What I really wanted was to stop using the needle, but not stop using Smack. I just wanted to get my hands on better Smack, and cheaper Cocaine. I had my own problems. I needed a range of solutions, not just the one that she was offering. It took a while before I realised that the problems I thought I had, were not the ones that needed solutions.

Part of me wanted to stop. Of course, I wanted to stop. But it was hard. Every day I wanted to quit the same deteriorating ritual and every day I made excuses why today wasn't the day to stop and every day I would cave in to my addiction and I would get my fix. When I failed to achieve what I wanted, which was to drastically change some small parts of my life (see, I'm still in significant denial at this point in my journey) and stop using, every day I would have to make excuses to myself as to why I wasn't as worthless as I believed I was. That sort of thought process was debilitating. Every day I would feel stupid, worthless and weak and the only way to feel better would be to use, to tell myself that tomorrow I would be stronger, that today was just a bad day. And again I would go back to doing exactly what made me feel so lousy in the first place. I would be getting drunk and getting high even when I didn't want to be. For three years I had made excuses to myself every day just to justify my behaviour, and to talk myself out of throwing my useless body in front of a train.

Do you understand just how crazy that is? Of course YOU do! To be doing precisely what I don't want to be doing, because I know it do be the only proven method to escape the dreadful feelings I was experiencing because I felt my life falling away, out of my grasp. And then being filled with sadness, self loathing, shame, guilt and remorse, and yet the only way to escape these feelings is to do the very same thing that I know is killing me and causing me to feel so dreadful in the first place. Then, reflecting back on how terrible I feel because this is killing me and I know it, but yet then, once again doing what I don't want to be doing, because I know I can escape feeling like this for a short while. What an ever-decreasing circle of tragedy aka insanity! True madness. This is the trap that addicts and alcoholics find ourselves in.

This feeling of uselessness, this feeling of self-loathing and self-pity is the nature of the whole illness. This is the very essence of addiction. This is what needs to be addressed when working with addicts. These days, I help alcoholics and addicts to develop more reassuring attitudes and behaviours when I work with them. For addicts who are as extreme as I was, abstinence is the only place to start. I was informed about abstinence at the very beginning of my journey into recovery. I experienced enforced abstinence, first hand. I was put into a place where I was unable to get my hands on anything. I was locked away from it all. While I was there I saw many people leave, who couldn't cope with that. But I had a determination and after three years of trying to find my own way I realised the enforced method was the one that was going to work for me. I couldn't have done this on my own. I needed someone else to take the reins.

For a long time I believed I could just tweak a few things, stop using Heroin or stop using needles or maybe get a job and I would be fine. But that wasn't how it worked at all. That wasn't what I needed. My recovery started with the letter that I wrote to God. From there I can track clearly my path to recovery. A few weeks after that I began my own detox, then into an institution, then I relapsed, then I made the final change. The first steps I took were shortly after I wrote the letter to God. The first was meeting the girl, the girl who told me about these people who had stopped and stayed stopped. As that information set in my mind, things began to change.

9. What happened next was out of my hands

I was due to be evicted from my residence due to my non-payment of rent and all my bills (I had much better things to spend my money on) on December 27th, 2000. Two days before, on Christmas Day, for dinner I had had a Mars Bar, and a half packet of crisps, which I shared with Adam. We also shared half a £10 bag of Heroin (which is a very small amount for those of you who don't already know) then we resigned ourselves to the eviction, and once again, I was homeless. On Boxing Day I took as many of my belongings with me and I left.

I knew my parents were away over Christmas and that my little sister was still living at their house. So I went to her and told her I was a little bit poorly and needed somewhere to stay for a few days. My sister, bless her, took me in. She had no idea that I did my last cluck and my last detox there in the house while my parents where away. She took care of me, my little sister, completely naive to what I was going through, thinking I had the flu. It wasn't the hardest detox I have ever done and it wasn't the longest detox I have ever done, but God willing, it will always be the last detox I have ever done. That doesn't require a round of applause; it wasn't the last time I used, but it was the last detox I ever did.

I love my sister to bits and she has been with me since that day. She took the time to nurse me through that detox so gently and kindly with all the love and good heartedness that she has. The last alcoholic drink I ever had was with her. It was 6th January 2001. We had two bottles of vodka - the first a full litre, of which she had a glass and I had the rest, the second a smaller 70cl bottle. Again she only had a glass. I was clucking (experiencing cold turkey) and I was in such a severe physical withdrawal from the Heroin that I managed to crash out for an hour and a half before I woke up clucking again. My detox was a long one and over the fourteen days of painful, self-monitored withdrawal, I managed very little sleep as my legs and arms underwent involuntary spasms, bouncing up and down. I shook, rattled and rocked myself through those sleepless days. It was tough. But I was determined.

My parents had Sky TV, which had some movie channels. Right at the beginning of my self-controlled detox, I watched 'Merry Christmas, Mr. Lawrence'. Have you seen it? It's a great movie, made in 1983 and staring David Bowie as the commander of the Allied Prisoners of War in a Japanese POW camp. I won't go into details here, although I'd strongly recommend seeing it if you haven't already. Anyhow, during the film, David Bowie's character is buried up to his neck in ant infested sand and earth, and left out in the sun for a few days without food or drink, as a torture for non compliance in the Japanese Commander's orders towards the allied prisoners. And while watching this film, I thought about the types of pain and torture these poor sods had had to endure at the hands of their captors. I figured, if these blokes could endure that sort of discomfort in the name of their country and out of loyalty to their beliefs and brotherhood, then I, this junkie scum, could endure a few days of discomfort while I go through my withdrawal pains. If they could do that, then I certainly could manage this. So, armed with this determination, I resigned myself to going through whatever the pain and discomfort of this detox threw at me. And that included almost no sleep whatsoever.

My parents came home on 6th January. They came home to me - a raggedy mess of bones and sickness and drug abuse with my lovely sister caring for me. I had been drinking solidly through the whole detox. I had used up all of my spare stashes of Subutex and Methadone. I had devoured all of my saved Valium and various other benzodiazepines. I had nothing left but vodka. I begged my father to let me stay for a few weeks. I promised him that I just needed somewhere to stay for a couple of weeks while I found a job. I told him I would get my own place then and everything would be fine. I told him it would be easy, I'd just get a good job straight away and get back on my feet; I just didn't have anywhere to sleep and no money to eat. My dad said "No", not surprisingly. Here I was, his 29-year old son, who had never done a day's work in his life, messed up, sick and strung out, drunk and all used up making promises that we both knew I wasn't going to keep. My dad, bless him, had the foresight to tell me that if I was going to stay in their house I was going to do things their way. My dad had the foresight to tell me that I was going to do things his way or he wasn't going to tolerate me in the house. It was his way or the highway! They weren't going to have me use them and I had to follow his rules. The first thing my dad did was to give me a brochure of a residential treatment facility and told me to call them. At this point, I don't know why, but I finally did what I was told. Having been asked to leave at the age of sixteen, here I was at the age of twenty-nine being told that I couldn't come back unless I did things their way. I knew that they would help me, and I knew that I needed help, so I decided that I would do it their way. At least I would try.

10. The Surrender

It was at this point that I finally surrendered. After years of fighting, after years of hanging on to my far-fetched idealism and dreams, it was this very moment, when I finally allowed my father to help me, that I surrendered. This was a very profound and hugely significant moment for me. Surrendering to his help meant letting go of so much I had held onto so closely since I was a teenager, particularly my utopian dogma, my idealism, and particular beliefs about living a counterculture lifestyle. It was finally admitting to myself that I was no longer that tough guy I thought I was. I was no longer carefree and high and having the time of my life. I had to admit defeat, complete unequivocal defeat. I had been defeated by the very culture I had promoted for so many years; a culture of free love, free drugs and free spirits. I had to admit defeat to a culture that I had helped to build. I had to let go of the Technivals, the Techno Travellers and many of the morals and values that had defined me my entire adult life. None of these things were serving me anymore. They had led me to this path of destruction that without surrendering from it meant I was going to die. I knew that now, at the age of twenty-nine, I could not keep up with this culture anymore and it was a desperately sad moment for me when I finally admitted this to myself. I felt, in so many ways, that on a personal basis like I had failed.

Please note, if you're reading this as an addict or alcoholic yourself, that this was just the way I felt at the time. This is not how things materialised and that in the long run I had absolutely maintained my place in my culture, my liberal beliefs and my attitude of self-reliance. Please, keep reading through to the end. There is a happy ending.

The process of change for any addict looking for a way forward must start with surrender. Recovery and rehabilitation must start by admitting that you need help, that you cannot keep living the way you are living, that the game you have been playing, however long you have been playing it, is finally over. You must concede that you cannot continue your drug use. You must realise that your cycle of use and abuse is dangerous to you, and you must admit that you want to make a change regardless of how difficult, sad and heart breaking this might be for you on a personal level. After surrendering, you as an addict are sure to find yourself directed to the path or solution, which will work for you and help you on your way to recovery. For me, the only solution that made sense after those three years of searching was abstinence. The only way I could see myself healing from all of this use and abuse was to remove myself from the situation.

It's Not About Me!

The only way to stop the cyclic use of drugs was to stop completely using drugs. This, for me, went hand in hand with surrendering.

I began to see the light. It was amazing to hear, for the very first time, the concept of abstinence. It sounds strange to a drug addict to tell them that the only way they're going to recover from their addiction is to become abstinent forever. It seems a little unnecessary. Not only being abstinent from the drug they're using but all drugs. That's rather extreme. Telling a drug addict they have to stop using all drugs - even the legal ones - is a big deal. Telling an addict they have to give up drugs including the ones they smoke, the ones they drink and even the ones the doctor could possibly prescribe is something that is hard for an addict to comprehend. Then telling them that they cannot have the ones that grow naturally (or unnaturally in the case of genetically modified skunk weed) in the ground or the ones imported from another country, or even the ones that aren't chemically induced, can be heart breaking. To be told that I had to abstain from everything was hard to hear, but I did hear it, and it made sense to me. I had a good, long run but the party was finally over. I listened to the stories that these people had to tell me and I decided to surrender. I was very lucky to be introduced to people who had recovered. These people were inspirational and took the time to help teach me what I needed to do to become sober, to get on with my life, to recover from my life-long party.

Once I was able to admit that I was finished with life my way, I could then step forward in my journey to recovery. So I did; I stepped forward.

I saw what was next. Once I had stopped using, I realised that I would have to change my environment. I realised quickly that I could no longer associate with my old friends and the crew I had grown up with during my raving, travelling, partying days. At least I understood that I needed to be away from them temporally, anyway. I would have to find a new group of friends and create a new crew of people around me. I knew that I would have to create a fellowship of people around me who were all on the same journey so that we could understand each other. Together we would be able to feel part of this new world we saw before us, and we would be able to help each other through the change so that we could understand this strange new world that was everyone else's reality but was so far removed from our past.

So I did just that. I surrounded myself with like-minded people who were on the same journey and this allowed me the gift - the freedom - of knowing that

I wasn't alone. Here was a group of people going through their own hard times, but they were with me, they were here to encourage me and to inspire me. A lot of the people I met were amazing towards me. They were so tolerant of this barking mad, starry-eyed kid. I began to consider this new group of people around me to be my new best friends as they showed great patience, love, kindness, tolerance and generosity towards me. These new friends would take me out for meals, buy me coffee and generally help me out, even if I didn't have any money. I was inspired by their kindness. This inspiration was to have such an impact on me, that I matched and mirrored their mannerisms and behaviours, adopting these in such a way that once I had a little bit of my own sobriety time, I would mimic their actions, showing the new person who came after me that this is how they deserved to be treated too.

The way I was treated as a newcomer to the world of sobriety is, to this day, the way I try to treat other people who are new to this world of sobriety. It is a cycle that keeps moving. Kindness gets played forward all the time. We pass on what we learn and we treat each other with more tolerance and kindness, easing newcomers into their new life with love and lightness. I was inspired by this new lifestyle and I began to dedicate my life to rebalancing my karma. I realised how badly I had treated people in the past and I wanted to make it right. I wanted to readdress all of my problems and build a new life that held more purpose and meaning. I called this process of making things right, "Rebalancing my karma".

It is very severe, the desperation you experience when you want to stop using drugs and you cannot. When you want to do something and you realise you're incapable of doing it. It feels hopeless to become so unable to control yourself that you do what you do not want to be doing because you do not have the self-control to stop. It's terribly disparaging. It certainly affected my self-esteem and my confidence, and I know that most addicts feel this way at one stage or another. When I began learning about abstinence and when I met these people who were on the same path, I was filled with hope and joy. I was given a reason to live. I was given hope for the future. I believe that nobody gets sober just for the sake of getting sober.

We all need a purpose in our life. We need to have a mission in our lives, and for people in early drug and alcohol recovery, this is as important as ever. For me, that mission started out as spreading the wonderful experiences I was feeling my way through as a result of this exposure to a magnificent world of a spiritual awakenings and recovery from my addictions. I wanted to tell everyone and save everyone. This later evolved through many different stages and guises, but ultimately it settled down to quite a simple mission in life - my higher purpose was to see how I could help other people, or how I could bring some sort of extra value to the quality of their lives; in essence, serving humanity.

The things I had done in my past, my feelings of guilt, regret and shame filled me with an intense sadness and desperation. But my new path was focused and meaningful, giving me outstanding hope, motivation and inspiration. All you can do is take what you have and turn it around; make the choice to take yourself in a new direction. With a little help, discipline and focus, anyone can find the way out. Kindness, generosity of time and spirit go a long way towards encouraging someone to become the best they can be.

Part 4.
RECOVERY
– rehab & the early years

"and...breathe"

1. Sleep please

Many of the traditional treatment facilities in the UK will mainly focus upon someone's Class A drug addictions, such as Heroin and Cocaine (in the form of Crack). Certainly all the Therapeutic community and CBT based models will exclusively focus on your drinking and drug problems. The traditional rehab will attempt to treat your particular drug addiction by simply addressing the one specific drug that you may be struggling with at the time. I believe they fail to see the whole picture and are missing the point of addiction - what it means to be an addict. They will not give you the tools to help sustain any period of complete abstinence; in fact, many of them will encourage you to learn how to control your drinking and some will attempt to teach you how to drink and use drugs (including the ones that may have gotten you in trouble in the first place) safely. This attitude stems from the 'service user' empowerment, by accepting that drug addicts know what's best for themselves and then encouraging them to practise whatever it is they want. Unfortunately, this is missing the blindingly obvious point, that a drug addict wants more drugs and has no desire to actually stop - just a desire not to feel so dreadful quite so much of the time.

Let's explore this. If you had asked me what I wanted, I'd have always told you I want cleaner and cheaper Heroin and Cocaine. That's what the problem is;

It's Not About Me!

it's cut too much and it's too expensive. If you reduce the price, I won't have to commit so much crime. If you improve the quality, then I won't need so much to get high, and thus I won't have to commit so much crime. This is, of course, completely bonkers. Simply reducing the price means I can buy more, and improving the quality doesn't mean I'll use less. It simply means that my body will become dependent upon a higher dose with each hit. So, please don't ask a drug addict or an alcoholic what the solution to their problem is, and most certainly do not form government policy around it. That's absolutely bloody nuts!

Most of these rehabs across the UK are therapeutic communities where you are taught new skills like gardening, plumbing, carpentry or things to do with your hands to keep yourself busy and to attempt to distract your mind. They have rather shockingly poor success rates, which when combined across the whole field of addiction treatment drag the statistics right down to around a 30% success rates. This, ladies and gentlemen is not good enough. No one should be allowed to run a business based upon such dreadful success rates. You wouldn't eat at a restaurant that only got your order right a third of the time. You wouldn't buy a car that could only do a third of the things the brochure told you it could door did a third of the speed or mpg. You wouldn't keep taking medication if only on a third of the days you weren't feeing unwell. I'm sorry, but recording 30%, or even anything under 50% in any form of business model is a massive failure!

So that being said, I was very fortunate that my dad had picked a centre that was a committed 12-Step facility. I had no idea what a 12-Step facility was, or even what any of the others were, meant or stood for, but I did remember that girl who had come into my place and told me about this programme where she had gone to get off the Smack. And I remembered how she had told me about this group of people who had stopped and stayed stopped. And I also remembered she said something about it being a 12-Step 'thingy'. And all I knew is that I wanted to do that 'thingy' that they had done and she had spoken to me about. 12-Step what???

I was very lucky to end up in a 12-Step programme. Without their commitment to teaching abstinence, I don't know where I would be today. With their help, I began my life of abstinence. Do not applaud though, it wasn't my sober date, but it was the next step in my journey to reach recovery. It was 9th January 2001, and when I arrived at this facility in deepest, darkest Kent, with my parents along to ensure I got there and to see with their own eyes just where I was going (making sure I didn't balk too, I guess). I had been clucking for two weeks by now. My sleeplessness was driving me crazy. In the past 14 days, I had honestly never caught more than three straight hours of sleep in a row, and on many days I wouldn't sleep at all. After only getting 16 hours over the first 10 days, I had now managed 12 hours during the next 4 days, so things were improving, but I was still going crazy. I asked them for help. I told them I needed to sleep. I told them it was my only priority right now. I absolutely must get a few good nights' sleep. The doctor prescribed me sleeping pills for two nights (how many GPs give you such a small prescription?), which, of course, the nurses made sure I took at the right times, i.e., spread over two nights and not all in one go, as I would have preferred. Remember, I was an addict and we are not known for doing things in small doses. The doctor also told me something that was backed up by the nurses, the counselling staff and all the other patients I checked it out with; they told me that would be the end of my drug use. After the shock of hearing such a strong statement, I sighed and resigned myself to agree with them. I let go. I stopped fighting. I put my hands up and accepted my fate. It was the best agreement I ever made!

My father had previously met a guy who had himself recovered from alcoholism and had done this through a 12-Step recovery programme. Dad had the foresight to see that this was the type of treatment programme I needed; abstinence, followed by a psychological process that would clear my brain long enough for my inner self to kick in and see the light - metaphorically speaking. My dad had insisted I call this guy and then go and visit him at the treatment facility he worked in. I made the appointment for the next day, 7th January.

The day I met them at that centre, was the day I met a truly sober and free alcoholic for the first time in my life, Adrian Lee. At first I didn't believe him. I thought he was just saying that sort of stuff as a sales tactic. Well, he'd missed out on selling to me, because I never wanted to actually, totally stop. I just wanted a reprieve. But as we continued talking, and he shared some of his own stories with me I began to like what I was hearing. And when he told me that it would be possible even for me to stop and stay stopped. Well, I actually believed him!

I began treatment on 9th January 2001. When I entered the facility, all I had were the clothes on my back, a pair of shoes with a hole in them and an unhealthy appearance. My skin was grey and I weighed in at slightly over 8 stones. I couldn't bend my elbows, my knees or my ankles from where my injecting spots were weeping or had become infected. I couldn't walk up a flight of stairs. I had a beard, my eyes were sunken and my demeanour was sullen. I certainly was not a pleasant vision for you! I resembled a ghost, or at least a 'dead man walking'. But I truly believed I just needed a good night's sleep and everything would be fine.

During my first day in the centre, I had a moment of clarity. I heard something for the first time that was sure to change the very fabric of my life. I heard the answer I had been searching for during those past three years I'd been trying to get clean by myself. Yet, even reflecting back, I would never have believed it possible, even if it had been spelt out or explained to me in plain English before this very moment. Even though it's so obvious now, it's just one of those things that's so far removed from the possibilities of addicts while they're in the madness of their addiction. When you hear it for the first time you can't help but think, "That's so obvious", but it's almost amazing that addicts can't think of it for themselves. It was so simple. It was so obvious. Do you know what they told me? Can you guess what this profound statement was? One of the counsellors looked me in the eye and said in very easy to understand English:

"If you want to stop using drugs, you have to actually have to stop using drugs!"

That was it. It had never occurred to me in all the years when I had tried to quit using Smack by various methods including geographical relocations, change of social scene, different methods of consumption, substitution for alternative drugs (my favourite being Ketamine mainlining for a week) or attempting to manage my doses in diminishing levels. That simply going cold turkey, and not using anything at all would actually have been the right solution all along. Who'd a thought of that? Not using drugs at all was the best way to not use drugs at all. Durrr!

I had certainly never begun to consider that drinking booze continuously wasn't helping. Smoking ganja was simply one of those things that always improved my life and mood. I had never considered these substances were simply driving me back to madness on a daily basis. In fact, alcohol and ganja hadn't been serving me well for a very long while indeed. As difficult as it seemed, it made perfect sense and I committed to it there and then!

I had seen lots of people try to quit drugs over the years, and yet being completely drug free and sober never seemed to be anyone's first choice. Even the girl who had referred me to a 12-Step meeting was coming to me to score weed and would hang out with me and get drunk sometimes. She hadn't stopped using drugs. But she had stopped using Smack. The staff at the facility explained to me that I had to abstain from all drugs. To be honest, I was five miles from the nearest pub and too weak to walk up a flight of stairs, I couldn't bend any of my limbs; so really, I didn't have much chance of scoring anyway. So, I resigned myself to doing what I was told to do.

I was an anarchist, a free-spirited lover of life. I had always done just about whatever I wanted. I had lived a life of travelling between countries whenever I wanted, committing any crimes that suited ME or my purposes and making my own choices regardless of what society said was good or bad. But here, at this residential facility, one step away from an inpatient psychiatric hospital, I made the choice to surrender and that's exactly what I did. I sat still in those counselling rooms, I participated in the various group therapies, I listened and I contributed, and I took the next steps along my journey towards recovery. I finally let go and allowed myself to get help. As I watched the healing happening around me I found myself attracted to the process. Right there in front of me was a group of people who had done the same shit I had, used the same drugs as I had, had similarly insane stories like I did and we were all here, in it together. Instead of talking about what party we were going to next, I was with a group of like-minded people discussing how to live a drug-free life, but we were still hanging out and having fun together.

I thought, "This is perfect; I can still hang out with the same sort of people as I did before. I can make friends with guys who like the same stuff and we can talk about what we are going through together." It seemed like an excellent solution to me.

When I first turned up at the rehab, everyone was talking mystically about the guy who owned the facility and took us for certain groups. The way everyone talked about him it was as if they were expecting me to have some sort of trouble with him, and that he would sort me out. When I met him, however, it was quite the opposite. When I met this guy, I knew right to my very core that he was about to change my life. He was genuinely sincere and serious, with plenty of good-natured humour coupled with compassion and enthusiasm. I felt star struck. His name was (and still is) Dr. Robert Lefever. The strangest thing about this guy for me was that he always wore exactly the same grey suit and Cambridge tie, yet we still found a common ground. He always wore this same suit and tie and, to the naked eye, he completely represented, in a physical sense, everything my mind told me were the parts of straight society that I should be avoiding at all costs. He was always dressed so impeccably and respectably, yet I found

It's Not About Me!

myself drawn to him, despite coming from such opposite ends of the cultural spectrum. Me having lived my adult life as a crusty punk and raver and Robert working right in the middle of the upper-middle classes and rubbing noses with aristocracy, colonialism and everything pomp and circumstance (so it appeared to me). He was, in fact, the first person dressed so formally that I had ever connected to. No man who dressed so 'straight' had ever interested me, or as he did, tamed me. Robert was different from other suits I saw in the street. He had a certain spark in his eye that spoke to me. It told me he knew what I was experiencing. It told me that he understood and that he was right there next to me during my journey. That look in his eyes was slightly manic and crazy, and I connected to that instantly. I trusted him implicitly right from the very beginning. I was, indeed I am, always willing and keen to listen to what he has to say, so that I can learn from him. Robert, despite all his professional qualifications in a whole manner of things, stands out to me as my greatest teacher. He taught me how to live and how to behave in order to live a better life.

Robert exposed his faults and fears alongside us as we struggled to share our own and when he spoke it was always with authority, knowledge and transparency. He possessed empathy and sympathy and, by following his lead, I was inspired to learn how I could feel the same. I wanted what this man had; I wanted it for my own even though I'd never tasted anything like it before. When he spoke, I listened, evaluated and absorbed. During our group therapy sessions, sometimes Robert would speak in humorous little riddles. But however complex they may have been, they were never so difficult that I couldn't understand exactly what he meant. It felt like whenever he was talking, he was talking for my benefit. Everything he said felt like it was being said to help me personally. The outstanding lesson he taught me was that I needed to make recovery my new mission in life. He taught me that nothing else was more important, and I listened.

If you had met me previously, I would have told you about my personal mission to change the world through psychedelics. My mission would bring about a change of my generation's consciousness and go on to create a planet of peace as we all grew up together. My mission was indeed a far out and crazy dream to bring a positive change to the world, but it had also failed and gone horribly wrong. As twisted and misguided as my mission had been, the desire to bring about positive change had been sincere and the cause was certainly a noble one, I had just been going about it all wrong. Robert inspired me to carry on my work, just in a different way - a completely opposite way.

Now my mission in life was re-ignited. I was to spread the gospel of recovery in its simplest spiritual way. I would start by working with addicts and learn my craft. My craft was to turn the world on to positive and healthy ambitions, by engaging and behaving in the simple spiritual values I was learning with which to deal with my addiction; honesty, hope, support, encouragement, forgiveness, compassion, sympathy, understanding, generosity, willingness, gratitude, charity, contribution and many, many more that keep occurring to me as I grow and change and develop. I became armed with a full arsenal of reasons to maintain my personal sobriety and, with that power, my life was about to change forever!

It was changing like a new volume in a story from an epic book. Everything was going to be different from here on in. Everything was going to be about serving the greater good. I was back on track with my life's purpose and I felt as if I had a place in the world again. Feeling that way made me feel invincible. Similar to the way I felt when I was using Cocaine - similar, but very different. This feeling was pure. Now I was connected to Mother Earth and my duty was to serve humankind and the planet. In my opinion (which is what matters here), this was a very noble cause. I was happy to accept this duty with open arms.

2. Abstinence? Seems a bit extreme!

Let me give you a quick example, which summarizes the type of poor decisions I'd been making for many years previously. When I smoked a cigarette, I would consume it in 3 or 4 minutes. I wouldn't smoke it slowly, but I'd take long drags on it and hold the smoke down in my lungs as deeply as possible for as long as possible. I was effectively getting high on the oxygen depletion as much as any nicotine buzz I could create. Around the age of twenty-eight, I began coughing in the mornings. I began coughing up phlegm and constantly using my asthma pump. I was always short on breath, unless, I was smoking Crack, in which case I miraculously managed to restore my lungs to full capacity for the duration of the session (often lasting 3 or 4 even 5 days). I don't know how, but I was always able to smoke Crack. But I knew the cigarettes were causing me to struggle with my breathing and were the source of my cough, which was just getting worse and worse, and being noticed by just about everyone. The obvious solution to most people would be what? Stop smoking altogether, right? Pack it in. If eating bread and jam were causing me to come up in a rash, I would stop eating bread and jam, even if I really liked raspberry jam flavour, right? I would stop doing the very thing that was causing me such harm and distress to my body.

However, I wasn't ready to stop. I was nowhere near ready to stop. That conversation was still a very long way off. Stopping smoking? Out of the question. I am a smoker, by definition. That wasn't an option I was prepared to consider. I began making plans to accommodate this cough by constantly carrying my inhaler around with me (which was later to become my Crack pipe), and buying lozenges to suck upon. After a while though, my cough just got worse and my breathlessness was becoming a serious hindrance to even sleeping and to just walk. It seemed like I needed to be smoking Crack just to be able to breathe properly. Even at this point I didn't even consider not smoking cigs, even though I knew smoking was the reason. I negotiated with myself and moved to a lighter brand. I would check the tar levels versus the nicotine levels and I sought out brands with a higher nicotine level but lower tar level. And so, smoking what was a lighter cigarette, I went about my business. But here's what happened, yes my cough did subside for periods and it became less unmanageable, though it never really subsided totally, and I then began smoking more cigarettes than ever before. I went from being a 15/17 a day person, to going up to 30 a day - almost double. Yes, I addressed the problem in sorts, but no, I would not actually do what I really needed to do. I wouldn't ever consider stopping and getting abstinent. That wasn't to happen until I was 5 years sober.

Talk about denial. I wonder if you noticed it? There I was blaming my cough on the cigarettes, and I told you how I was fine whilst smoking Crack. I actually had the audacity and the unconscious denial to blame the fact that my lungs were dependent upon Crack, on the more logical and socially acceptable cigarette smoking. Somehow it seemed a better way to justify my continued Crack smoking, but not address my nicotine addiction. Now that, is really rather screwed up, don't you think?

So, when I went into treatment, I actually had no desire whatsoever to stop using Cocaine. I wanted to stop injecting Heroin. But I didn't have any desire to actually get clean. The only desire I truly had was to get off the Smack and try to stop using needles. While I was in treatment, I had heard all of this abstinence talk thrown around and, although it made sense to me logically, I still wasn't buying it 100%. Abstinence seemed like a pretty extreme way of treating a little drug habit. Abstinence is certainly not the first thing any addict thinks of. When I wanted to treat my little drug habit, I never once considered that I would have to stop using all drugs. What about the drugs I used just for fun? What about the drugs that didn't do any damage? I didn't think I would have to stop using Cocaine as well as Heroin. I certainly didn't think I would have to stop using Es or whizz (amphetamines) or barbiturates or tranquilisers or benzodiazepines or all the good psychedelics, DMT, STP, DOM and DOET. And I really didn't think I would have to stop using the prescription drugs I could get off the doctor. What about drugs that grow out of the ground that we smoke or eat? Surely they were okay? Isn't that a bit extreme? I really didn't think it was necessary to stop drinking, the legal drug any one of us can buy pretty much anywhere. I could not understand why I was being told I wasn't allowed to drink. Then I was to discover why the hard way; I had been drinking non-alcoholic beer just before I overdosed…again!

I was committed on my road to recovery. I took my treatment seriously, though it was a tremendously enjoyable time, despite being very intense and filled with its own dramatic moments, when someone or other would leave campus to go get drunk, or someone would arrive in a blackout, or someone would try to self discharge in order to go and use, and the group would rally around them to try to persuade them to stay. But the disciplines and this new way of living were good for me and the things I was learning were really speaking loudly to me. I had completed eight weeks of primary care there at a facility out in the middle of nowhere before I was moved to a secondary care facility in Kensington, London for an additional seven weeks.

I wanted to make the recovery process as easy as possible for myself, so I did what many people do in treatment facilities and early days of recovery - I paired up with another patient and began an attempt at a romantic relationship. I was flattered that she would be with me, and I think (hope) she felt the same. Together we served each other's needs and although misguided, and by no means suggested by anyone else, I genuinely think it helped me through some of those early days. I found that by forging this relationship, my experience during treatment became much easier to tolerate. We naively, of course, believed we could be in love and that we could live a romantic life together in the long run, making plans to live together and meet each other's parents (her Mother was an Oscar winning actress, so I was really excited whenever I did get the opportunity to meet her).

Now I'm not condoning this sort of behaviour. Most rehabs forbid 'exclusive' relationships, and for good reason. In more cases than not, one or both of the parties is highly likely to relapse or not even begin their recovery journey. So, I'm not condoning it, but I will tell you that my treatment girlfriend and I effectively used one another to cruise our way through rehab. When it came to process groups and sharing, I managed to deflect most of my own issues with her. We would talk about these things outside of the formal structure of group discussions, and I thought that this was very healthy. It was (so I thought) a relationship where we helped each other work through our issues. But the reality was quite different. She became a scapegoat to ensure that I never had to delve too deeply or emotionally in front of the counsellors; you know, the people who were actually qualified to help me deal with my issues. Durrr!

I was about 15 weeks into treatment, and I was working my way through the treatment centre's version of the 12-Step programme and I was on Step nine. It had taken me quite a while to get here because I had come into the facility so unhealthy in the first place. But I was here and I had been working the Steps effectively so far. However, regardless of how successful treatment had been up until this point in my mind, Step nine had me stuck. I was ahead of many of the others in my group - a 2senior peer', so I was frustrated at being in a position that I couldn't just check the Step off my list. I kept telling myself there wasn't long to go, just check it off the list, get it done and I'll be cured and I can get out of here and get on with my life. But, oddly enough, it really doesn't work like that.

Step nine is about making amends. I was supposed to make amends to my aunt. When my grandmother had died, I had been extremely obnoxious and rude, insisting that I could play loud Techno music through the Hi-fi at my parents' house. I was absolutely insensitive and self-orientated, taking no regard of anyone else's feelings. Furthermore, I had come to the funeral armed for life like any other day - completely intoxicated and stoned on Heroin. My aunt had been quite upset by my behaviour, understandably so, and working this Step meant I was supposed to make my amends to her while she was in the country. But I wasn't willing to make the amends. My arrogance wouldn't allow me to be that humble. I was still far too concerned about my own personal image. I was obviously still caught up in my own character defects of selfishness, arrogance and self-centeredness and I was not willing to deal with these personal issues. Nor was I willing to make the changes necessary to move past them. I couldn't even admit that I was being selfish. I was only admitting these things to my girlfriend, which wasn't really helping my process much at all. I had created a written inventory of the things I had done, but there were still far too many things that I didn't care to share in-group or with my counsellors.

We had been taught early on in our treatment process that a higher power, or a God that we can understand, is in our lives to help us. We're taught that we are not powerless in our own lives and that our decisions are still ours, but we're also taught that during our addiction we were powerless over using and that the decisions we thought we were making were, in fact, not choices. We were taught that our addictions render us powerless, and this is why they need to be controlled and understood. I was not able to comprehend any of this. I had not really grasped my own take on whether there was or was not a God yet, and if I should be turning to another power to help me find strength and guidance. Confused? Well, to make matters worse, I still thought that I was in control and had the power to choose. Nuts! Powerful? I had no understanding of the powerlessness I had when it came to my addiction. That is, until I slipped.

My girlfriend and I were in a bar in Camden. We were drinking non-alcoholic beer because we were in recovery and those were the rules, right? But we were drinking non-alcoholic beer alcoholically! Between the pair of us we consumed nine bottles in an hour (I, of course had the extra one). While we were sitting there, she gave me the 'Dear John' story and told me she wanted to separate! I believed it was because she wanted to drink something stronger but didn't want to drag me down with her, so she wanted to cut the cord first.

I was shaken and shocked. I left her and headed back towards West London, going back to an old squat I knew I had left some of my tat in. Upon arrival, I headed for my old bags of stuff that I'd stashed before I'd headed back to my folks almost three months earlier, and I pulled out an old inhaler pump, the kind you use when you have asthma. I had asthma (presumably bought on largely because I was a smoker in the first place), and I had various plastic pumps I used to smoke Crack out of. I could easily justify and disguise this great portable Crack pipe as an actual inhaler (sic) if the police ever stopped me. A little bit of foil, an elastic band and a pin that's all you need. I checked it and there was residue on it – I'd often been in the habit of stashing pipes for rainy days. Part of the addict's protection of supply and the worst-case scenario, desperado mentality I had. I dumped the bags out and started sifting through the stuff. Soon I found enough of these old pipes with sufficient residue to make a smoke. Within a minute and a half I had scraped out the resin and smoked it. When I had that Crack pipe in my hand there was never a question of "Shall I or shall I not?" There was never, a hold on, I am in recovery now, I don't do this stuff anymore." I had a Crack pipe in my hand, I scrapped out the resin and I smoked it, no questions asked. Why? Because that was exactly what I did any time I had a Crack pipe in my hand. Old habits die hard - really hard.

Once I had smoked what was left in those pipes, I was off. Within moments my mentality had shifted. I was seized by my head and its immediate obsession to go do this properly. I needed to score and I needed to score right now! I was back to my old way of thinking and, to make matters worse or improve the situation depending upon how you choose to interpret it, I had cash in my pocket and nothing could stop me. I scored a half-gram of white (Crack) and a half-gram of brown (Heroin). And I was heading over to a girl's place. It was like nothing had ever changed. There was always a girl involved and this wasn't the same girl I was in Camden with - my (now ex) rehab girlfriend. This was a different girl I was going over to see. Someone I knew from rehab who, as a day patient, wasn't taking her treatment very seriously. We all knew she was using throughout her rehab and so we all knew where we should go should we ever choose to use again. She offered us a sanctuary. She wouldn't judge us. She wouldn't give us a hard time. She'd simply expect us to split it with her. I needed somewhere safe to use this and I needed to use it with someone who was going to be discreet. I figured I'd be safe at her place, since she was unlikely to tell anyone what we were up to.

So, I am at her house, I put all the Crack in the spoon at once, and before taking the hit, I added a small amount of Heroin - about a 16th of a gram (this is a relatively very small amount - about £5 in value). I had more than a couple months of clean time under my belt and my veins were coming back. I was pretty healthy and it was easy to get the vein the first time. With that single jab, I felt myself going up and up and up and then - this time I seemed to know - I was going over. But as always, when you know you're about to go over it's always too late. Comic Relief 2001 was on the TV and I remember Posh and Becks being interviewed by Ali G. I saw their faces but couldn't hear them or make sense of what was happening and then it went black. The girl called an ambulance and promptly nicked my remaining drugs! The ambulance guys came in, found me and resuscitated me on the spot. I guess I was unconscious for an hour or so. It's hard to tell, except that I never did see the Posh and Becks interview. That was the last time I used. I say that was the last time, but obviously, I had to go back to the spent filters from my hit to see if I could squeeze anymore out, since the girl had nicked the rest of my Smack. However, after that very nearly tragic experience, I had a severe and profound wake-up call, and no illegal narcotics have entered my body since that day. That was 16th March 2001. That was my sober day.

3. Powerless

It would appear that when I drink alcohol I have a reaction that manifests itself with one-millilitre syringes full of Class 'A' drugs. Even when I am drinking non-alcoholic beer, the pattern of behaviour is still the same -identical. Not only did I not get drunk, but I still almost died! Now, that is really screwed up. What I finally understood from that episode was that once I started drinking (non-alcoholic) beer in a bar (or anywhere for that matter), I was drinking it alcoholically, and I had already relinquished my control over how much I would drink (five bottles in an hour) and when I would stop (after being resuscitated by paramedics). I had already put the wheels in motion to set off my prior patterns of behaviour. So for me, alcoholic or non-alcoholic drinks seemed to have the same result. It reminds me of a time when some of my friends arrived at a warehouse rave we were having somewhere near Toulouse, Southwest France, with a few ounces of novocaine, which they told us was Cocaine. Novocaine is from the same family as Cocaine, except it doesn't give you the same effect. It tastes the same. It smells the same. It even numbs your mouth, lips, nose, muscles when applied which is why dentists use it before pulling your teeth out; but it doesn't give you any sort of high. However, once snorted, it makes you want more. I craved more novocaine, even though I wasn't sure if it was very good Cocaine or not, even after the third line. I was craving something that only tasted like a drug. It wasn't even actually a mind altering chemical, but yet I was convinced I needed more. Doh!

By the way, the reason they had a few ounces of novocaine was to cut their Cocaine with something that completely resembled Coke, but is a fraction of the price - medicinal grade novocaine purchased from the same place that a dentist practice would buy it. Personally, I think that's one of the more genius cuts to use. Certainly it's less damaging than some of the stuff I've seen and I even resorted to using from time to time.

So, it seems I have no control over substances that even reassemble the real stuff. I can't control non-alcoholic beer, like I can't control non-narcotic novocaine. Damn it! This is leading me to understand that I have some sort of physical intolerance to these substances, which is kind of strange because I always believed I had an enormous tolerance. I suppose in an odd way I have both types - tolerance and intolerance. This could be understood to mean that due to my inability to control my substance intake, I've lost the power of control.

So, looking back and reflecting once again on this relapse to where I retrospectively believe I was baulking on my treatment centre's 9th Step from their workbook, I now realise that I was baulking because I had not really and truly become humble enough to ask for help in removing my shortcomings. In fact, I had not become entirely ready to have them removed. I had not been fearless and thorough even though I had read it out in Step five after having written about it earlier in Step four. I hadn't actually made the decision at all in the third Step based on the fact that I didn't genuinely believe that any of this was going to restore me to sanity. What I had failed to grasp was right back at the beginning. What had failed me in my recovery was my own lack of commitment and understanding right back at Step one. The reason I picked up that Crack pipe that night and scraped it out was because I hadn't understood the very solid foundation lessons and teachings of my recovery programme. Step one talks about being powerless over your addictive substances. This powerlessness that it refers to is what I understand today as choice or lack there off.

So now I'm really in trouble. I have neither control nor choice. I'm doomed!

Or at least any drug and alcohol use is doomed - doomed to leave me in a wreck - doomed to rip from me any ability genuinely to enjoy myself again.

I didn't have the choice to leave that pipe when I found it. I didn't have the choice to say "No". In a broader sense, this lack of control and inability to make healthy choices could be referred to as powerlessness, which is how it's referred to in the 12-Step programme of recovery. This powerlessness can also be translated to godlessness. In Step two, we are taught that a power greater than oneself can restore one to sanity and that God will give us the power to resist. But I didn't have that power. At least I didn't have that sort of power at this early stage of my development. I hadn't completed those first nine out of the 12-Steps successfully at all.

But there was something different about me after this overdose episode. Maybe, some of you reading this will identify with me? After my overdose, over the next

24 hours, I had a period of inspired thought where I had the realisation of this understanding around powerlessness. That actually became the foundation for my recovery. I finally understood. I understood that I couldn't simply have a drink. I couldn't safely use a line. Smoking one pipe will never be a reality for me. Even drinking non-alcoholic beer will lead me back to one mil syringes. I have not drunk or used drugs since that day.

This wasn't my first moment of clarity, and it wouldn't be my last, but it was a very profound one. One of my first moments of clarity had come the first time I had been drug and alcohol free for a few days. I'd attempted various methods of detoxing myself, but when I did that final self-enforced detox at my folks' home, I did it by myself and was then enrolled in this treatment facility to finish it off. I went through the worse of it at my parents' house before I was institutionalised. So, it was a few days after that when I had a moment of clarity when my head popped out of my arse (where it had been for a very long time) and there was the realisation that having come this far and being entirely drug and alcohol free for the first time in 13 years, I did not want to turn back. I knew that this was the path I wanted to take. What I did not know was just how difficult it was going to be.

Another 'blindingly obvious' moment of realisation came to me when I understood just how much of an expense sending me to rehab was costing my parents financially. And I met quite a number of other patients who were back for a 3rd, 4th or even 5th or 6th attempt at rehab. I knew that I couldn't treat my parents like that. I was grateful for them having spent a small fortune on my treatment, but I wasn't going to fuck it up and not get it right first time. I couldn't put them through this financial burden a second time. It wouldn't be fair. So I had to get this right first shot.

I became willing to do anything and everything to change my life, even though my attitude, my habits and the changes that happened in my life were to be a much more gradual process. So, even though I had the willpower never to use again, my story proves that this isn't enough. Simply having the desire not to use or drink wasn't enough actually not to use or drink. I required more than just my own willpower, since I proved to myself that I was using even against my own will or desire. It was after my relapse, after having to be rescued, resuscitated and revived that my whole self truly committed to the changes that needed to be made. I had seen the light of recovery and it's possibilities. I had tried it and I had liked it, but for some reason I had this 'just one more hit' syndrome going round my head. I had been unable to successfully shake that nagging thought of what it would be like just to have one more hit - the perfect hit, the right dose, in the vein first time with good gear and a clean body - 'just one more hit' syndrome.

I made a decision when I came back from being resuscitated that I wanted to get back those few months of relative stability I'd just thrown away, and get clean again. I mourned the loss of those first 60 or 70 days of clean time (depending upon how you calculate it) and I was disappointed in myself when I went to expose myself to the group at the rehab and back to the 12-Step Fellowship rooms. However, I think that was the moment I became willing to do anything and everything to change my life. On that day, I fully conceded to my innermost self, that I was an addict and I could not only never drink or use safely again, but unless I got serious about my sobriety, I wasn't going to keep it. That hasn't changed since that day.

My sobriety date is 16th March 2001, and that includes weekends, holidays, birthdays, weddings, warm Summer nights and cold Winter nights, tragedies and successes, leap years and any other excuse you can think of - no matter what.

4. Unmanageability – the longest word in my vocabulary

I believe that 'unmanageability' is the longest word I know. Before I got sober, the longest word I knew was 'wheelbarrow' which has 11 letters. Not bad, eh? Maybe longer than you'd expect; 11 letters is quite decent. But as I got sober I discovered new words. Words that were new to me, such as patience (8), tolerance (9), discipline (10) compassion (10), generosity (10), forgiveness (11), spirituality (12), contribution (12) understanding (13), powerlessness (13), and unmanageability which at 15 letters is a pretty good double-word score in scrabble, if you ever have enough letters, Looking back at the length of my new words, 'wheelbarrow' really wasn't too shabby a long word to know.

I think the first obstacles on the road to recovery are emotional. I have said before how using Heroin strips you from your emotional self. You lose all feeling. When using Heroin you may understand logically that a situation is happy, sad or funny but you don't actually feel it. When you remove the drug from your system you start to feel everything again, and this can be unbelievably overwhelming. You start to feel things so intensely as you take a journey through emotions you haven't felt in years - some you may have forgotten even existed - that your feelings appear quite extreme. Personally, I experienced emotions that I was sure I had never felt before. It was certainly stuff that I didn't recognise. These feelings were unusual, they were not necessarily unpleasant just unfamiliar to me. It can be a tricky minefield to navigate through for someone who is already feeling raw and vulnerable.

When my rehab girlfriend and I split up, I was thrown into an emotional whirlpool of anger, rage and resentment. It was so intense, and yet this girl and I had only been seeing each other for four or five weeks or so. Regardless of the short duration of this relationship, I was incredibly hurt by it. I had not experienced a reaction like that for a few years. The last time I had felt that level of hurt and betrayal was when my relationship with Lolette had ended after four years because she cheated on me during my final weeks on Guadeloupe. That had cut me up so badly that I wanted to kill her new man and then kill myself. It threw me out of kilter for over three months. The only escape from those sorts of feelings, that I knew, was to get obliterated and stop feeling (and thinking) anything. After I had passed through the grieving process, it dumped in a place of extreme recklessness. It was from here on in that I adopted the needle as my preferred method of drug delivery. It was here that I went into the larger scale trafficking and wholesale distribution. It was here that I became truly soulless, and by that I mean that my spirit was so damaged that I didn't care anymore. I only cared about me and my next hit. I only cared about ensuring that my needs were met on a daily basis and I began to trample across anyone who crossed my path.

But here I was after just a month long, cosy relationship and it was genuinely profound to experience that sort of emotional extremity again. In fact, during my early years of recovery it began to happen time and time again. Each new relationship seemed to last just a few weeks and leave me feeling dreadful all over again, despite the insignificance of the relationship. Actually, these displays of extreme emotion still exist in my life today; I'm just not as shocked or rattled by them these days.

I cry watching TV sometimes. I recently cried on the plane on a trip to the USA and I openly cried in front of the other passengers. I was watching Invictus, which is about Nelson Mandela's attempts to win over the hearts and minds of the white South African people after his election, as well as the black support, but it's told through the tale of the South African Rugby Team, The Springboks. I don't have a problem with that. I'm not ashamed of my emotions. I'm not ashamed of crying. I'm not ashamed of laughing either. In fact, I love to laugh. It is one of the most wonderful things about being sober, being able to truly laugh and enjoy myself. Since I started my journey along the road to recovery, music and comedy have been wonderful tools for me to express myself emotionally at all ends of the emotional spectrum. To this day, I need to surround myself with music all the time, at work, in the car, when I am thinking; I am always playing music. I still love comedy too. My wife and I sit together and watch comedians all the time. It's one of our favourite nights out; it always feels good to laugh. And a quick note about smiling - smiling is infectious. If I smile at someone else they're likely to smile back or avert their gaze because they're too self-conscious to deal with someone (a stranger) smiling at them. I'm smiling right now, reading and writing this. When we smile, we feel good. Unless we're acting or being sarcastic, a smile will almost certainly raise someone's mood. So, the easiest way to make someone feel better is to smile at them. What a gift!

"Keep smiling because life is a beautiful thing and there is so much to smile about"

– Marilyn Monroe

After my overdose, I went back to the 12-Step recovery meetings that I had been introduced to via my rehab. Everyone had come back from their annual convention and had the most amazing energy from what they had seen, heard and experienced. They were carrying a message of hope and they delivered it directly to me with a friendship and a camaraderie I had never experienced before. This group of people seemed to love me unconditionally. They tolerated my behaviour despite the fact that I really didn't know how to behave as a part of civilised society. They gathered around me, encouraging me to come back to the meetings. They helped by guiding me and encouraging me to make the right decisions. They explained to me when it was appropriate to change my behaviour and when it was appropriate to change my clothes. They reminded me of that fairly often. I had obviously picked up a few bad habits over the years, and not caring about hygiene was one of them.

RECOVERY – *rehab & the early years*

One of my first recovery mentors said to me "Ian, you're going to go far... because you have so far to go!" All of my new found recovery friends, mentors, sponsors, fellow newcomers, etc. were always gentle and kind, nudging me in the right direction. These new friends would take me out for coffee and buy me meals. Some would even come and pick me up and take me to meetings. They wouldn't take me anywhere else, only to meetings. They carried me, and my spirit, to meetings. People have asked me about the dilemma of carrying addicts. At what point are you enabling or carrying someone? This is as far as anyone carried me. They carried me to meetings. So, if you want to carry an addict, or you feel like you are carrying one, encourage them to go to meetings. It's the best place for any addict to find identification with others who are on the same path as they are, thus developing a connection deep enough to build trust and building a healthy solution-based relationship. These 12-Step Fellowships loved me like no other camaraderie I had ever experienced. I have been in many different kinds of Fellowships, in recovery and in the tribes, communities and crews that I moved around in for so many years. The groups I was exposed to in 12-Step recovery were every bit as much my family and friends as anyone else I had ever been associated with.

When I started going to these meetings, I was still very new to my own recovery and I really didn't know how to fit in. But I opened myself up and allowed myself to learn. I was more than willing to be inspired and I'm sure it is because of this that I was motivated very early on. I wanted so badly what these people had. I wanted to feel the way they did. So, when I spoke to them, I did my best to adopt their behaviours and patterns and find a way to adapt into their lifestyle. I was trying to assimilate. It was a successful strategy. I opened my arms and my heart to those who were prepared to listen, and then I did what they advised.

One of the first questions an addict needs to ask when embarking on their recovery path is whether or not they have had enough pain. Are they ready to become abstinent yet? Abstinence is always the biggest block to a permanent sober lifestyle. It's easy to say you have a problem with Cocaine but you want to keep drinking. My experience has shown me that if I have a problem with Cocaine, one drink will switch my brain into party mode and those little voices in my head will tell me to go and get some Coke, just to help me with this little drink I'm having. It will tell me lies and it will deceive me into thinking that the two substances aren't related. It tricks me into believing that I can drink and/or use without consequences, despite all the experience I have to the contrary.

It's Not About Me!

For some reason, I believe that this time it'll be different. In my case, even a non-alcoholic beer is a trigger for my more dangerous addictions. It's not necessarily the first drink or drug that I use initially that's the problem. It's where that very first drink or drug will lead me to that's the real issue. So why risk it? Why risk using the very things I don't want to be doing because of the old limiting belief that this other less intense drink or drug won't cause me any harm? Get over it. Get over myself. Learn how to be happy and content without believing that the drink or drug that I first take will give me sufficient pleasure. Learn to be happy, joyous and free through life. Like those 70s hippies would say, "I'm high on life". I don't like that slogan, but it's kind of true. Let's learn to be happy, joyous and free just by living life on life's terms and without trying to improve upon it chemically. That's why abstinence is the only option for complete recovery.

As I went through this process of determining whether I was ready to live a drug and alcohol free life, and I asked myself if I had suffered enough pain, I realised that I wanted the pain to end. I realised quickly that I was ready to do whatever it took to take that pain away. It seems to be quite a universal phrase, effective change can only occur once the individual has experienced such significant emotional pain that they are ready to go to any length in order to change.

It works in all areas of life. Recently I realised that I was putting on too much weight. I was sick of the pain of looking down at my ever-expanding gut and finally I said, enough! I have to do something about this! So, I changed my diet. I was already exercising four or five times a week, so I had to change my diet quite radically to get the results that I desired. It took me enough pain to be able to commit to that decision and the pain wasn't physical, it was emotional. That is where it has to start. By the way, I recently successfully climbed Mount Kilimanjaro! More about that later.

It is this level of unmanageability which ruled my life before. So caught up in emotional baggage i couldn't get rid of because of my suppressed emotions, I was caught in a never-ending cycle of addiction trying to feel better about the way I was feeling by using the very things that were making me feel dreadful in the first place, all the time believing they were helping me deal with the lack of happiness in my life. Ah yes, very unmanageable indeed.

5. A brief explanation of Recovery

Getting clean and sober, stopping and staying stopped is difficult. There is no doubt about that. As an addict it may be the hardest thing that you will ever do. In my experience, it was certainly the hardest thing I had ever done up until that point in my life. But you can do it. It involves every part of your body and your mind. It's not just a physical addiction that you have to kick. It's more than that. Much more! It's an intellectual process of thoughts that you have to change because, without making those changes, you are sure to fail and fail again. This is because it affects our emotions. When I feel lousy I use, and I don't feel so lousy. When I feel great I use, and I feel even greater. If everything's just 'OK', then I use and I don't notice just how 'OK' it is. I like to feel fantastic, and I found that I could use drugs and alcohol in order to ensure that I was feeling fantastic as much and as often as possible. So, take away that opportunity to artificially change the way I feel to improve my emotional state and I'm left with a bunch of unsatisfied feelings, which suddenly start speaking very loudly in my mind.

I knew what I was doing was killing me. I had track marks running up and down my arms. I was sick to my stomach. I was dying and I knew, logically, that I had to stop. But there was another voice in my head, another mind-set, and another attitude that justified my behaviour. I was able to talk myself out of getting help by telling myself I was just having a bad day. That tomorrow, things would be better. I kept telling myself that what I was experiencing was just a bad patch and I would sort myself out sooner or later, whatever that meant.

I was brought up to believe that doctors would help me to preserve my health. Culturally, that is how we are all born and raised. You get the sniffles, you go to the doctor. You have something wrong with your body, you go to the doctor. Doctors are there to help you, right? I believed that my addiction was a health problem, so I went to doctors. I asked for help and the doctors would put me on drugs that they promised would help me. But my drug addled mind convinced me that these drugs being prescribed were just as good as those I got off the street, even better, they were free! So, here I was, dying, addicted and messed up with a concoction of drugs going in and out of my body, and in and out of my possession. Drugs were drugs as far as I was concerned, and as long as I wasn't feeling the pain of not entertaining a mind-altered state, I was happy enough. I went on like this for a while, pretending to try to get clean in order to qualify for free prescription drugs, and then scoring off the street to 'top myself up'. Either way, I was always high. Thankfully, eventually my head popped out of my arse and yelled at me, "How did your life become this?"

That is where my whole journey to recovery started. Not with trying to get help from doctors and nurses and drug-toting professionals. My recovery started on the day my head climbed out of my arse and I managed to shake some sense into myself.

In England, the National Health Service (NHS) is a service the government provides to complement the welfare of its residents. It's a fine effort at allowing anyone with any sort of ailment to receive treatment free of charge, though sometimes there's a long waiting list. Its primary function is designed to help people in need of treatment for health problems receive the appropriate treatment without unnecessary or prolonged pain. But my experience with the NHS and their attitude towards the treatment of alcoholism or addiction is not a positive one, and it is an area that I am quite opinionated about because of what I have directly experienced.

The NHS does a great job at patching up the problems that are caused by someone's affliction. They cover up the symptoms of someone's drinking (liver disease, malnutrition, jaundice, etc.) or someone's drug use with prescriptions. It's the same with tobacco smokers. They receive treatment for the harmful effects that smoking causes (cancer, lung disease, etc.) but, up until recently, they would not receive adequate help actually stopping smoking (note: This has since changed over the past few years; the government is now pumping plenty of money into smoking-cessation efforts, to wonderful results). Very often, the attitude is to help the people feel better...but just for today. Let's prescribe something that treats the symptoms of your ailment, rather than the ailment itself. But what the NHS fails to do - or has failed to do in the past - is actually to treat the root cause of the addiction. This is where the NHS has gone wrong in its attitude towards addiction treatments. When I needed help and went to the NHS, they simply treated the symptoms of my diverse addiction problems. I found that incredibly distressing. When I asked for help with my Crack habit all I got was free condoms and some advice about safe sex. When I asked for help with my Heroin habit I was signed up for free Methadone. When I asked for help for my drinking I was given no help whatsoever, aside from suggestions that I should try to control the amounts I drank (notice they never suggested I should actually stop - just drink less). It was all inappropriate, wholly inappropriate. An alcoholic cannot possibly 'drink less'; with any addiction, it is all or nothing (abstinence). This is why I have worked in the private sector since

I got sober. Remember I mentioned the man in the suit who had inspired me into recovery? Dr. Robert Lefever had installed in me the importance of finding a reason to get clean and so I intuitively knew that I had got this far in life for the purpose of helping other addicts break their own habits and find a way out of the downward spiral. But because of my experiences with the public sector, I could never have imagined working for them.

The problem, of course, with the private sector is that regardless of how good our work is, we aren't free...so we aren't able to help everyone. That said, I don't endorse the government and I don't stand against it. It is true that the government has been more vocal recently about adopting more changes towards better abstinence models as effective treatment methods. Unfortunately, there just isn't the money to support it. Politics and money, at the end of the day, can be what saves or what destroys a person when they decide they want to recover. They either get the help they need and they recover, or they don't and they die an addict, sooner or later.

The other concern I have with the government's attitude towards the drug problem is their insistence that it be criminal related and not health. You're more likely to receive help if you're referred through the probation services because you got nicked, than if you're body is shutting down due to your alcoholism and you go see your doctor. Why this insistence that drug addicts get treated through the criminal justice sector and not the health sector is the biggest crime of all. It means that law-abiding drug users and alcoholics must break the law before they receive any treatment. What sort of a message is that?

When I started noticing that I had become a person I didn't want to become, I tried to stop what I was doing. I tried to turn my life around. But that is a difficult process. Getting clean and staying clean is the hardest part of any addict's life story. When I stopped using drugs I couldn't help but ask myself, "Have I stopped behaving like a drug addict?" This is why there are therapies to help; because it is not just recognising the behaviours, it's also trying to stop them from reoccurring. It is certainly a difficult process. Once an addict has developed a selfish, obsessional mind-set of "I want this drug/drink/behaviour/ attitude, etc. for me", and most addicts develop this at some point before or during their addiction, it is a very difficult emotional and intellectual habit to break. Addicts who don't have help changing their thought processes can still look at life through a selfish lens, even long after assumed recovery. There's a saying that 'you can take a drunken horse thief and you can sober him up, but you're still left with a horse thief'. So, we need to stop being horse thieves and we need to start being cowboys.

The early stages of recovery are hard; there is no easy way to get through them. When working with a recovering addict you are helping them tackle a disease that is telling them what they can do (in fact, what they should do) exactly what it is they are trying to stop doing. Relapse is fairly frequent, though by no means a certainty, and happens to the majority of addicts at some point during their recovery process, normally at a very early stage. All this being said, I want to be very clear that any addict will recover if they adopt the right mind-set and are prepared to go to any length necessary to make the change that they want to see in their lives. The message is one of hope; the hard work is always worth it - you can recover!

In the 12-Step environment you're encouraged to get a sponsor (a coach or mentor) to help guide you through your recovery and beyond. This person is someone who is there to help the new person learn and reflect on a life of sobriety. Your sponsor becomes your most useful friend who has your emotional and mental wellbeing when times are good and when times are bad. A good sponsor encourages you to behave well, teaches you what to do next and how to protect your body and your mind. Once you've progressed through the programme and are strong enough yourself, you will be encouraged to sponsor the next newcomer that arrives behind you.

I have been through the process myself and, for a long time, have been sponsoring addicts myself. As a sponsor I never make up things and I always lean on my own experience to help guide my new friend through their own recovery. It's all about learning from other people's mistakes and experiences, finding a way to connect with each other on a difficult part of life and find hope even in mistakes and slip ups. When I was in my early stages of recovery it helped me a great deal to know I wasn't alone, that the way I was feeling wasn't weird or different or unusual. I got this reassurance and faith from the stories of how other people coped during the beginning of their recovery.

Before I entered recovery, I had absolutely no concept of what it would take to achieve it. I really never considered I would recover. I had no idea that I was going to become abstinent. In fact, I didn't have a clue I was going to stop much before a few days before I actually did stop. Something happened, the levy broke and I made a decision to make a profound change in my life. Once

I did see it was something that suited me and something I could fit into, I just immersed myself in it and dedicated myself to it fully. It felt right and good and like it was exactly the thing I should be doing. It was then that I knew I would survive as long as I stuck with it. As I began seeing changes in myself and in other people, I knew that it was working and my faith in the programme solidified even further.

Physically, I transformed, and it was quite incredible. When I started the journey, I was under 8 ⅛ stones. Within a year I gained around 30% of my body weight, going up to 11.5 stones, I looked like a completely different and much healthier version of myself, one I had never seen before in my adult life. The other changes I noticed quickly both in myself and in others were the psychodynamic changes. During recovery, people become able to communicate much more freely. We talk together much more openly and we are far more comfortable talking not only about our own but also about other people's emotions and journeys. Recovering addicts go through a process where they are encouraged to be more relaxed when it comes to expressing themselves and, when the lights come on, you finally see these people for the first time, with their eyes truly open. These people then gradually become employable, or ready to return to work, for they are now functioning members of society again and can be engaged in interesting conversation and relied upon to make sensible decisions. The miracle is that if you were to write what you wanted to achieve in one year's time, you would achieve that and significantly more. The final results will always be well beyond what you could have possibly imagined. The goals you can achieve are endless because, through this process, you become powerful.

I guess what I'm trying to say is that recovery isn't simply about no longer drinking or using. It's about so much more than that. Recovery is about regaining the reins of your life and doing something fabulous with your destiny. It's not about sitting still watching the world revolve around you. And it's not about waiting for life to happen. It's about setting a new pace and making changes in your life which not only affect you in a positive way, but which also go on to contribute something back to society as a result of your doing the right thing more often. Obviously everyone's got different levels of interaction with the rest of the world, but recovery is a second chance. What are you going to do with your second chance? Please make sure your second chance isn't wasted on you! Please make sure your second chance is of benefit to more people than just yourself. That's what recovery is. It's about understanding that your life mustn't be only about you ...anymore.

6. A little history lesson

I am quite strong minded and strong willed. I truly believe that the only solution for a true addict and alcoholic is one of abstinence and the discovery of some sort of spiritual attitude in order to successfully recover. What do I mean by spiritual attitude? I mean to come to understand that there's a whole world out there and that listening to your own head will no longer serve you until you accept the rest of the planet's existence and their right to exist - nothing too deep, religious or confining. Everyone can make their own judgments as to what spirituality means to them, but this is a good place to start.

There is a distinction in my mind between an addict who uses drugs and a person who is addicted to drugs. Someone who is merely addicted to drugs can with sufficient reason (marriage, new job, relocation, children, etc.) make the choice to stop using regularly. This sort of person has the ability to use socially from time to time or drink casually with friends without falling back into the stronghold of addiction. Most of my friends I used to run around with fall into this category of people. These people have moved on from their addictive drug days to a normal, healthy life. They have settled down and taken on responsibilities, and found their vocation in life, maybe a good job or career, and yet they still they manage to use drugs socially and recreationally without any ill effect on their lives.

But an addict who uses drugs, someone who has the addictive disease, which manifests itself through sheer selfishness, greed, obstinacy, etc. (like myself) clearly comes up short on the spiritual front, and therefore could be considered to have a spiritual illness which manifests itself through these thoughts and behaviours and finds personal salvation through using drink or drugs (to find inner calm). So, I believe there has to be a spiritual solution. That's not to say I'm the only person with such beliefs. Almost all of my elementary spiritual practices and teachings came through the 12-Step Fellowships, which were born in the 1930s.

The founders of the 12-Step recovery programme were members of a strict Christian sect called the Oxford Groups, founded in 1908. These groups were focused on changing the world, one man at a time. They held meetings at members' homes and encouraged new members to 'surrender' on their knees, whilst explaining to the group their 'sin' such as their alcoholism. The Oxford Groups had strict principles known as the Four Absolutes.

1. Absolute Honesty
2. Absolute Purity
3. Absolute Unselfishness
4. Absolute Love

It was considered a necessity within the Oxford Groups to share with the group. It was perceived that this sharing allowed for healing and it was a blessing to the members, since it bought relief and victory over the sin they were sharing, or so they believed. They stressed that members shared to the group with total conviction, stating that half measures will be as fruitless as no measures.

The two founders of Alcoholics Anonymous, who wrote the original 12-Step programme, were both exposed to the Oxford Groups, until they were asked to leave and to take their alcoholics with them. They then designed the AA programme based upon the 6 Tenants of the Oxford Groups.

1. Admission of personal defeat
2. Taking of personal inventory
3. Confession of one's defects to another person
4. Making restitution to those one has harmed
5. Helping others selflessly
6. Praying to God for the power to put these precepts into practice

As you turn to the back of this book, you'll find I outline the actual 12-Step programme in detail and you'll be able to see how they've evolved from this original process. In many ways, keeping things simple, these 6 Tenants can still be interpreted extremely effectively to bring about change for whatever process you're working through, so long as the individual believes they'll work.

Anyhow, I believe everyone is born a spiritual being, and whilst being exposed to modern civilisation they become torn away from their natural spiritual essence to various degrees. It's the old 'nature versus nurture' question again, and I believe it's a mixture of both. The more one is exposed to negative sectors of modern civilisation and a totalitarian, agriculture-based democracy, the less likely one is to remain pure. It takes a great deal of substance and personal integrity to remain in line with the 4 absolutes of the Oxford Groups, which are a great way of considering our levels of spirituality.

Please be clear with me here. I am in no way endorsing any form of religion or cult or particular faith. But I do believe in the essence of what all religions appear to be encouraging us with. I do believe in the very simple message that's shared by all the various religious figureheads such as Jesus, Buddha, Moses, Allah, and even some of the more mortal incantations such as Dalai Lama, Gandhi, Mother Theresa, Nelson Mandela, Thich Nhat Hanh, Deepak Chopra, Krishna Das, Swami Ramdev, Rabbi Debbie Young-Somers, or [insert your own personal preferred spiritual teacher here, if you wish]. That message is simple. "Be nice."

I have my own understanding of spiritual theory, which may or may not be universal. However, regardless of what particular faith or lack of you are taught, or what you are encouraged to believe, every person with addictive disease, and a spiritual shortcoming will need to take some form of spiritual restitution if they are to ever fully enjoy life again, without the continued companion of their destructive addictive substance or behaviour. We can all help guide an addict down the various spiritual pats, but they will need to begin by surrendering to their illness or addiction first. One thing I am sure of is that the Oxford Groups were spot on when they required their members to firstly admit personal defeat or the rest of the journey to recovery. Well I know what's worked for me, and I know what works for the men and women that I work with, but I am certainly not closed minded enough to believe that there is only one right pathway to recovery. There are many different journeys and I'd like to encourage people to find their own, particularly if they choose not to adopt one similar to mine. I absolutely do not have the monopoly of the only one righteous method - absolutely not.

7. Truly an Addict

As the parent or friend of an addict, one might try to understand the difference between a recreational drug user and an addict in order to try and classify their loved one. But I'm here to tell you there isn't much point in doing that. If someone needs to stop using, we can help him or her, whether they are a recreational drug user, heavy user or full-blown addict. It's down to the individual to make that decision, although we can certainly help point them in the right direction. No one can force an addict or alcohol user into recovery, but we can help guide him or her in, and we can certainly put enough pressure on them in order to assist them in making the right decisions, "No, not by torture, but by the way of a Family Intervention, managed by my company". Making the choice to get sober or drug free is never a process that can be forced upon someone, so unless they make a decision to get sober or clean, the programme is not likely to be successful. Our Interventions allow them to make the right decision and accept the help that's on offer to them.

Some users will undertake many different processes and recovery efforts before they are ready to concede to their doomed reality. Someone else may have been on a path of destruction for many years and wake up one day and realise they want to change their life, and their journey to recovery will start on that day. If someone is using drugs to the extent they are damaging their lives in any way; if they are spiralling downward, hurting themselves or the people around them, then they need to be guided towards recovery. For most people, stopping using is all they need to get their life back on track. They can stop performing the daily damaging ritual and turn their life around. You'll never really recognise these people, because they simply get on and do it. They don't really need any outside help or assistance. They simply go about changing their lives. For maybe a 10% minority, it involves far more than just stopping drugs. It involves complete restructuring of one's attitude and outlook on life. So, if you're asking yourself whether a particular person you're worried about actually needs outside help, then they do! The reason I know this is because you're asking the question. If they didn't need outside help, then they have probably made that decision already, or they're about to.

Sometimes, during the preliminary stages of an Intervention I'm asked "How do you know what type of help 'so and so' needs? You've never even met them!" Whilst I think it's down to the individual to discover that for themselves; when I've been asked in to examine a case by other family members, there's usually good reason, and it's normally because the addict/alcoholic hasn't decided to accept help or admit defeat yet, even though the family know what's going on. It would be judgmental of me to start saying, "That person is definitely an addict, or that person is a problematic user" without actually getting to know the client first. But in the case where we've been asked in, there's genuinely always good cause to take the word of the concerned party, rather than wait to find out and prove the point. Furthermore, it's worth pointing out that I am very well qualified to make a remote assessment of someone, based upon the description of his or her behaviour and attitudes, as relayed to me by, for instance, a loving parent or spouse. I've been doing this long enough to see the little behavioural traits and patterns that every addict seems to betray.

So, when the question arises whether they are an addict or not, the best answer is "Yes", since the treatment for addiction works on everyone whether they're an addict or not. Even if they're just a small time user or part-time binge drinker, or they receive the same treatment as a full-blown addict or alcoholic, then their chances of successfully changing their lives are 100% more likely than not receiving any treatment at all.

Don't bother questioning whether you are an addict or not. If you've got a problem with drink or drugs and you're unable to sort yourself out and you require outside help, by simply accepting the same treatment as an addict, you're much more likely to get a successful resolution to your situation. Why mess around with semantics? Just accept the help that's on offer, and make the change on offer to you count!

Let me put it this way to you. Are you that convinced you're not an addict that you're prepared to risk your life on it? It's like if you have cancer, would you want to take the risk that it's not malignant and it's actually benign? Or would you prefer to treat it with everything you can to make sure you zap it out of your system, just in case it is malignant. You don't pussy foot around, do you? You take the harder most effective and permanent form of treatment. Well problematic versus full- blown addictive drinking and using should be treated the same way. But don't worry, the treatments we have on offer are actually really pleasantly healing. It's not like you're poisoning yourself with toxic chemotherapy or radiotherapy. This is the easier, softer option.

So, there I was on 16th March 2001, returning to life after that almost fatal hit, and I understood at that very moment as my senses began returning to my body after that over-dose, that all I truly wanted to do was to get back my sobriety, which I could now see I had lost. Those first few months of recovery experience had had a profound and ever-lasting impression on me. In such a relatively short time I could already see that life could be so much better than ever before. But yet, I'd not been able to shake that 'one more hit' syndrome. Aha, but no that 'one more hit syndrome' was out of my system; the question was would I ever need to have another one? Well the answer to that thus far, and I trust forever more is "No, never again".

Something happened. A few days later I began to sense that something strange and permanent was occurring. I actually felt better than I had ever felt previously. All it seemed to take was that full surrender and final acceptance of what had happened, and what could now happen. The future looked so bright. I had hope, profound optimism and gratitude in a full-frontal pose!

Here I was, back at the beginning of my clean-time journey, with a near-death experience to cheer me up, but I felt safe; I felt welcomed, loved, tolerated, forgiven.

I understood intuitively, at that point, that when I drink non-alcoholic beer or any other substance, I lose control over where I'm going to end up. It's like I become possessed. I don't act like myself. I don't behave like myself. I don't treat people the way I normally would. I don't react to people as I normally would; the 'Dr. Jekyll and Mr. Hyde' syndrome. I get it! I have no control over what is going to happen next. All bets are off as to what's going to happen. I have lost the power of control. I am powerless. It is really screwed up when you think about it; that when I start I can't stop, and when I stop I can't keep myself from starting again.

That's the kind of dilemma that we find ourselves in before we are exposed to the tools we need to combat the issue. When I start I can't stop; and when I stop I can't keep myself from starting again. The only way I found it possible to stop was through a power that wasn't available to me until I had surrendered to the fact that I was screwed. Once I was able to see, believe and accept this powerlessness, help seemed to arrive from an external energy, that I was then able to start owning. How crazy is that? Or rather, how much evidence is there for me in this fact that there could be a power greater than myself (God?), and that most importantly, it isn't me!

This external power was able to give me such a big gift. It gave me the power to control my own life through love. It allowed me to begin to choose my destiny once again. Rather than being led down whatever mad path the drugs and alcohol led me, I began to set my own destiny. In the beginning, as I was finding my feet, people around me (family, friends, etc.) loved me through those moments when I was shaky and people tolerated me as I discovered how to live such a life.

I found myself back in the 12-Step Fellowship meeting rooms and I came to understand that I truly was an addict. I was truly an addict from whatever angle I looked at it. I was truly an addict who required an external source of power so powerful that it was stronger than my addiction, just to begin restoring me back to sanity again.

I'm an addict, even though my head tried to persuade me that I was no longer an addict or maybe I wasn't a real one, and possibly I could do it all again with impunity. Perhaps I could be a social Heroin user once again, and Cocaine was never really that bad for me. Maybe drinking booze would help me in my professional life, etc., etc., etc. My head speaks bullshit to me; so reminding myself that I'm truly an addict who cannot control my narcotic consumption is a healthy place to be if I want to maintain my current life of abstinence (which I honestly do).

I'm truly an addict and, based on my life experiences ever since I came to understand this, I'm very grateful to truly be an addict.

8. Recovery through osmosis

There is recovery through osmosis. It is possible to get clean and sober through osmosis. I am experienced at that. Initially, when I attended 12-Step Fellowship meetings, I got clean and stayed clean just through the recovery of the other people in the room. I wasn't working any sort of therapeutic programme to address my addiction issues. My friends inspired me to keep coming back to meetings and to not drink or use between the meetings and that seemed to be enough. That seemed to work. I looked at these people and admired them. When they said to me, "Do 90 meetings in 90 days," I thought, "Yes, I can do that." I looked at what they were achieving and I thought. "If I do what they do, then I can have what they have." So I did it. My experience is that most of the people I did 90 meetings in 90 days with are still sober today. Not all of them, but certainly most of them. So I did lots of 12-Step meetings.

Something else I had in common with those people I hung out with and got clean with was that most of them were 'service junkies'. A service junkie is actually an endearing term or nickname used to describe people who truly go that extra mile in 12-Step Fellowships. These people will take on many more responsibilities than most. In fact, it has been said that 10% of the Fellowship do

90% of the work. It can also be noted that 90% of service junkies stay clean and sober in the long term, which is not a something that can be said for those who aren't as committed to contributing.

Being of service is one of the major principles towards maintaining emotional sobriety, since it takes the individual out of their own headspace while they are busy focusing on someone or something else. I think Anthony Robbins say's it best:

"The secret to living is giving"

The act of 'being of service' is one of contribution and volunteering. It permits the individual to bring their energy into the mix of the larger body, and by simply trying to help, they receive the great lessons they need to become accomplished. Alternatively, they'll bring the knowledge to the pack of fellow volunteers, and be the gift to others in such a way. It is this ultimate act of sacrifice that is so essential for someone with a selfish background, like an addict or alcoholic. This is one of the cornerstones of anyone's recovery, hence the success rates being recorded clearly lean in favour of those who contribute towards others and towards the Fellowship.

My group of friends and I did 90 meetings in 90 days together. During this period I had a lot of time to just look around the room at the people I was going through this journey with. There was something that struck me intensely every time I would look at the elders - or rather the people that had been here a while and to whom I had gravitated. I was spending so much time with these 'recovered' people that, as I got to know them, I noticed they all seemed to have laser beams coming out of their eyes - a profound and attractive stare and glare, it spelt wisdom, and self assurance, as if they knew something I didn't. Would they share it with me?

So, I gravitated towards the people who had laser beams coming out of their eyes; those who had this kind of Ready-Brek glow (like the cereal advert from the 70s/80s) thing going on, which is a bit of a cliché but I am sure you know what I mean. These people had huge grins on their faces and they carried themselves with elegance and a sense of self-determined achievement. They had passion and an enthusiasm that was palpable. I found myself drawn to these people and they gave me that osmosis recovery. They encouraged me and loved me and tolerated me enough (even though I still often smelt really bad - personal hygiene wasn't my forte at the time) to keep me coming back. Believe me, they tolerated my smell and me in those early days, whilst I learnt new behaviours and new ways to live. I remember asking my first sponsor (like a mentor of recovery), One-eyed Tim (the reason we called him One-eyed Tim, strangely was because he only had one eye?) how frequently I should bathe? He suggested that I do so as often as I changed my underwear, but that didn't really help much. I now needed to ask One-eyed Tim how frequently I should change my underwear. He laughed as he realised my general innocence and ignorance around such matters. I needed to start learning these social skills. I needed to start learning how to behave differently. I needed to start learning how to live differently. I needed to start understanding what it was that was going to give me power to stay on the path I had chosen to recovery. I needed to learn that I was going to be more powerful than the powerlessness I had felt that day after drinking that non-alcoholic beer. I needed to regain my right to choose. I needed to regain my control over my own decisions and my own actions.

Or maybe I didn't; but what I was taught by those who came before me with Ready-Brek glows and laser beams coming out of their eyes, was that there is One who has all the power I need, and that one is referred to as God! May I find him/her/it now, or even, "May the Force be with me", if you're a Jedi.

The one thing all these people with laser beams coming out of their eyes and big grins on their faces had in common was that they all were quite comfortable talking about God. The reason they were all quite comfortable talking about God was because they all had a working knowledge of the 12-Step programme. They were all talking about the Steps. They were all talking about this newfound freedom and newfound happiness they got as a result of working the Steps. Put quite simply, I was blown away and inspired. I wanted what they had so much I was inspired into the next stage of my recovery, the post-osmosis stage. Until the point when I began actually working the Steps and doing what they'd been doing, I was getting clean off the people I surrounded myself with through osmosis. They were the ones who were giving me the energy to stay clean. I can say this with absolute certainty, you can walk into the 12-Step Fellowship rooms and you can stay clean just by entering them and staying very close to the healthy ones there. But you won't get it all from just entering the rooms. You will never get laser beams coming out of your eyes, which is seriously an amazing achievement, without joining in and working the Steps. You will not get that Ready-Brek glow without working the 12-Step programme.

This is a 12-Step programme. Don't be confused. If you go to a gymnasium and you watch someone on a treadmill, the simple fact that you are watching someone on a treadmill means that you are not eating and, during that time, you are losing weight ever so slightly. But the real benefit of going to a gym is when you get on that treadmill yourself. If you join a boxing club, you are expected to go boxing. If you join the library, you are expected to read books. If you attend a karaoke evening, then you're expected to sing. These 12-Step Fellowships encourage you to work the 12-Step programme. It's not rocket science or brain surgery, but so many people seem to miss that point (sadly).

9. 12-Steps explained (the personal version)

One-eyed Tim, my first sponsor, began to take me through the first few Steps - one, two and three using the experience he had. And then he took me through Steps one, two and three a second time. When I asked him if we could do Step four, he said we couldn't do Step four because he hadn't worked it himself yet! This was a disappointment to my system, because it meant that I'd need to find someone else to sponsor me, and through transference I was kinda fond of One-eyed Tim.

I had been attending a particular meeting on Monday evenings that took its name and structure from the original Alcoholics Anonymous textbook aka 'The Big Book' with a guy called Nick the Stitch, who wasn't called The Stitch because he was a grass, and he wasn't called The Stitch because he would make you laugh so much that you were in stitches (though that was certainly true), but he was called Nick the Stitch because he was (and still is) a tailor. One of the regular members at that time was Nick the Saint. The reason we called him Nick the Saint was because he was a very good person, but he wasn't actually a saint! Although One-eyed Tim really does have only one eye, and Nick the Stitch is a tailor, Nick the Saint is just a really nice guy, not an actual Saint. Anyway, Nick the Saint was talking to me and offered to take me through all of the 12-Steps. I had listened to him many times and I wanted what he had within himself (kindness, calmness, knowledge and alleged Jedi powers) and so I became willing to continue my 12-Step journey with him.

One Sunday morning, around 10 am I arrived at his offices in Clapham, and putting aside how foolish we both felt, together we knelt on the floor in an effort to display humility and said the Third-Step Prayer, which taken from the Big Book of Alcoholics Anonymous reads:

"God, I offer myself to Thee - To build with me and to do with me as Thou wilt. Relieve me of the bondage of self, that I may better do Thy will. Take away my difficulties, that victory over them may bear witness to those I would help of Thy Power, Thy Love, and Thy Way of life. May I do Thy will always!"

I sat up and took in a deep breath bringing forth God, as I understood God at the time, into my consciousness and sub-consciousness. God, as I understood God at that time was 'Good'. I put an extra 'o' in the word 'God' and I channelled my thoughts and feelings into a 'Good' energy. I wanted to be a 'Good Guy' not a 'Bad Boy'. That was my earliest concept of God; just the Good energy inherent in humankind. God is Good. So I was praying to the Goodness in the Universe to permit to lay aside myself, my own thoughts, my own agenda, my own self centeredness and my own best thinking, so that the Goodness of the Universe could enter my spirit and allow me to do the 4th Step work without worrying about whether I was doing it right or not, since it was God's work through me - if that makes any sense?

But let me start at the beginning - I find most people prefer it that way.

i. Step One

Step one of the programme is to admit that you are beaten. It is a step in which you must admit that you need help. I initially asked for help when I wrote that letter in despair to a God that I didn't understand. I then admitted I was beaten when I asked my parents for help and, at that point, became willing to do whatever it took to recover. It is written as "We admitted we were powerless over our addiction and that our lives had become unmanageable." Though I also find it easy to reverse that sentence and consider that I myself had become unmanageable and that my life had become powerless, that is to say that I couldn't control my destiny and I have no ability to retake control - I was out of control. I had no personal power left. Please note this isn't a question of will power, but more a challenge to my own essence and the power of my spirit. I was defeated. I surrendered to the fact that I was done!

Essentially step one is about admitting that you are at a point where drugging and drinking has beaten you and you simply cannot continue this way any longer. You must admit that your behaviour, due to your addictions is having such a detrimental effect on your life that you are out of control and unable to cope. I was completely out of control and my attempts to manage my addiction had failed. As a result of this lack of control I felt totally insignificant and my life felt completely meaningless.

When we talk about being powerless we are talking about the inability for an addict to use their drug of choice safely and without consequence. Powerlessness for me refers to my lack of control and combined with my lack of choice. When I start I can't stop and when I stop I can't keep myself from starting again. I am unable to choose to drink or not. I have lost the ability to choose whether to get high or stoned on any given day. I simply cannot "Just say No", even though I don't want to be doing the very thing I'm about to do. I'm unable to choose not to do the exact thing I'm doing. I'm powerless to stop doing what I don't want to be doing in the first place.

Unmanageability refers to my feelings about the world I live in, the feeling that I have lost the ability to design my destiny, the feeling of worthlessness, helplessness and hopelessness. It's a crippling place to be in and leads to thoughts and feelings of depression, paranoia, inferiority, insecurity and ultimately suicide. Being unable to achieve the things I want to achieve leaves me feeling out of control and unsuccessful with myself. Feeling restless with myself, easily irritated or antagonistic, and ultimately absolutely discontented with oneself. This is unmanageability in its essence.

ii.   Step Two

In Step two, I found a way to believe in a power greater than myself, and I found enough faith to believe that it would restore me to sanity. I was very lucky to be surrounded by other people on their own recovery journey who embraced me, encouraged me and gave me confidence on a daily basis. They helped me back down to earth as I learned more appropriate ways to live and socialise. I was taught about my insanity and from that configured my own version of a lifestyle considerably saner. Every day when I had the urge to use I would pick up the phone and call one of the members of my group. They would restore me to sufficient levels of sanity by reminding me what I was working towards. They were a power greater than myself. These people were my energy and my determination when I didn't have any of my own. These people reached out to me on a day-to-day basis and encouraged me to stay dry and clean. They taught me that just because I felt anxious and nervous a lot of the time, it was no reason to start using again. They taught me that when I felt like a drink would improve my emotional state, to pick up the phone and go to a meeting. And, when I did, there was always someone there to look after me and bring a cheer to my mood. They never let me down.

Step two is about finding a power greater than yourself to restore you to sanity. Some people turn to God, I turned to the members of my group and in them I found sanity, forgiveness and strength enough to make it through to Step three.

iii. Step Three

The understanding that I had gained in Step two made Step three an easier transition for me. Step three requires that you turn your will (your self-centred and selfish thinking) and life (or at least the results and the consequences) over to the care of God. Not necessarily a religious God (and in my world it certainly is not a religious one), but a God as you understand it or him or her to be.

Even though I didn't know much of God before this, it was not a difficult step for me to take. It wasn't a big jump from believing in the power of my group to a Higher Power, something that is higher than all of us. I also used the concept of a Higher Purpose, since this seemed to fit into my personal values. I would listen to the members of my group, as they would talk about God, and as they understood God to be. No one member had the same God. Very few of these members appeared to be referring to a religious God, though there certainly were some. My sponsor let me borrow his God for a while, just during the time I was figuring out God for myself, but made it very clear to me that it was only a loan, that I would have to discover my own God soon enough. The nicest and possibly easiest concept of God I heard was from Nick the Saint, as he took me through my Steps. He was and still is a Star Wars fan (aren't we all?) that used the Good Side of the Force versus the Dark Side. He considered himself a Jedi Knight. I understood what he meant and I enjoyed this interpretation, and even used it for a while. So you see, any interpretation of God will do, so long as it's not me (or in your case, not you, etc.). It wasn't that hard to do. I recognised a power in my life that was not human and, in that power, I discovered my own Goddess.

Step three was not just a step in recovery for me. It is a Step I have worked again and again throughout my life. Recently I set myself a large project goal and I had no idea how I was going to achieve it as it was based on something I had never done before. I had no idea how to even imagine the end result. So, instead of stressing about it, I remained calm and I wrote myself a task list spread over many months. I then broke this down into monthly targets and weekly challenges. When I woke up each morning I had a list of things I had to achieve that day and I would just get on with them. At night I would go to bed, my list completed and I would let my God take care of the results. When I woke up the following morning I wouldn't think about the things I had done the day before, I would just get on with the tasks I had for the new day ahead and leave the rest up to God. I just had to do the work. So that's what I did. I did what I needed to do and assuming I was doing something that God (Good Energy/Higher Purpose/Spirit of the Universe) approved of, I then left the results to God to manifest in Her own way, in Her time and with Her consequences. I guess you'd call this 'letting go'.

I frequently asked myself if my God would want me to achieve the particular path I had chosen, and if She did and I did the work to a certain standard, magic would happen. And it did. It was as simple as that. I still use this Step three belief in my day-to-day life. I have a white board by my desk with daily and weekly tasks to achieve.

When I asked Nick the Saint to help me, we began by saying the third Step prayer together. The third Step prayer is about asking God to work God's will through you and that by simply applying the principles of doing the right thing, right things would occur back at me. It allows me to become open minded to whatever God may want me to do or to be. So, it is because of this prayer's quest to open me up to the concept that God would help me if I allowed God in to help me in the first place, that it fits in so well just prior to the fourth Step.

iv. Step Four

So I said the third Step prayer, and still feeling quite nervous, I began with the writing. The fourth Step is a written Step and it requires a great deal of self-examination and truthfulness. Its purpose is to reveal to you the truth about your past behaviours and patterns, thus allowing you the opportunity to reconsider how you're going to behave in the future, by realigning your attitudes and principles. It's often considered challenging, particularly by those people who take their time writing it. But so long as I had God helping me write it, I was determined to get it written in a day. And so I began.

The purpose of asking God to help me with my fourth Step is so that anything that drops into my mind can be explained as something God wants me to do work on and therefore should be examined. It's to stop me from thinking my way out of writing about certain parts of my life and behaviour that I'd still rather keep secret, which would defeat the object of this step, since it's a cleansing step. All the aspects of my previous moral code must be revealed, so that I can be completely refreshed with new healthy values and operating systems within my mind. It's a get-out clause for the intellectual.

So, I did the writing in a day; it took me about five and a half hours. I did it in columns. When I looked to see if I had short changed myself on anything or to check to see that I had made a full disclosure on everything, I was certain that "Yes", I had made a really good effort and "Yes", I had done a searching and fearless attempt at taking my own moral inventory.

v. Step Five

Step five is to read Step four out loud to someone else, usually your sponsor, and before God, similar to confession, I guess, though I've never been a Catholic, so I wouldn't really know. I read it the same day of my fourth Step to Nick the Saint, after the writing was finished, before it got too late.

Nick took a look through what I had done and helped me with some of the harder aspects of my personality to calculate. He helped me assess my own character defects, and he wrote them down for me, just so I didn't miss any. Thanks Nick.

He told me to sit still and contemplate my work for a short while, making sure that nothing further sprung to mind that God might still want me to confront. When I was finished and I was sure I had completed my list. I was expected to read it all out loud to Nick.

As I began reading it out loud, I realised that this was harder than I thought. He assured me of the absolute confidentiality of this experience, but there was stuff in there I had never wanted to think about again, let alone say out loud to some guy I hardly knew. However, whenever I stuttered and stumbled, he would approach me and hug me like no man had hugged me before. He loved and supported me through the process. He tolerated me and encouraged me and pushed me and squeezed me for the little bits that I was hesitant to say.

At the end of the day, I knew that I had written the very best Step four that I was able to do on that day. I knew that I had genuinely brought God into my life and I had asked God to help me write that fourth Step and I knew that God had given me the power to say what needed to be said on that day. That fourth Step was as good as it needed to be and it was as good as it could be. My fourth Step that day was simply the very best fourth Step I could have possibly done. Phew, it was over.

That was my fourth and fifth Steps, and these days I take the people I sponsor through exactly the same process. They arrive for ten in the morning and they write everything they can in one day. Then they read it out loud to me later in the afternoon.

A lot of people are scared of Step four - really scared, but there really is no reason to be. Step five is far more challenging. It addresses my vulnerabilities and asks me to humble myself before someone I admire and look up to. It's tough saying some of those things that I did in my past out loud to another bloke. It requires courage, trust and faith.

So look, my whole experience of working the fourth and fifth Steps was one of relief. It was an incredibly freeing process. It felt like a weight had been lifted off my shoulders and when you talk to other people who have been through the steps, you will find that once people have completed this stretch of work, it always has a very positive effect upon people's lives. No matter what you may hear about the difficulty of Steps four and five, the relief felt afterwards clearly over compensates for the difficult challenges that one day may have put you through. And if I'm honest, it really wasn't that difficult, and most other people you'll ever meet who have done a fourth Step correctly in this manner will agree with you - nothing to worry about... get on with it.

vi. Step Six

To begin Step six Nick asked me if I was entirely ready and willing for God (even though I didn't understand God) or my Higher Power/Purpose to remove all of these defects of character that had been revealed to me previously through my fourth Steps.

I was scared. I told him, no, I wasn't ready. I was willing to let go of most of them, but I wasn't ready to let go of them all. There were two reasons I was resistant towards letting go! There were two behavioural attributes that I possessed that even though we could be judged as negative manners, I wasn't actually willing to stop doing.

The first character defect I wasn't willing to let go of was lust. I had just come out of a seven-year opiate habit where my libido was significantly challenged at times. Certainly the last three years it had been seriously minimised and not truly functional, particularly in the past year or so since Leticia had left me, so I certainly wasn't willing to let go of lust after only having just gotten it back!

It actually took me an additional five and a half years to let go of lust, by the way. It was a long process of discovery for me. But there is, of course, a happy ending to that story, since I have now been happily married and completely monogamous ever since I met my wife. She is a very cute, recovered alcoholic, and she works her own programme of recovery entirely separately to me and mine. We have a really healthy and loving relationship. I tell you, ever since we got together, I have been head over heels in love with her, and just as soon as I committed myself to her, the lust was removed from my life. I didn't need it any more, I had something much better; I had love. Lust is selfish and love is sharing. I was asking God to remove the lust when she was introduced to me, and we got together. Not that I'm suggesting for even a moment that God is a pimp or anything, but that's just how it went down. But more about that story later.

Neither was I willing to let God take away all of my dishonesty; at least not just yet. Being dishonest was a part of my lifestyle and as a practising junkie it was a required part of my occupation and a very necessary way of making it through each day. Deceit and dishonesty had progressively become larger and larger parts of my personality over the previous years. It was the way I had survived most of my adult life up until this point. It was one of my tools of the trade, so to say. I was terrified of letting it go.

I was very happy for God to take all of the other shit away, since I certainly didn't want any of it hanging off me anymore. But yet I wanted to keep some of the dishonesty. I believed I still needed it. I believed that my life still required me to lie, cheat and steal, because no one would ever trust anyone like me, nor would anyone ever give me any chances or opportunities. I needed to steal them.

My sponsor Nick told me to go away and sit with it for two weeks and see how it goes.

But yet, within 48 hours I was on the phone with my sponsor begging him to help me let it all go, having come to the very sudden realisation that I really didn't need any of it anymore, ever!

On the Tuesday just two days after having written my fifth Step on the Sunday, and having contemplated the Step work I'd done thus far throughout Sunday night and Monday, I found myself getting arrested!

Of course, before you ask, I was innocent.

They were arresting me because they thought I was committing debit card fraud, which I wasn't, as it was my own card. I do appreciate that I must have looked pretty dodgy using my own card because I had such limited experience using my own card previously, since I'd always found it much easier to just use yours! But, here I was, attending a job interview (which I actually got) so I was wearing a shirt, a tie and a suit, and since I don't enjoy being dressed up in such a formal manner; I was rather uncomfortable both in my appearance and myself. Anyway, I had some time to spare after the interview before my next train back into London (I was in Maidenhead), and I found myself browsing the local shopping mall. I was in a newspaper shop purchasing a book, some sweets, and a few sundries, when I found myself being confronted by the shop security guard challenging me on my true identification and whether I matched the person on the card. For some reason, knowing that I was innocent played into my arrogance and I became rude and threatening. I soon found myself being escorted off the premises by two local policemen and introduced to the local police station holding cells.

It was there, sitting in that cell, knowing that I was innocent, that I felt God winking at me. God was teaching me a lesson. God was showing me that dishonesty was a lifestyle choice that I needed to let go of. God was suggesting that if I failed to change my ways, this is the path I could be taking e.g. jail. My fear of prison is much more intense than my fear of a life with no drugs. I would have gone to fairly extreme lengths to ensure that I had drugs, but I would literally skip countries and go above and beyond the realms of possibility to keep myself out of prison. So, can you understand that I had such a fear of prison that God decided to use it to show me I needed to trust the process and have faith that I'd be OK, and that my life would work out fine, so long as I have the balls to begin a life lived on honest principles. There was God winking at me telling me to let go of dishonesty, and I'm so very grateful that I caught Her eye that day. In that very instant I made the decision to let go of all my dishonest attempts at living.

And so, I am pleased to publically announce that since that day, I have been as honest a person as I could be. Well, at least I've made a significant effort to adjust my ways. I have only shoplifted once more since that very day, and even on that occasion I was caught by the Mall Security. It was a service station on the way back from Glastonbury Festival, and tired, dirty and exhausted I couldn't be bothered to wait in the very long queue, so technically speaking, it was actually my lack of patience that got me into trouble - though they let me off without any consequences, aside form having to pay for the item I'd nicked. Well this path is one of progress not perfection.

vii. Step Seven v1.0

After this happened, I called my sponsor in a panic. I was ready to let go of dishonesty. Over the phone he told me to sit still and find a place to say a prayer acknowledging that God was going to take care of the results of my future actions, so long as I did the right thing. And that as long as I did my best to behave appropriately, She would help me move away from my negative personality traits. She would help me recover and help me regain my sanity. She would allow me to become the man I was always meant to be. He told me to try to get in contact with my God and see how She would help me. Low and behold the light came on in my eyes.

Now I have the privilege of sending people off to do their Steps six and seven today, and one of the miracles is seeing someone at the end of Step five coming back to you a couple of hours later with the lights on in their eyes having experienced Steps six and seven ready to do Step eight. It's like watching a living, breathing miracle - live and direct, right before your very eyes; one of the true gifts between the person working their Steps and yourself. Over a matter of hours the lights come on. It's truly a beautiful experience.

viii. Step Seven v2.0

There's a more practical version of Step seven that I'd like to mention. The Step asks us to 'Humbly ask God to remove all of our shortcomings.' It's been my experience that by going to 12-Step and other communities of contribution-based meetings on a regular basis, I counterbalance all my character defects. As previously mentioned, we know that left to my own devices I'm selfish, self-centred, dishonest, self-seeking, fearful and anxious, to name a few. I lack in patience, tolerance, understanding of others and I am unforgiving, just for starters. But by going to contribution-based meetings and particularly 12-Step Fellowship meetings, I have to actively act the complete opposite. I have to be patient around newcomers or other members with different opinions or ideas. I have to learn tolerance and display empathy and consideration for others. I have to offer to help without expecting anything in return - selflessly. I have to be giving of my time and energy. I have to behave in a manner that's respectful of others. These are all new ways to behave for me. I had rarely used these behaviours previously. These are some of the new tools I picked up in this programme, and these are some of the ways I managed to change my patterns of behaviour.

It was very important for me to learn this. What I had to do was change the way I behaved and, as a result of changing the way I behaved, I was able feel more confident and comfortable about myself and my behaviour. When I am more confident and comfortable about the things I do and the way I do them, I feel better about myself as a person and my personality evolves in a positive way. I am still evolving using this process every day; I am a constant 'work in progress'.

ix. Step Eight

Step eight requires making a list of all those we had harmed and through that process become willing to make amends to them all. I took the list of harms that I had written in my fourth Step and added more names as memories surfaced. Maybe God didn't need me to be so detailed on that particular day, but just to get to grips with the process so that I could do it more thoroughly later on in my journey. During the weeks between Step four and Step eight (Did I mention that this is a slow process?) I had had many revelations and was aware of other mistakes I had made and harm I had committed that all needed to be added to the list. In fact, the longer I waited before getting on and working the eighth and ninth Steps, the longer my list of harms to other people was going to be. The question for me was whether I was willing to make amends to the people I'd harmed and, if I wasn't, then I needed to ask for help with my willingness.

My problem wasn't really willingness. At this point, I was so convinced of the need to make things right from my past that I was very willing, almost chomping at the bit, and ready to go, which were certainly famous last words, because when I was actually in the situation to make the amends, often they were a real struggle. The point is that I was willing in my head, and I was able to discuss all of my amends with my sponsor beforehand, and my God seemed to help us devise the most suitable way to make each particular amend. It was now time to rebalance my karma and try to make right the wrongs I had caused others and myself.

x. Step Nine

If you were scared of Step four (which you have no real reason to be scared of), then you are sure to be terrified of Step nine. There is honestly no reason to be scared of Step four, but there is every reason to be scared of Step nine. Step nine is a very scary process. But it is also, without a doubt, the most rewarding and the most healing. Going through the motions of making an amend is one of the most beautiful experiences. I'm absolutely shitting myself walking up to someone's house, knocking on his or her door saying, "Hi, do you remember me?" Much of the time they didn't know who the hell I am, because so many of my resentments were all in my own head. Many of the people don't even know you owe them an amend. Most people didn't know the actual extent of my behaviour, or didn't truly realise the harm I thought I had caused them. Most of it was conjured up in my own imagination. Although, obviously, there were also people who didn't think I went far enough in my attempts to make things right.

My experience is that about 80% of the formal amends I made have personally had favourable results. There were some I came out of and felt unsatisfied, not having received the closure I wanted. But you know what, it's a healing process and this is precisely the process I required to grow from being the scared little boy I felt myself to be, into the man I was to become. I can talk quite openly about becoming a man with honour as a result of the Steps, but my genuine experience was that I truly became such a man as a result of working my way through my Step nine list of amends and repatriating the past to rebalance my karma for the future.

As I was going through my list of amends and confronting my fears, I found myself praying. While I had been working the other Steps, I was on the phone with my sponsor almost every day, but here I was experiencing a genuine reality check, facing my own past like that, and I required more assistance than my sponsor or any other human being may have been able to give me. I sought the strength from a Power much greater than myself or any other human being. I needed God's help and whenever I asked for Her help, She always seemed to show up.

This process began to reveal more and more things to me. I realised that I was really dying when I was using. All of the fear, the self-hatred, the obsessive behaviour, the addiction, the depression I had felt during my worst days, was lifted from me around this time. The obsession to use was completely removed from my psyche. As a result of the obsession being removed, I didn't have the first hit, smoke, line, glass, etc. If I don't have the first hit, smoke, line, glass, etc., then the compulsion to consume even more is never triggered. If I do have the first hit, smoke, line, glass, etc., for instance when I scraped out the resin of my old pipe, I will drink booze and I will be leading myself down a path of self-destruction almost immediately. And, one day (it may come quickly or it may come slowly), I may have that one hit that's going to be the 'one hit too many'. I will die! There are far too many people out there dead, who don't know they are dead. Because once you die, it's over. I've never heard of an 'accidental' overdose that was planned. Relapse after a period of abstinence is very dangerous for the body. Our minds assume we can consume similar amounts as before, but our body isn't on the same page. There are people in coffins and they don't know they're in coffins. I see people go out and use again, except they don't return to us afterwards. People I've known for a few years while they've been getting clean and sober, decide that this time they can drink and/or use without the same problems as before and yet they often don't return to us. They end up in a place far worse than before very rapidly, leading them into an early grave, and far too often without even knowing it, due to overdosing.

But people I see taking these Steps, paying particular attention to their fourth, fifth and ninth Steps, seem to have a very solid ground from which to recover. These are the people who seem to free themselves the most sincerely. Where the fourth and fifth Steps are freeing, the ninth Step is very healing and it got me to a place where I had truly changed. Step nine was the freeing process. It was where the obsession to use was lifted from me. It was really here I learned what it meant to have dignity and integrity. It was here that I began to start practising true honesty and showing the world that I was maturing and becoming a man. I humbled myself and permitted myself to become vulnerable before the eyes of other people and before God, as I understood Her. And I allowed myself to heal! I grew up as a result of this ninth Step!

xi. Step Ten

Step ten is essentially doing Steps three through nine on a daily basis. This is where my relationship with my sponsor is most active still. I love my sponsor so much, which is a very convenient truth, because otherwise I'd struggle to be honest, vulnerable and straight with him. I still communicate with him fairly regularly (via Skype these days) and ask for his help around a certain episode I may have misbehaved around, or felt my reaction to be unpleasant around. This action of restoring my negative behaviours in the eyes of God and the person affected is called the tenth Step amends. My sponsor will then look at the situation from a different point of view and he'll offer me counsel on the situation in a way that I can't quite see for myself. Or he'll offer me direction based upon the spiritual choice, rather than my self-centred point of view. He offers a second pair of eyes on a situation, removed enough to be able to see how God would best have me behave, rather than my own potentially misguided opinion. This is the purpose of our relationship, looking at how I can be a better man in every way, every day.

Step ten is not too hard in theory because you already know the Steps well by this point. Once you have the experience of already working through the Steps, then you just do it every day as a discipline. Sometimes I get two or three resentments within a short period of time and it's really not a big deal. It's not a tall order to deal with at all, especially when you think of the amazing freedom you receive as a result of putting in the work and getting through these resentments. In fact, these resentments are like nursery slopes in the school of life. By figuring out how to deal with them, I learn how to be the best me I can be.

xii. Step Eleven

Steps eleven and twelve I love. These are my favourite parts of the programme. Step 11 reads:

> *'We sought through prayer and meditation to improve our conscious contact with God as we understood Him/Her, praying only for knowledge of His/Her will for us and the power to carry that out'.*

The only thing I am asked to pray for is knowledge of God's will for me. Oh, and can I have some power to carry that out with, too? I am not asked to pray for a new car. I am not asked to pray for a new house. I am specifically not asked to pray for a new girlfriend, (I think I've mentioned this before - God isn't a pimp). I am even not asked to pray for world peace, or an end to famine, or education for the world's children, though all of these things would be nice. And although sometimes God is happy to oblige in some aspects of my life - I've certainly felt I've received a great number of gifts in life as a result of accepting that God exists in my life and figuring out how to best serve Her Higher Purpose - the only thing I am actually asked to pray for is knowledge of God's will for me. What is God's will for me? Step eleven is the search for the knowledge of what God would have me do. What is the right thing to do in God's eyes?

Let's break this down to understand it better: In Step eleven I needed to figure out what God's will for me was, by using both prayer and meditation, and once I had figured that out then I could ask for the power to carry out God's will.

It's Not About Me!

So what is God's will for me? The easiest way to answer that is to say that my God wants me to be happy, joyous and free. If your personal God doesn't want you to be happy, joyous and free then for God's sake, get yourself a different God! If you need to borrow mine, although She's a little busy at the moment, She would be very happy to help you out too. Just put your name on the list, or stand in the queue and She will get around to you sooner or later. Just remember that She's ever so busy helping out those who are truly desperate (victims of war, famine, abuse, neglect, etc.), so you may find yourself quite low down in her order of priorities, but if you're able to practise patience in the meanwhile, I absolutely promise you that She will get around to you in due course, and that the result will be beautiful, even if it's not what you were expecting. Oh, and by the way, if you're uncomfortable with me referring to God as a woman, just consider my God to be your God's mother.

To supplement my own understanding of God's will for me to be happy, joyous and free, I understood that I needed to behave appropriately to qualify for such feelings. After all, if I carried on using drugs, then I would not be feeling happy, joyous and free (for much longer than the duration of the high e.g. 15 minutes when smoking Crack). Those states only came about as a result of my doing the right thing. So, this is the beginning of God's will for me - quoting Spike Lee's wonderful film 'Do the right thing' which if you've not seen, you absolutely must, and if you have seen it then go watch it again and enjoy the lessons told through such a great story.

My sponsor suggested that I go and explore religion. He said I didn't have to join any of them, just have an open mind and look into them. Just see if anything floats your boat. See if there's anything that sits in line with your values and if there's anything you think you can use to your benefit. Now let me stress something. He didn't tell me to shave a hole on the top of my head and join the Brotherhood of Monks. He wasn't suggesting I start wearing a habit of colourful robes and start hanging out in cathedrals, churches, temples, synagogues, chapels, monasteries, mosques, etc. He didn't encourage me to go and starve myself and live my life on meagre rations as some sort of hermit. He wasn't suggesting I dedicate myself to wearing purple and giving away flowers. He was simply suggesting I open my mind to what the other established religions had been preaching for hundreds and thousands of years to see if there was anything of any use in there for me to use as concepts of God and spirituality. He simply encouraged me to explore religious dogma and see if there was anything I liked.

In a funny, cosmic, roundabout way, the one theology I was most drawn towards during my religious research strangely enough involved the Dalai Lama, the leader of the Tibetan Buddhists. The Dalai Lama is the spiritual leader of the Tibetan people living in exile from Tibet because the Chinese have invaded his country and decimated his culture and his religion. So, he has to live outside his own country preaching love and tolerance to his people in foreign lands where they are all refugees. The Dalai Lama expresses such forgiveness, such compassion and such human kindness despite the atrocities he has witnessed and despite what his people have witnessed. And yet despite everything that's happened to his race and religion he remains positive, serene and optimistic. I was really inspired when I began reading about him. The Dalai Lama was using the same words I was picking up in the 12-Step Fellowship meetings and in the recovery programme literature; really long words like 'forgiveness'. That is a really long word. It's got 11 letters. I remember when I got clean and sober the longest word I knew was wheelbarrow. It's got 11 letters too, you know. Now I am pleased to say that the longest word I know is unmanageability, it's got 15 letters (we covered this earlier, right?). I probably still couldn't tell you what it means exactly, but I certainly know how it feels.

So here was the Dalai Lama, living in exile in Dhār masala, India, where I had overdosed on my birthday a few years ago. I had been researching many different theologies, but something the Dalai Lama said resonated with me. Something he said just seemed to be perfectly aligned with what I was learning through the 12-Step programme of recovery. It fitted in perfectly. The Dalai Lama said,

"A spiritual life is one of being of service to others."

and the penny just dropped! Where had I heard that before? Here I was in a spiritual programme, exploring many different ideas of spirituality, and here's the Dalai Lama telling me that a spiritual life is one of being of service to others!

Could it be that simple? Could it be that obvious?

xiii. Step Twelve

Step twelve reads:

> *"Having had a spiritual awakening as a result of these Steps, we tried to carry this message to other addicts and to practise these principles in all our affairs."*

Having a spiritual experience as a result of prayer or meditation or some other soul-searching exercise, we realise that our destiny is to receive enough power to carry a message of hope (hope that we can recover) to others. So, just like the Dalai Lama said, "A spiritual life is one of being of service to others." In this programme we're taught to be of service to others as part of our understanding of a spiritual life!

That is God's will for me. My divine purpose was so simple; I was here to take what I had learnt, to take all the kindness that had been so selflessly given to me and to return the favour to other people in service. Most people who go through the Steps have a spiritual awakening and they try to carry this message to addicts and practise these amazing principles in their everyday life. It's not always easy, but it is always rewarding. God's will for me was to carry this message to other addicts and, in doing so, try to learn how to behave appropriately and practise those same principles in all of my affairs. God's will for me was to learn how to behave by surrounding myself with positive people and doing whatever I could to develop a spirit of contribution and charity by learning how to be of service to other people. A spiritual life is one of being of service to others. Being of service to others took me down a positive road of recovery, and I know to this day this is still my God's will for me.

The knowledge I've been searching for is that God's will for me is to help other people. So, as long as I'm doing my best to improve the quality of other people's lives, then I am serving God's will and guess what? God makes sure that I'm happy, joyous and free! That's how simple it is. To be happy, I simply help others. As I said earlier, Anthony Robbins says it the best when he says, "The secret to living is giving!" It is beautiful and simple.

I look at all the spiritual principles I've learnt through all of these 12-Steps and I discover that I need to practise these principles in all my affairs. I work with others and help addicts and alcoholics to understand that there is an exit strategy. There is a way out of addiction, but it involves caring about others and doing the next right thing on a daily basis to improve the standard of life on this planet, rather than destroy it. I know that sounds like a heavy burden but please keep it simple. You just need to generate a little bit more goodness for humanity on a daily basis, rather than drain their resources and then you're heading in the right direction. But every day I am also working on myself, changing my own attitudes and behaviours, so I, too, may become a better person on this planet.

10. WOW!!

For me, after three ravaging years of wanting to get clean, I was finally living my dreams. It had been a massive struggle, but once I'd begun to see just how simple it actually was, it rapidly worked in automatic. My programme ran itself on autopilot. I was clean and I was sober by God's grace and by keeping my life simply about contributing towards other people's welfare. Instead of thinking about me and whatever my selfish needs may be for that day, I was tuning into to a bigger picture. I was working on my future, by considering how it served more people than just me. My future had to be one inline with the spiritual principles of this programme, combined with discovering something to do that enabled me to feel enriched in life. After all, I never got clean to be a miserable bastard. I got clean to have an even more fulfilling life. So my life evolved into something profoundly different. I moved into my first house. I began working in different parts of the country. I had a whole network of friends around me. I began travelling around the world again. Life just evolved and took on new meaning with every amazing experience that came my way. About eighteen months into my sobriety I woke up one day and realised that I had recovered. I understood that I no longer needed to drink or use drugs, in fact, I didn't have the urge and I knew I wasn't going to. The obsession with these things left me. It was a beautiful moment in my life, to realise I was finally free.

It's Not About Me!

Part 5.
RECOVERY
– onwards & upwards

"Life's in session and I'm showing up"

1. Work: re-joining society

I became willing to work. I had never had a job before and I really didn't know much about working at all, but I was willing. I was lucky that people I had met along my early recovery journey started to offer me cash-in-hand jobs to keep me afloat and ease me into the whole working life experience. I did all sorts of different things. I did painting and decorating, demolition, refuse collection, site clearing, handyman jobs and other similar jobs that didn't require too much experience or skill. This sort of work was perfect for me in early recovery because I didn't need to think about it. I just needed to show up on time and get the work done. I adopted a principle of being self-supporting and never being reliant upon others. I was determined that I would make my own way through life and finance my own lifestyle, and I have done so ever since. I never signed onto the dole or collected any sort of welfare from the state - I was fully self-supporting entirely from my own contributions - for better or worse. I hadn't even gone on the dole back in my darker days whilst I was using, since I was just too paranoid, believing that the police state was looking for a badass criminal like me, and that they were ready to pick me up should I ever show my face at an Unemployment Office collecting some money. So, I had always figured out how to make a little money here and there, but absolutely entirely from dishonest means, aside from playing my records when I was a DJ and getting paid by club owners or rave organisers (when they pay me in drugs and booze). But, in recovery, I found honest ways to make my money and pay for the things that I needed, and I have never turned back to any criminal pursuits to raise cash.

I was inspired to change. I saw other people who had been on this journey longer than I had and I watched what they were getting from their lives. I mirrored their behaviours and their conduct and in doing so I developed a brand new attitude of my own and learned appropriate behaviours that would serve me well amongst society folks, rather than the anarchic and libertarian outlaw elements I'd previously immersed myself in. Please note I don't use those terms to describe my previous communities in a derogatory way. I believe there are many lessons that society can learn from these methods of tribal living - where the security of the whole is of paramount importance in order to see the security of the individuals within. Imagine yourself living as a circus entertainer. Everyone's welfare depends upon the success of the show. So long as the circus is making money, everyone gets fed and all the vehicles have fuel to roll on to the next location. That's tribalism, and that's how I used to live. Unfortunately, there isn't a tribe currently able to manage my, or rather its members' recovery. At least, there isn't yet. Hence, it's why I needed to return to society to restore my mental, emotional and physical health. There are Fellowships and there are recovery communities, but there certainly aren't any tribes of recovery folks that I know of, though there potentially could be in the USA.

So, I put myself in the proximity of people who were succeeding; people who were achieving their goals and getting what they wanted out of their lives whilst living and maintaining their recovery. I mimicked them so I too could learn from their success. I was inspired to change my own life and I realised that I wanted to be employable. I wanted to have a good work ethic and be a responsible member of society. I realised that I wanted to remain drug and alcohol free on a permanent footing. I realised I wanted to contribute to my friends and family. I realised I wanted to make a difference in the world. I realised I wanted to bring a woman into my life on a full-time basis, rather than one-night stands (although this attitude did fluctuate over the first five years or so - it takes time!). These realisations led to change. And the change led to a rewarding lifestyle I still enjoy every day of my life.

I got my first job within the first thirty days of becoming sober. I got my first legal (through the books with tax and NI etc.) job at six months clean; buying and selling chocolate – wholesale! Possibly not the best role for a self-confessed chocolate addict, but at the time I was starry eyed and keen to work. By the time I was 18 months clean I was working in Telecoms in the City of London wearing pinstripe suits.

But something happened and, by some strange twist, I came to realise that money had become my new God. I had somehow lost the principles the programme had taught me. I was no longer focused on a Power greater than myself that would help restore my sanity. My life was focused on making enough commission to buy a new suit, a new pair of trainers, a new of electronic gadget, a new phone, or whatever. I wanted things, material things, and I wanted them now. I had completely lost sight of those principles I had held so dear.

I became lost and depressed and was unable to put my finger on it. I couldn't understand why I was becoming increasingly unhappy. I would talk to my sponsor, asking his guidance. He would tell me to "Shut up and pray!" Now, however rude you may consider this reading it on paper, it was always said to me with love and compassion. I began to understand what he meant.

When he was telling me to 'shut up and pray', he was referring me to Step eleven to help remind me to consider what my God's will for me may be, and then request the power to carry it out. He was sure I'd see the way out of feeling sorry for myself through prayer.

Or, when I was feeling especially depressed, or particularly miserable, he would tell me to "Piss off and help someone else" (he had a certain way with words). In these instances he would be referring me to Step twelve, which was basically to get grateful about my life and go help someone less fortunate than me. He would be telling me to go and help a newcomer, or help someone who was struggling with some part of his or her life, and through helping someone else I would begin to remember just how great my life had become over the past 18 – 24 months.

Then, finally, if I were ultra upset about something on a given day and not responding to his suggestion of me helping someone else, he would simply resort back to telling me to "shut up and go and pray", knowing that through prayer I would realise that God's will is for me to help others, thus leading me back into the solution, learning the same lesson but in a slightly different way. The way out of negative behaviour and destructive patterns was always the same. It always came back to helping other people. The solution to virtually all of my emotional turmoil always seemed to be the same - go and help someone less fortunate than yourself and discover true gratitude. That's how I changed the very essence of my emotional and spiritual life; simply by focusing on the person in a greater spot of bother than me.

That was the answer to my problem of selfishness and my problem of fear, and my problem of depression, and sadness. He was reminding me that this process is gradual, and it is constantly changing. He was reminding me that I needed to expand my mind even more.

Oh, and of course, I needed to pull my head out of this money-chasing God and return to a God whose desire for me is to be happy, joyous and free. Not necessarily wealthy and hard working.

2. Recovered?

Now some people will say that using a word such as 'recovered' is quite strong language and I am aware that in some 12-Step Fellowships this is frowned upon, preferring to refer to themselves as perpetually recovering; which is cool, if that's the language or belief pattern you prefer. Indeed, whenever you see recovery discussed on the TV or in other forms of media, usually they'll use the term 'recovering alcoholic or addict'. So, to explain what I mean by using the term 'recovered', and it is a personal choice, I am still recovering from my addictions. Believe me, I am. There are still two areas of my behaviour that require attention. I have not yet mastered obsessive shopping or compulsive sugar consumption. However, I have mastered lust and nicotine. I have mastered caffeine, and I have absolutely mastered alcohol and narcotics. But, I am still recovering from my addictive disease, and I probably always will be in some form or another.

I haven't recovered from my addiction as a whole but I have recovered from drinking and using illegal and legal drugs, and I have evidence to support this:

I was going through some old vinyl records when I was a few years into my recovery, and I pulled out about half a gram of Heroin. I opened it up; I intuitively knew it was Heroin; I didn't need to dab it and taste it; I didn't need to put it in foil and see it run; I didn't need to see how it dissolved with citric acid before cooking it in distilled water in preparation of a hit. I intuitively knew it was Heroin and I was able to throw it away under running water in a sink.

Another time, as I was going through some other records in preparation for a DJ set at a 12-Step Fellowship Convention. I found five grams of Coke. I intuitively knew it was Cocaine. I didn't need to dab it and taste it; I didn't need to discover how finely it chopped up in lines; I didn't need to see what it was like when mixed with bicarbonate of soda and water; I didn't even need to see how it dissolved with ammonia, before heating it over a small flame. I even knew it was one of the five-gram packets that I used to sell, because there were only about four and a half grams there (remember the .8s?). I was able to throw it away in the toilet basin and pull the flush with zero resistance.

I found hundreds of LSD trips (strawberry blotters) wrapped in cling-film, stashed away in my stuff on another occasion and was able to destroy them without testing them to make sure of their potency. Actually, destroying those trips was very easy over a candle flame.

I even found some cherished, high-grade quality Hashish (Cannabis resin). It was from a specific location known to yield incredible quality crops of Cannabis in the Manali Valley, Himachal Pradesh, in India. It was most likely from my journey to India before I got sober, and therefore smuggled back into the UK inside my own bowels. I knew that this was the best Hashish in the world and oddly I found this one drug harder to let go of than any of the others. I found it difficult to simply throw away this Hashish, so I gave it to my younger sister, (such is brotherly love!) who I must say is not an addict in any interpretation of the word. She enjoyed it, and it probably took her a couple of months to consume what would have constituted just a few spliffs for me. That said, in support of any concern about my sister's integrity, I have absolutely no evidence that she smoked it at all, and I'm sure she actually handed it into the police for destruction, like any good citizen would do. Although this could just be another example indicative of the current generation's relaxed and accepting attitude towards drugs, specifically Cannabis?

Today, I can go into bars and I can go into pubs and, assuming I'm there for the right reasons, I find I don't need to drink or do anything naughty. I find myself quite comfortable drinking spring water with plenty of slices of lemon, and recently I've even begun drinking Coke - Coca-Cola, I hasten to add - I especially enjoy that over crushed ice.

It's Not About Me!

Is this recovered behaviour? I think so. But let me explain my terminology with a simple metaphor. If you shoot me with a pistol and the bullet lands in the shoulder, I am left with a gunshot wound. With time, this wound will heal. I will recover from a gunshot wound. But, I am not bulletproof! You could shoot me again and once again I would be wounded, or even killed. That is how it is with my addiction. I can't start because when I start using drugs, I can't stop. When I do stop, I can't then stop myself from starting again. I discussed this in detail earlier. So, the best thing for me to do is to refrain from starting in the first place. And, because of the work I did with this 12-Step programme, and other personal development I've done undertaken, this idea of abstinence has been incredibly easy and straightforward. I have - simply put - recovered.

This is my understanding. I've recovered from my drink and drug addiction, just like I've recovered from my caffeine and nicotine addictions. I have recovered because I have tapped into an external Power in my life and I know how to make the right choices. I choose not to use any substances because I have made a conscious choice for my life. I have the power to choose not to use and I do so on a daily basis. I have recovered from my powerlessness, which is what my initial problem was. "Lack of power was my dilemma" to quote from the Alcoholics Anonymous book. I was powerless around drugs; I couldn't stop using them. I had no choice not to do it and when I started doing it I had no control over not doing it again. I now have more than enough power, which I found through a relationship with my own Higher Power, my Higher Purpose and my God as I came to understand Her.

One of the problems I now face is battling with chocolate; I'm not even in recovery from it. I attempt to control my use by restricting it to night times only and other similar techniques, but it isn't working. So, although I am still in recovery, and I have already recovered from drinking and drugging and caffeine and nicotine, I can still struggle with other parts of my addiction. I'm on a journey to recover from my illness in its entirety, but for the moment I am still recovering from some aspects of it. I do know that I'm able to choose not to drink or use on daily basis simply because I'm able to tap into things that I talked about earlier like gratitude, understanding and self-awareness. I have an understanding of a power greater than myself that I refer to as God, who works hand in hand with me in my life and gives me that power on a daily basis. Without this spiritual dimension, someone like me would be in big trouble and never recover. Sooner or later, I will ask for help around my chocolate addiction - probably when I've had enough pain.

I'm still an addict. I have never recovered from being an addict, my addiction is my disease, and I live with it every day of my life. I used to find comfort in drugs and alcohol. They gave me emotional and mental tools that allowed me to be who I thought I wanted to be just to get through each day, but this is really no way to live and certainly no longer an option for me. So I have found other solutions that work much better for me. I use lots of different methods to induce the same sense of ease and comfort in my life. Different things that help me now include; water, fruit, exercise, walking, talking, laughing, singing, company, friendships, and even business - all types of things. Yet, I am still an addict. I am just not an addict who's actively using drink, drugs, caffeine and nicotine to change the way I feel today. I choose less harmful and more positive behaviours to change the way I feel. I'm perfectly comfortable being an addict. These days I am just an addict who has been in recovery for a long time and one who is very happy to have recovered from drink and drugs and stimulants.

3. It's not about me

During my recovery journey, I explored my spiritual energies and learning outside of any formal church, temple or religion. I discovered a God of my very own, and every day I am discovering more and more about Her, as She reveals Herself to me more and more, permitting me to absorb a better understanding of Her will for me, and what Her plans are in helping me live a more successful life, happy, joyous and free.

When you consider how I behaved before I came into recovery, it's obvious to see how corrupt I was without even realising it. I was a bad boy, I was not well behaved, I was a bully at school, a serial cheater on women (well, whenever I could!!!), and I had no self-constraint, rarely ever behaving myself at all. I used the excuse of free love, freedom and hippie values to do just about anything and everything I wanted, and to explain away my lack of respect for other people and for society. I was not just a rebel but also literally an outlaw. I had to go into exile from the UK because I'd been arrested so many times and I didn't fancy jail time. That would just cut into the amount of fun I was trying to have. I was a badly behaved person.

My journey into abstinence turned me into a spiritual person and that has allowed me to change and develop good qualities that now I can say I am proud of. The measure of my life is no longer selfish actions, but rather selfless ones. Instead, the quality of my life is reliant on the quality of the lives of the people around me, and how I can help improve our quality of living. That was the profound behaviour I adopted and is the underlined message of this book. It's not about me; the world is no longer about me. My world as an addict was always all about me. This recovery has been, and continues to be about other people, and the whole thing has to have been about readdressing my karma, rebalancing my energy with the universe by contributing towards the quality of other people's lives. These days, I'm about making things right, for the sake of making things right, and no longer contributing towards making things wrong.

If I see a woman struggling with a pram, a couple of kids and a load of shopping, I realise I have a choice. In previous times, I would grab her purse and run away, perhaps gaining myself £50 and the possibility of happiness or even obliteration for a couple of hours. Whereas today when I see a woman like that, I know I can offer to carry the pram up the stairs, help her get the shopping in the door, or help her across a road safely without an ulterior motive. I do these things now and feel great without looking for any payback at all. I feel great just because I have had the chance to make someone else's life better or easier, even if it is just for one small moment of the day. When you steal from someone you don't feel good about it. Sure, there's the initial adrenaline rush and thrill of having achieved your goal but there's no long-term feeling of wellness that comes from taking things that don't belong to you. When you give to someone there is a feeling of generosity and gratitude that stays with you long after the event has taken place. I know which feeling I'd rather have. This feeling is what I talk about when I talk about spirituality. I'm talking about my own kind of spirituality, a little something I like to call Bubble-gum Spirituality.

4. Bubble-gum Spirituality - part 1

Bubble-gum spirituality is my own version of spirituality, put very simply for anyone to understand. It's not complicated. In fact, keeping it simple is the whole point here. You don't have to commit to following any particular religious dogma; you just need to have a willingness to do the right thing.

It's a simple spiritual understanding of the world and suggests appropriate ways to behave. The main message from this sort of spirituality is that a life lived along spiritual lines will offer you far more internal happiness than anything material ever could. Happiness comes from a sense of global human connection and participating in humanity on Earth today. This is best practice 'Spirituality for the Masses'.

Its key messages are twofold:

1) Always do the right thing.

This is about no longer being quite so selfish and self-centred; instead, think about how best to serve your community, family, fellowship, society, humanity, and the planet. What is the right way to behave? What's the right thing to do here? Put yourself to one side and decide to do the right thing for the majority and not for yourself. I am part of a movement called 'The Pay It Forward Movement'. It's based upon the film 'Pay It Forward' with Kevin Spacey, Helen Hunt and Haley Joel Osment. The kid (Haley) prompted by his teacher (Kevin) designs a social action, which if followed through is designed to make the world a better place. It's simple in its design - simply, when someone does a good turn for you, don't pay them back, but pay it forward to three other people. Please watch this film if you're not already familiar with it. Well, 'The Pay It Forward Movement' aims to carry this message into practice. By taking responsibility and doing the right thing as often as possible, asking only that the recipients of our kindness or generosity 'pay it forward' to the next group of people, we aim to make the world a nicer place to live.

This is Bubble-gum Spirituality.

2) Contribute to others without expecting anything in return.

This is about serving others without asking to be paid, expecting recognition, or demanding they do the same for you. In fact, the best way to do this is to contribute anonymously. Every 23rd December, I participate in something called 'Basket Brigade'. We fundraise throughout the year and come together on 23rd December to make Christmas hampers that we assemble ourselves and decorate with a card, signed anonymously. About 200 of us come together and find our roles in this massive production, which creates around 600 family-sized

Christmas hampers within four or five hours. That afternoon we distribute these hampers all over London to people whose details have been collected from various charities (dealing with poverty, or victims of domestic violence, etc.). As we deliver them, we simply announce ourselves as the delivery driver and insist that we have no knowledge of the origin of the basket, aside from the card inside which says, "From a friend". To see the recipients' eyes well up with tears of gratitude - nearly always with children who would otherwise have had a very difficult Christmas, often going hungry and lacking many simple things is the real gift. To know you've helped someone else without expecting anything in return.

This is Bubble-gum Spirituality.

These are the two cornerstones of Bubble-gum Spirituality. Embrace these principles into your lives and see the change in how you feel. I've highlighted just two of the ways I bring Bubble-gum Spirituality alive and kicking into my own life. But imagine living your own life along these principles. Now you can begin to see just how magnificently your own life can improve, just by doing the right thing without seeking any rewards.

Bubble-gum Spirituality can be accurately summarised in two sentences; 'Always do unto others as you would have done to yourself.' And, 'Do for others what they cannot do for themselves.'

5. Employed and Employing

About the time I came out of my primary depression at around two and a half years' clean, I made the decision to leave the city job and began working at the rehab I had gone through. I worked at this facility for a year, during which time I learnt from some of the very best in the addiction treatment industry about how to run and operate a rehab. I worked alongside the great Adrian Lee, who was the first sober man I ever met when I turned up at the treatment facility for an assessment. He had effectively persuaded me to accept my father's help, come in and have a rest from my addiction. He told me a little about his own drinking and, in doing so, had connected with me in such a way that I knew he had my best interests in mind.

During that year, I learnt how to build and run a treatment centre by watching, working and learning through doing. I was taught how to market treatment programmes and how to operate an admissions department, but I learnt so much more than just what I was taught. I learnt about the nuts and bolts by watching and asking questions. I have always been very perceptive at watching the way others do things and then mirroring them for myself so, in that respect, I'm a great employee. However, I'm not really a very good employee at all. I'm an entrepreneur. I have a spirit in me that says, "I can do this myself." I fail to see the reason I wouldn't find my niche and set up my own facility. The staff there never knew what I was dreaming about. They just saw an incredibly efficient and dynamic young marketer. I was very effective at what I was doing, but any entrepreneur among you could see it was only a matter of time. Certainly, it came as no surprise for the owners, Robert and Robin Lefever (father and son) to see where my future lay. I simply wasn't cut out to be an employee. I had bigger dreams in mind. It was really just a matter of figuring out the right time. The right time for me came in a most unpredictable way.

I attended a workshop between Alcoholics Anonymous (the original 12-Step Fellowship) and the Buckinghamshire Probation Service and suddenly it dawned upon me that there was something missing in the UK. Treatment centres that incorporated the 12-Steps had largely only been available to the wealthy in the form of private rehabilitation centres. Now, some of these centres had been fairly successful at selling beds to the NHS, but there weren't enough to be truly making a difference. I saw a gap in the market. I started thinking, "What if I could create a centre at such a low cost that we could sell beds to the NHS and offer them much better value for their money?" and suddenly, by selling treatment at a much lower price be able to effectively open up the 12-Step recovery programme to more of the population? No longer was spiritual treatment for addiction only going to be available to the middle and upper classes. I wanted to make it available to the working class and those families with a more limited budget. So, that is exactly what I did.

I had a wealthy businessman friend in the 12-Step rooms around North-West London, who boldly said one day that he'd like to open a treatment centre as a way of making amends for some of his past. This was totally in line with my own values and my own amends - to help rebalance the karma of my own past - that of turning on so many people to drugs they may never have been exposed to and the wide distribution of drugs I was involved in. Nameless/faceless harm to others required a massive effort to help many others in return.

It's Not About Me!

The first facility I opened took seven months to build from scratch, and it was loosely based upon a model I had visited in Bournemouth, combined with the US models of sober living accommodation around a central therapeutic counselling centre hub. It wasn't the nicest of places, but it was nice enough. Although the clients often complained about the poor accommodation and the lack of luxury facilities, it was low budget and still considerably nicer than the standards that many of the clients were coming to us from. They would come from sleeping on cardboard in a squat, and complain about having only a single bed and no TV. My target had been to build a functioning centre with 24 beds, and I well and truly exceeded my goals.

Within six months we were at capacity, and we began opening up more accommodation facilities for the clients, allowing me to grow the number of clients. It wasn't long before I was operating the facility at 150% capacity, running at 36 beds with a decent-sized waiting list. I thought I had enough momentum now to make some changes. I wanted to reinvest profits into the client accommodation and facilities. I put my foot down and told the investors that the profits needed to be reinvested in the accommodation and the quality of care that was being provided. Our staff were overstretched and it felt like the shareholders didn't care. They refused to reinvest in the housing stock or the amenities. To further complicate the balance of resentment I was carrying, the clients were by now being housed in shared rooms while kitchens were being turned into sleeping accommodation, and the staff were simply overwhelmed with the massive task of maintaining three consecutive groups with daily new intakes and graduations. The shareholders then asked me to discharge my deputy manager Gavin, so they could save on his salary. I realised I was working 70+ hours a week and the shareholders had all bought themselves nice new cars. I pleaded my case, and I warned them of my intentions. I was a man of principle and unless they were to follow my vision and reinvest in the clients' welfare, I couldn't manage to support them any longer. They didn't believe me and they didn't buckle. So, I quit! I split! I stuck to my values and maintained my integrity. After just over a year, I left and took part of the staff with me, including my deputy manager, who'd they'd insisted I let go of.

I stood up for my own principles and I knew that I had proved I could do what I'd set out to do, even if it appeared that the people I'd done it for hadn't appreciated precisely the same vision as me. I left and set out to do it all again, this time with my previous deputy Gavin as a co-owner in our own rehabilitation facility alongside a couple of property guys, one of whom was in recovery himself and had become a friend. We built our centre in line with the vision that Gavin and I shared. It was completely client focused and results driven. With this in our minds, we believed it would be successful; and it was.

It was to be the best move I ever made. Our rehab was opened within four months and was instantly successful growing larger, much quicker, with industry-leading statistics of successful outcomes of over 70% and over 90% in the third-stage housing environments. It is one of my proudest achievements in my life thus far; one of my legacies.

But after two years of running the admissions and intake side of the company, operating two mobile phones and rarely turning them off, always talking to families and addicts and alcoholics and various referrers from both the private and the public sectors, I was burning out. I had been operating like this for almost four years now, and I was very tired. As my performance slacked off and I began to make sloppy mistakes, I came to the realisation that there were other people better suited to do my job than I was. Our company had outgrown my skills and it was bigger than me. It was time for me to set out and do something else.

This was the time Sober Services was conceived, and I'll share more about that later.

6. **From Nicotine to Sugar** – The difference between obsession and compulsion

I stopped smoking cigarettes without even having the desire to stop. I had smoked for so long and I never considered that I would ever give up the habit, but I did, and without any real effort at all. It was most incredible, and an event that really could only be referred to as divine intervention. I was in a guided meditation session and, during the session, I was faced with the question, "What is the decision I don't want to make?"

At first, I thought that what I really needed to focus on was doing an even better job at my work, therefore working harder would be the decision I hadn't wanted to make. I thought that I needed to commit more and give more time to ensure that my company grew bigger, faster. But the voice that came back to me from

It's Not About Me!

God was telling me that this was a decision I did want to make, not a decision I didn't want to make. Again, I was faced with this seemingly strange question, "What is the decision I don't want to make?"

My thoughts turned to my girlfriend at the time and I started thinking about how I really should be a better lover and a better partner to her. I made the decision to please her more and take better care of her, but God turned back to me again and reminded me that this was a decision I really wanted to make! So, what was the decision I didn't want to make?

I was deep in this guided meditation when, all of a sudden, it occurred to me. It came to me intuitively and I was so sure, without a shadow of a doubt, that the decision I really did not want to make (even though I knew I really ought to) was the decision to quit smoking cigarettes.

I knew that I didn't want to make this decision; it was a decision I had been avoiding for years. I knew I hadn't ever made the decision before, because I didn't have the desire to stop. Even though I knew I should, I really didn't want to. I still associated great pleasure with smoking. I simply didn't have a desire to stop doing something else I still associated with pleasure, despite the knowledge that it was killing me (albeit slowly).

Then God told me that if I stopped smoking right there and then, that She would take care of me and that I would be fine, it wouldn't be so bad. She informed me that She would be there for me, to help me every step of the way and to take care of the withdrawals and the obsession. God told me that if I made the decision to stop smoking, everything would be all right.

So, I took out the cigarette packet that I had tucked inside my jacket, I opened it and there were still 17 or 18 cigarettes staring up at me. I broke each and every one of them and threw them on the floor followed by both of the lighters I had on me. I knew that I would never smoke again. I knew that I had just quit and I wouldn't go back. I knew that this time God was going to remove my obsession and allow me to slide through the withdrawal without much fuss and that I never would pick up a cigarette again, even though I had already smoked that day and therefore my body was craving more nicotine. I just knew!

I went outside to my car and found four packets tucked in the door pockets and glove compartment along with three more lighters. I gave them all away to people walking past me in the car park. I went back to the hotel room where I was currently staying, opened my suitcase and pulled out another six packets, which I gave to some friends in a nearby room. When I got home after the weekend away, I knew that there was a massive hoard there that needed to be removed. There were 2,150 packets of cigarettes; eleven and half cartons! You can see just how serious I was about smoking, just by my stash protection of supply! I had been stockpiling them, careful to ensure that I never ran out. I sold them all in one go to a buddy at the great price of £200 all in. I even chucked a couple of lighters into the deal. A massive reduction - less than 20% of their price! Why? Because I just knew I was never going to smoke again. I knew I was done!

It wasn't easy, going through the withdrawals like that, but cold turkey is the only way I know that works, because it allows me to associate the pain of withdrawal with the substance, despite making it difficult for me during the process. That said, the process of detoxing through cold turkey is considerably shorter than a medicated one, even though the pain may be significantly more intense during the actual process. It's still my preferred method. None of those cutting down attempts to stop seemed to work for me.

I knew that God had effectively removed the obsession for me to smoke and I'd never choose to do it again. I had regained my power to choose. I chose not to use! So long as I never decided to give God the finger and try to 'have just the one', then I would remain in power over my smoking addiction. But I knew that if I had just one, then it'd be game over and I would smoke again. Abstinence is the only way for me. I haven't smoked since that day, more than six years ago.

Now let's consider sugar. I have thoroughly enjoyed a close relationship with sugar, particularly chocolate, ever since I got sober. When I look back over the years I see that I even tended to enjoy particularly sugary alcohols. My favourites were drinks such as Southern Comfort, Baileys, Malibu and Midori, all of which I enjoyed drinking neat, from the bottle. So, suffice to say, I have always had a rather pronounced sweet tooth.

A few years ago now, I became concerned about my growing waistline and what I was dubbing 'my serenity belly'. The happier and more stress free I was, the larger I was becoming. So, I took the drastic action of cutting out all sugary drinks specifically those of the canned or large plastic bottle variety. I cut out all kinds of squash and cordial. Since that day I have virtually only drunk water.

It's Not About Me!

I drink between two and five litres of water a day and I love it. I drink spring water and it revitalises me. I try to avoid the distilled or purified stuff. I consider water to be a healer for many of the symptoms of life. Headaches, restlessness, insomnia can all be cured by water, it makes up 97% of my body, and my body screams for it.

My theory was this. If I don't put sugar in my body then I won't crave it anymore. If I don't crave it, then I won't eat chocolate. So, here we should probably introduce my chocolate habits. They are pretty serious. I don't do this love by halves. I don't buy small bars of chocolate; I buy slabs. A 400-gram slab of Dairy Milk, a 390-gram slab of Galaxy or 400 grams of Toblerone is pure gastronomic heaven to me. There is a pouffe to put our feet on in my lounge room, which opens up to store large books, blankets, and comforting things. Inside there are usually two or three slabs of each of my favourites and I would easily eat one of these in a sitting. If I were controlling myself I might be able to hold myself back and only eat half ...but it was always 200 grams minimum in a sitting. To this day, despite trying to work on this addiction, I still eat a cool 125-200 grams daily.

The theory of not drinking sugar and thus taking away my sugar cravings works in theory. But I never talked to my God or asked for help around my love for sugar. I've simply tried to do it on my own. Every time I get the overwhelming obsession to eat chocolate, I am completely powerless to stop myself from devouring it. Chocolate is just like Cocaine and other drugs for me. When chocolate creeps into my thoughts, I'm already powerless. I could be walking down the street, minding my own business, and happen to see someone take a bite of a chocolate bar, or see a chocolate advert or even just pass a store I know sells chocolate and my mind takes off on a chocolate rampage. I become obsessed with it, I will drop what I'm doing and go and buy some (plenty), immediately eating it, and I love every minute of it. So, even when I don't drink sugary drinks and my body doesn't crave it, my mind obsesses about it all on its own. I am unable to beat my obsession, despite not triggering my compulsion. And then, just like with Cocaine or booze, once the first bites passes through my lips it's game over. I keep going back until I've devoured the equivalent of a full three-course meal of nothing but chocolate. Powerless! Godless! Hopeless!

I admit that I'm powerless over chocolate and that my life (my weight) has become unmanageable.

I admit that I'm unmanageable over chocolate and that my life (my body) has become powerless (to stop it). So, my challenge is to allow God in to help me with my sugar addiction. I need power! Unlike my smoking, in which I clearly accepted God's help and was able to break that habit permanently, I haven't even approached God yet to genuinely and seriously ask for help. For sugar, I need Step two: Came to believe that a power greater than ourselves could restore us to sanity. I need God to help restore me to sanity. Then in step three, I need to make a decision to turn my will and my life over to the care of God (as I understand Her). And that's where I am stuck. I have failed to admit complete defeat and ask for God's help. I have Step one, but not Steps two and three.

Why? Because my belief system tells me that I enjoy chocolate. I tell myself that the pleasure associated with it is more powerful than the pain I associate with it. Therefore, I still want to find a way to eat chocolate like a gentleman, like I used to think I could use drugs and drink sociably again, drink like a gentleman and use with my friends. Right? However, just like all my addictions, abstinence is the only way I can stop doing what I don't want to be doing in the first place. There is no middle ground.

God did, once asked, freely help break my obsession with smoking. God could and would, once sought, help break my obsession with sugar. In the same way as all other drugs, if I don't put the first cigarette in my mouth, then I won't have the compulsion to smoke the second or third. Like if I don't eat the first piece of chocolate, then I won't eat the following 200+ grams! It all starts with breaking the obsession. There's only one way I know to do that, and it involves asking for help from a power greater than me, greater than my addiction and ultimately, greater than anything material. It needs to be spiritual. I haven't found the strength yet. But I will...I will.

7. Bubble-gum Spirituality - part 2

During the tail end of 2005 and throughout 2006 I watched as my father slowly lost his life to a brain tumour. I watched him die slowly and painfully. He successfully completed two operations where his skull was cut open and the tumour cut out, but sadly it was too aggressive and, after the third operation, he never recovered. The path downhill post that third operation was fairly rapid – a

It's Not About Me!

couple of months. He died 1st January 2007 around 3pm. It was desperately sad and depressing watching him lose his aura those last few months, and it affected me (as it did all of my family) considerably more than I cared to let on. Certainly, until writing this passage, I realised I'd never truly expressed just how difficult it was for me to say a permanent goodbye to my dad. He and I had become very close during my sober years and I considered him a business and life mentor, as well as my father.

When I was making my ninth Step amends, where I go about making right the wrongs I had caused people during my addiction and rebalancing my karma, I had approached my dad to offer my apologies for being an absent son and so unavailable to him during my 13 solid years of madness. I asked him how I could make it right, and he requested that I join him by his side in supporting the Saracens – the Rugby team that he had been following for many years. He bought us both season tickets and I almost never missed a home game alongside him for the last five seasons of his life. We both wore the Saracens colours and our Sundays together were certainly the best times I ever spent with dad. They might have been even better days if the Saracens had won a few more matches but that was asking my God for too much!

So losing dad was tough. Losing a parent is always one of the toughest challenges in our lives and, now that I was sober, I literally felt my way through the difficult last 13 months and into his passing. A huge wave of responsibility hit me as I realised I was now the oldest male member of my family, and I slipped into a new position of family protector. I'm the oldest of all my cousins on my father's side and, with that knowledge, most organically, fell a certain maturity upon me.

At his funeral, there were more than 200 people in attendance. The room it was held in overflowed as more and more people arrived. I could see just how loved and respected my father was. It was for his eulogy that I first wrote the words that went on to constitute my Bubble-gum Spirituality passage. My father had taught me the way to treat people and he taught me the importance of bringing value to other people's lives. I also caught his optimism and jolly demeanour. In fact, my default emotion is jolly. Some days I'm jollier than other days and some days I'm slightly less jolly, but by and large, I'm somewhere around the jolly zone on a daily basis. I got this emotional state genetically transferred by my father. But as I was delivering the eulogy, I began crying. It really was the first time in my life I ever began crying out of genuine grief and sorrow. I've cried during many an emotional film, where I'm taken on an imaginative journey and through empathy I cry with the characters, but here I was crying from profound grief and sorrow, overwhelmed by the absolute loss I was feeling.

And I cried shamelessly. I was conscious that there was an audience of well over 200 people there, yet I let go of any stigma associated with crying and just let myself go. It was an experience I shall carry with me forever. Crying in public for the first, and thus far only occasion, was a profound experience for me, as I truly felt my loss and pictured dad looking down on me, as I was speaking to his audience of friends, delivering his words about how to be the best person he could possibly have taught me to be. But it took my addiction and my recovery to get to that place, right there, right then.

I knew dad was proud of me and I knew, at that moment, he knew just how much I loved him.

Never someone to shy away from the teachings of any experience life can throw at me, I took the loss of my dad and learned how to help others going through their own grieving process. I had been given a gift as my life suddenly began filling up with friends and acquaintances revealing to me that they, too, had close relatives who were losing their battles with cancer. It was almost as if God put people in my path who were dealing with something I had just dealt with so I could use my own experience to help them.

Well, actually that's exactly what God was doing and I knew Her too well to think any different. My dad had already taught me that while I'm helping someone else with his or her difficulties, I am improving the quality of my own life. The 12-Step recovery programme revealed that to me too.

Bubble-gum Spirituality - It is a circle of giving and receiving and it's what I committed myself to as I made my deal for my sobriety with God, back in 2001 - God, keep me happy, joyous and free, and I'll be a servant of your will and desire. Since your will and desire is to bring more happiness, joyfulness and freedom to your subjects, allow me to deliver on your behalf. And thank you for giving me the gift of being jolly on a daily basis. Amen.

8. Falling in love

Throughout my life I have liked the ladies and I've never had too hard a time attracting new ones into my life, even if just for a few hours. In order to respect their anonymity and to attempt to be a gentleman about the whole affair (pun intended), I haven't gone into too much detail in this book to tell you about the girls whose hearts and sometimes virginities I stole during my school and college years and the great many different liaisons (romantic or just plain lustful) I had during my raving and DJing days, but aside from a few years where I attempted monogamy, being with just one woman was always unappealing to me.

Once I got sober, trying to pull girls and build romantic relationships became difficult for me for the first time in my life. Anxiety around women became overwhelming. I was virtually always nervous around girls, particularly ones I found attractive. I started believing that every woman I engaged in conversation with, would be thinking that I was doing so purely to get into her knickers and that they would be judging me, so I must be on my best behaviour and not actually genuinely attempt to get close to her, to make sure she knew that I was really a nice guy who meant her no harm, even though, secretly (or so I hoped) I did actually, most likely, want to get into her knickers. All the relationships I entered into for the first few years of my sobriety were instigated by the woman, as I felt too ashamed and scared to risk offending her in case she didn't fancy me back. But once they made their intentions clear, I would then follow up and obsess about her until, in most cases, I would scare her away.

I realised that being scared of girls because of my perceived reaction that they may feel that I was merely talking to them for ulterior motives and their forthcoming rejection was both projection (time travelling) and blatant paranoia! Paranoia of what I thought females would think of me, should they know how I thought they thought about me thinking about them. This was probably only true about 75% of the time, but I found it increasingly difficult to chat up girls in case they thought I was actually attempting to groom them for sex.

I'd lost any moves I may have possessed before I got sober and I had no idea how to handle myself without blushing or turning into a jabbering wreck anymore. After all, there's one thing you've got to hand to booze – it certainly removes your anxieties and limitations about being intimidated amongst the fairer sex, and vice versa I imagine, based upon the sights we see around every town centre of the British Isles every Friday night. I actually learnt the French language just by getting pissed with Frenchmen and not caring whether they understood or not - just pushing on through until I found the right words and expressions. And as for Heroin and Cocaine ...well they're the masters of bringing confidence to a person - at least that's my experience. Alcohol and drugs are very good at installing false confidence, e.g., 'Dutch Courage', and giving me the ability to talk to just about anyone I wanted to. Women seemed to be drawn to such overt confidence.

Sometime around 2004, when I was three or four years sober, with a newborn self conviction, brought about by the clarity I gained about myself and my own power, matched with the faith and courage restored to me by my own relationship with my Higher Power, the Goddess Herself, I overcame my fears by rediscovering my influence and authority over myself.

I did some work on my own inner Power, self-confidence and Qi (pronounced "chi") aka The Force and discovered my balls (technical term, you understand) once again. I began dating and fooling around with women. I became a successful and prolific character on the Internet Dating scene, and I successfully found myself entertaining different women on an almost weekly basis.

I rapidly became focussed (some would say obsessed) around women and then quickly reverted to being the very same dog I had been many years before. I felt the charm and influence that I had over women and I exploited it for my own amusement. Sex became my drug and there was no way I was giving it up. I would make sure I had a different date every weekend (online dating is a useful tool in this realm) and, when I went away, I would have multiple partners in any given weekend. It reminded me of the days in France, when I was a DJ travelling all over the country and, indeed, my time in Europe back when I had a female companion in every city and always somewhere new to hang my hat. At a large rave in Paris around 1995, I actually had seven girlfriends in the same venue, and had to seriously be careful not to upset any of them.

You see, I had never really worked on the character defect of lust. I wasn't a traditional pervert, or an obsessive masturbator. But I certainly sought my thrills through the highs of one-night stands, and the best part was always the actual pulling part - not the sex. The sex was the consequence and trophy of the obsession to achieve this lady or that. Just like with drugs, when very often the best part was simply the process of scoring or preparing the hit. The actual ingestion of the drugs and the subsequent euphoria was short lived because the real power came in the control (imaginary or real) of being able to have that hit whenever I wanted it. Is this making sense? Basically, I was all about the thrill of the chase. The sex wasn't important, which is how I was able to so easily distance myself emotionally from the sex act itself and immediately move on to the next conquest. Indeed, on a number of occasions I wouldn't follow through with the sex act at all, preferring the power I could wield over the woman who would now be chasing me. Not really very nice behaviour at all, but yet justified by the self-explanation that they were all willing players - just like everyone I turned on to drugs was a willing participant.

But, at five years clean, I had a moment of enlightenment and a breakthrough where I realised I no longer liked the person I had become ...again! Even sober this time, I knew I couldn't continue to live with myself behaving like that. I broke down to ask God, as I understood God, for some help. I was feeling dreadful and shameful again just like I had when I asked for help to stop using drugs. The guilt and remorse was a more powerful force for change than anything else.

There had been a cute girl I'd been sitting next to in a Big-Book (Alcoholics Anonymous) study meeting I attended on Thursday nights. She was ever so cute, but she didn't seem to realise just how cute she was, which honestly just made her cuter. We became friends as she used to feel safe sitting next to me. She would phone me up just to discuss TV soap operas or other daily mundane things in her life. I was amazed. Nobody had ever engaged me in such simple and down to earth conversation before. Everyone I knew talked to me about drugs, or how not to use drugs, or music or politics or theology or philosophy or other equally intense subjects. But this lovely girl called Emma used to talk to me about the simple things in life. It was an entirely new dynamic and experience for me. I kind of liked it. I kind of liked her.

So, when I was asking God for some help around my sexual behaviour and my treatment of women, imagine my surprise when God kept putting Emma's face in my meditation and visions. Now I'm not saying that God is a pimp, or even a dating agency, but when her face kept popping into my thoughts, I knew I ought to take some action. Her mother was in hospital and she was grieving, so I invited Emma over to my office for a chat. We had our first kiss while she sat on my lap behind my desk. Our first date was a couple of nights later at a Thai restaurant. We instantly became inseparable.

Emma is a very kind soul, who dedicates her life and her recovery from alcoholism to working with sick animals. She was working for the Blue Cross with rescue dogs when we met and has spent much of her career working as a veterinary nurse since then, although these days she has her own website www.whyilovemydog.net. Please come and have a browse of it when you get a moment. Especially if you love dogs!

One of the reasons we were attracted to each other was our desire to help those less fortunate than ourselves - in her case animals and in mine, humans.

We were engaged nine months later and married thirteen months after that. I've been monogamous ever since that first kiss, and for that I'm very grateful indeed (and so is my wife).

The past six years (and counting) have been a blessing in my life. Do you know why? It is because Emma is a constant source of amusement to me. She honestly makes my life better every day. We dance naked for each other in the mornings, and we design our own 'isms that only we get - little sayings and faces that we pull. I can honestly say Emma is the funniest person in my life and that ability of hers to make me laugh and her natural beauty are a constant source of interest for me. Neither of us has ever been happier and I am thankful to have her every day of my life.

9. Fellowship, in sickness and in health

I have had some amazing experiences in my life, and my post drinking and drugging years have been no exception. My life has been filled with exciting, surprising and wonderful moments. But life isn't always perfect, life isn't always simple and life certainly isn't always everything you dreamt of. I went through a really rough couple of years. I was severely let down by a very close friend who left me close to bankruptcy just a few months prior to my wedding, thus forcing me to significantly downsize the actual wedding event. This betrayal caused me a great deal of pain. Significantly, it crushed my self-confidence and left me questioning both myself and my own intuition. It could be considered an ego deflation, but it was actually much more sinister than that. I found myself contemplating suicide. I lost so much self-belief, personal faith and ultimately my own personal courage, that I sunk into a deep depression for a lengthy period of time - over 18 months. I felt weak and defeated. But I didn't go back to drinking or using drugs. I easily could have, and plenty of recovering addicts would fall back into their addiction at this type of hurdle, or when life gets particularly hard.

Even more recently, albeit on a much lesser level, which never led to any pronounced form of depression (more anger and resentment), I've been let down by a business partner who has taken advantage of my trust and manipulated many tens of thousands of pounds out of me and my company, before walking out and leaving my company close to ruin. Sadly, this was someone I'd taken on as a complete junior and virtual newcomer to recovery, fully trained and given company equity to as a reward. And once he'd got away with his scam, he then had the audacity to blatantly steal company equipment from me once I began confronting him about his disloyalty and disrespect as if this was his justification for his dreadful behaviour. It felt like a long time girlfriend had just cheated on me and left with my best friend. Fortunately I wasn't going to behave the same way I had in the late 90s when I'd set the Tahitian Mafia on to the perpetrator. The sad thing that comes from these experiences is they increase my own distrust of the very people that need my help and I choose to assist and help develop. Maybe God is giving me another lesson, along the lines that I should remain a sole trader and not partner up with people, but that's simply not in my nature. I like to share things, experiences, celebrations and results. I'm a people person and not a soloist.

Whenever I experience pain in my life, just like when dad slowly died over those thirteen months, I suffer and I struggle just like everyone else. I'm not invincible to pain and discomfort. No one is.

So I have also learnt through my recovery that I must allow people to help me. In times of sadness it is appropriate for me to allow those who I had previously helped, either directly or indirectly, to perform their own spiritual principles upon me. I have to ask for help and accept it when it is given to me.

So, I let people support me and I let them help and guide me. I have made some amazing friends in my local (and national and international) 12-Step Fellowship meetings, particularly in my home group, on Sunday evenings. This fellowship is my home, my support network and my guiding light. These were the people I trusted enough to allow them to see me be vulnerable. They are still the people I trust enough to share completely honestly with and to accept their love, support and suggestions. During this dark time in my life, I trusted them to help me get through it. I did this in the same way that my friends in the Fellowship open themselves up and accept my help when they are struggling through their own challenges and darkness.

A special mention must go out to Thomas McK. and Rob P. These friends, and my Fellowship stuck by me no matter what. When I wanted to run away and hide, they were there. In my heart, I knew I wasn't myself. I was feeling more and more isolated and I was using that isolation to escape the real world. But I didn't want to escape my life. I went back to basics and relied upon music and comedy to help me find my happiness. Of course, I now had a wonderful wife with me, constantly engaging with me and keeping my emotions just above jolly. But it is my Fellowship that really stepped up when I needed it to.

What I never did was turn to a mood or mind-altering substance to help me through my depression. What I knew was that I had to rely on my faith; I had to remember I could rely on my God to pull me through in Her time. I knew I had to allow my Fellowship to stand by me.

It was a humbling and difficult time and did much to remind me that my Fellowship is important to me, for my own wellbeing in both sickness and in health.

10. Stopping and staying stopped!

There are lots of reasons I was able to stop and stay stopped. I think the primary reason was that after three years of trying to stop using on a daily basis and failing at every strategy I could think of, that finally I realised the game was over and the party was finished. I realised that I needed help. I was alone, I was scared, I was dying, and I knew I had one chance to turn it around. Stopping and staying stopped is not easy. I tried to stop on my own but I did not know how. Every time I tried, I numbed my soul further and I slipped more and more into self-doubt and self-abandonment. When I finally found a solution, I grabbed a hold of it, desperate to make a change. I wanted to change. An addict needs to want to stop being addicted to make that sort of life-changing decision. I required more than just a need to stop. I required an absolute desire. And that desire had to have significant lifestyle changes attached to it. As much as your loved ones might want for you to stop and recover, if you do not appreciate the gravitas of your situation and you do not desire such change for yourself, it is simply not going to work.

Once I was taught a successful way to beat my addictions, I felt inspired and motivated. I felt elevated, which made such a positive impact on my life and my recovery journey. I allowed this path to be one of celebration, and not regret or resistance. I have never forgotten how miserable I was before I found recovery, just as I have always remembered how joyous I have felt ever since I stopped using. That continued sense of freedom and the knowledge that life is a wonderful and joyous experience is probably the primary reason I was able to stay stopped. There are many, many other factors, of course, and every addict will have their own personal journey, combined with various degrees of support, kindness and understanding. These are wonderful tools dispensed by friends, families, professionals, etc., that will help prop the person up as they find the right path for their own freedom and they all play their part. But, ultimately, it must be down to the addict to choose life. My company, Sober Services, offers drug and alcohol Interventions, where we go in and change the addict's emotional state just long enough for them to accept the help on offer to them. This must then be followed up with a full model of recovery (e.g. residential detox and rehab) that inspires and motivates them to want to stay stopped. Otherwise, it's a waste of time and money. There is no easy solution, but there is a solution. It's about knowing that there is a solution and then taking the appropriate course of action, rather than continuing to permit the addict or alcoholic to carry on killing themselves, because you're not strong enough to confront them with 'tough love'. Please get in touch with me if you'd like to learn more about how to help your addicted love one stop, even if they don't want to. Our interventions operate with honesty, tough love/bottom lines, and absolute love.

I've written some more about that a little later in the book, under the chapter "To The Families: Tough Love".

11. Healing the whole self

The therapies I was taught during my early recovery process were very useful at the time and worked well for me. They served me very well and they got me part of the way towards where I am today. These days, however, I feel that it would serve my clients better if I used some of my other experiences too, and therefore I'm able to offer even more holistic approach towards getting them on their own recovery journey. I tend to lean towards taking people through an immersion process where everything happens in a short period of time (anywhere from a few hours to a full weekend). I do this because it quickly shifts people's mind-set to a place where they can gain much more clarity of their situation and they often then get to experience a psychological change, profound enough for them to absolutely notice. The change is always evident and the reaction very powerful. It's a bit like people who enjoy very large lines of Cocaine - they do it because they appreciate the powerful effect it has upon them (or at least I did, anyway). So we do this immersion work because it permits a far more extreme and healthy change that restores the person's self-belief in both themselves and the process.

By going through this procedure in an immersion method, people can really feel the magical effects of the programme. This is something I'll always encourage. I would throw caution towards anyone who suggests you take your recovery at a slow pace, and sadly I see it all too often. People take years and years to go through the healing process and they struggle on through their lives never truly appreciating what's absolutely on offer here (freedom from the bondage of self limitations and low self esteem or fear of the real world). I don't think it's the client's fault, but often far more likely to be down to the teacher (sponsor/therapist/counsellor/trainer/mentor, etc.) who is simply passing on their own experience, through their own poor education from their own mentor. I will genuinely hasten to take on a sponsee or a client who isn't prepared to work this method in less than 90 days. Some people do prefer to go through the process slowly, but I believe that the profound and intense experience that happens quickly is actually so much more effective. Maybe that's how I am in my personal development world, generally. I like to have profound changes.

In my own recovery, I did recover fairly quickly, particularly in the physical sense. My body healed itself very quickly; as I believe it does for most people. The hard work comes when an addict must face their emotions and intellectual habits. The processes I employ today are much better strategies than those I was exposed to when I was in early recovery myself. That's not to say those strategies didn't exist; it's just to say I wasn't exposed to them.

When I take people through the processes and I see their lights come on I am always inspired by them. Then I witness these very same people take their power and use it to inspire others, helping them switch their lights on too; making positive changes in the world, one person at a time. 'Paying it Forward' allows us to show recovering addicts that they can greatly affect other people's lives in a positive way. I love to see how the quality of these lives are drastically improved by work that we did together all that time ago, and that they're still carrying on with that same energy of enthusiasm, still carrying the flame of faith, still waving the dagger of determination and destiny, defending their values with the shield of support and servitude. I see them behaving with that same gusto; eager to make a difference to newcomers' lives, just like they had done so many years before, and thus the cycle of helping the next person continues.

But this chapter needs more discussion than just the healing process associated with the mental recovery side of things. I am a great advocate of personal development in a holistic way. Recovery from my addiction requires treatment through a spiritual process. However, to be the best 'me' I could possibly be, I needed to spend a great deal more time working on myself. I have found the Personal Development Community generally very useful for this. I have greatly enjoyed doing other work outside of the 12-Step recovery programmes. I'm a great advocate of NLP (Neuro-Linguistic Programming), or Anthony Robbins and other such motivational speakers. I've personally graduated a great selection of courses, that have taught me about better health, how to manage my financial affairs, work with emotions, the Hero's Journey, Enlightened Warrior Training, mind over matter courses, public speaking, to name but a few types of courses. But probably the most important one was when I signed up with a group of people to climb Mount Kilimanjaro - the highest point of the African continent!

12. Mount Kilimanjaro

People had been suggesting to me that I join them on a trek up to the top of Africa and I didn't really have a good enough answer as to why I should say no. So I said, "Yes."

I'm not sure why I volunteered to go. I had no ambition to climb mountains. It wasn't on my bucket list. It wasn't something I'd ever even considered before. I genuinely think the real reason I said, "Yes" was because I figured I could probably lose some weight and thus allow myself to eat more chocolate. See, I told you I was still, and probably will always be an addict! Here I am facing some of the toughest and challenging tasks the world can offer, which I take on fearlessly just to justify to myself some extra sugar consumption. Durrr!

I turned 40 years old on 9th November 2011 and I figured I should actually start taking my training seriously. After all, I was leaving in less than three months time! 31st January was my flight departure to be exact. Thus far, I had attended a few training sessions with some of the team, on Sundays on Hampstead Heath. Now, I don't know how well you know Hampstead Heath, but it isn't known for its hills. It's got two hills to be precise. Parliament Hill, which we would walk up and down repetitively for an hour, and Suicide Hill, which is only 30 meters long, but rather steep. That was it. The rest was walking and, if I'm honest, I struggled with both aspects of this training. The walking up and down the hills always left me lagging behind the group, and the walking was also particularly difficult for such a lazy git as I was. By this point in my life, sitting behind a computer constituted work for me and after doctor's orders back in the beginning of 2011, I had stopped going to the gym entirely, when he told me I could run or swim - both activities I didn't enjoy. But walking up one of the world's greatest mountains was an OK thing for me to do, or so I thought. I must have been crazy!

I knew I had to up my training. Initially I took my iPad to the gym and set the treadmill to various steep gradients and walked uphill through seasons three, four, five and six of 'Lost'. If you've never finished watching Lost, take my word for it when I say it ain't worth it. It's thoroughly confusing, and rather pointless. As stories go, it absolutely missed having a decent ending. I really wouldn't bother with it if I'd a known the ending was so inadequate. Anyhow, I digress. So, I walked between two and three hours on the treadmill for a couple of months and, sometime after Christmas, but before New Year's Eve hit, I took my personal training outside to some real hills, and I really began to walk.

It's Not About Me!

It was different, really different. It wasn't nearly the same as training on a treadmill. Suddenly, here I was with a month to go and the realisation I wasn't particularly skilled at walking uphill.

I went on a test run of Mount Snowdon, just ten days prior to departure. It took me three and half hours to reach the summit. Not too shabby. This was the confidence boost I needed. So, when we left and arrived together in Arusha, Tanzania, under the shadow of Kilimanjaro, despite my body clearly being the most un-aerodynamic of the team, I had a quiet confidence in myself.

Now I could probably write a whole book about this expedition, but what I will say is that I successfully summited, and it was the toughest thing I ever did in my life. Walking on that crater of Mount Kilimanjaro six kilometres above sea level, with such limited oxygen absolutely exhausted, cannot possibly be described without experiencing it for one's self. The best I can do is tell you it feels like you're walking through a large bowl of treacle and each step can take 20 seconds or so and every few steps require a little lay down. It was just the most exhausting thing I've ever done. I had never been so utterly spent in all my life. I swore I'd never do anything so stupid again. What was the point? I reached the top and what? Yeah, and what?

Well, I think the truly profound part of the summit was just prior to reaching the top of the side of the volcano lid, before having to traverse across the crater to reach the very top at the other end. The sun began to rise as I was about three-quarters of the way up the volcano side and, as dawn swept across the land below, I had a very special vantage point. Because Kilimanjaro is an ancient volcano, and it isn't in a mountain range (there's just one neighbouring mountain, which wasn't in sight from this position), it is the world largest freestanding mountain, allowing for the world's farthest view. This side of Kilimanjaro at dawn is known for having the very best view in the world. I really could see for hundreds and hundreds of miles. I could see over one thousand miles away! There was nothing to hinder my view. Blue skies, and no actual objects within my eye-line, allowed me to actually see to the ends of the Earth. I could see the curvature of the planet. I had proof that the Earth is round. I've seen it with my own eyes. This was an incredibly humbling experience - seeing the actual shape of the Earth and realising at that very moment our insignificance. We truly do belong to the Earth. The world doesn't belong to us. We're here as participants, not owners. I had a profound spiritual experience, and if you find the videos of me taken shortly after witnessing this dawn, then you may be able to tell how overwhelmed I am with gratitude and the spirit of the universe. I talk about being in the presence of God (as I understand Her). This moment was the outstanding memory I have from my adventure. This is the gift I wish to share with others.

Our whole group of twelve people successfully summited! The average for a group is between 30 and 50%. I can tell you that another group on the same path as us, camping in the same locations, on the same days as us, summited three out of eight people. I can tell you that another group on the same flights out and back as us, summited no one out of their six climbers. So, it really was a remarkable achievement that we summited all 12 and scored 100%. I don't think I have ever got 100% before at anything!!!

What were we doing that was so different from everyone else? What was our formula for success? We believe the answer is twofold. Firstly, we had camaraderie and a great team attitude and spirit. We had been training together on Sundays for the past few months. Everyone wanted to do this together. And, though the group split itself up for the final push to the summit, based upon those who were faster than others (I was one of the slow ones), we all wanted to make it to the top for the team. The second reason we all made it was our mind-set. We were people who took our personal development seriously. We were all people who were constantly trying to find ways to improve ourselves and become the best we could possibly be. We were all engaged in various methods of personal growth, and we used these tools for ourselves and for each other. We were a walking group of people on a search for higher purpose, both personally and externally. We all had the Higher Purpose, Higher Power God bug. For us, it was an event that was far larger than we were. We were just parts of the whole. And to let the whole down by not achieving success was unthinkable.

So, we had a wonderful experience during the entire trip (we went on Safari afterwards). Despite the difficulties and hardships we endured in the summit, it was an amazing all round experience. So, there I was upon my return, telling some of my friends and colleagues in one of my other businesses, LivingBig [www.livingbig.co.uk] about the spiritual experience, and the absolute feeling of camaraderie we shared as a group going up together, and it soon became evident to me that I was going to have to go up again! Indeed, we decided that I should go up again only this time Id be leading them up to the top (despite swearing I'd never do it again), so that they could experience what I had experienced, and to see what I had seen, and feel what I had felt.

And so was born the LivingBig Adventure Club. Philanthropic in nature, all participants must be participating for a greater cause than just themselves. We offer our Adventure Club trips at absolute cost price - there is no mark up or profit. In exchange we ask that every participant is raising money for a charity of their choice. They must have a reason other than their own sense of adventure to reach the top. And, my greatest cause for the moment, is leading a team of 18 back up to the summit of Kilimanjaro - again! Training has already begun, and by the time you're reading this, I would have been up again for the second time in 12 months. We leave London on 19th January 2013. It's too late to join us on this adventure, but there'll be more. We intend on having annual trips, so email me [ian@livingbig.co.uk] if you're serious about helping others and having the time of your life! And if you are reading this in 2014, 15, 16, please go to the website and see if we made it!!!

13. God's in charge

People ask me if it is possible to recover from addiction without a spiritual dimension to both the illness and the recovery. Yes, of course it is. Some people are able to move through recovery without spiritual aid using reduction methods aiming towards eventual abstinence. It is an option. However, for me this was never a viable option, despite repeated attempts. I believe for me, I needed to first become drug and alcohol free, entirely, as quickly as possible. Then I needed to understand I was spiritually unwell; I was selfish and self-centred. I was full of anxieties and fears. I was angry, bitter, twisted, hurtful, and hateful and I was a negative person. I needed to be able to recognise these behaviours in a spiritual way so I could establish a need to change them. The way I changed these things about myself was through spiritual behaviour, spiritual practice and spiritual harmonies. There are, of course, some people who don't attribute these negative behaviours to themselves just because they are addicts, and that's fine. But the quality of my recovery is directly proportional to the amount of positive changes I've made in my character, behaviour, and thought processes, multiplied by my attempts to improve the quality of other people's lives and be of service to those less fortunate or still looking for personal growth and evolution. Without making such a radical shift in my whole persona, I would never have gone on to create the magic in my life that exists today. I do hope you can see that.

I would be wary of the harm minimisation and harm reduction programmes. I'm not a great supporter of them. I never experienced any real benefit from these types of programmes, aside from freedom from blood-borne viruses, due to the availability of clean needles in the UK and parts of Europe (mainly France) where I was injecting. One great example of the failure of the harm minimisation model was when I sought one out early in my search for help with my Crack use. I was given nothing but free condoms, encouraged to clean my pipe out more regularly and sent on my way. I thought this was naive, insulting and lacked empathy. It defies belief that the people who are attempting to help by suggesting various methods and strategies to help addicts and alcoholics with their addictions, rarely have any personal experience with it themselves. I do, of course, generalise here, and apologise if you feel like your case is different - I'm speaking from my own experience around East, West and North London mostly in the late 90s.

Maybe it comes down to the fact that, at the end of the day, I truly am an all or nothing person. I am either absolutely bang on it, using day and night, or I go to the other extreme and adopt an attitude and lifestyle of abstinence. Here's my real point; I don't believe you can be in a harm minimisation or a harm reduction programme and connect with that spiritual recovery in the same way. I was shut off from God and the Great Spirit of the Universe while I was getting off my head. I was designed for better things that only became apparent to me when I was drug and alcohol free, therefore receptive to the possibilities available when I allowed the spiritual side of life into my essence. Furthermore, today it just seems obvious to me that addicts are all spiritually unwell in some way or another. If I shut myself away from reality with drugs and booze, then what chance is there of me hearing God's message or any particular spiritual teachings, unless I'm experimenting with LSD and Magic Mushrooms, but that's really just an alternative reality and not one that can truly survive on Planet Earth, no matter how beautiful my hallucinations ever were.

When you work in an abstinence programme such as mine, you are given the option to make a conscious choice as to whether or not you are going to embrace a spiritual solution for your problems. Every person is different and every person will find out for himself or herself what works best for them. For me, there was no option other than a spiritual solution. It was the only way to get me to really listen.

14. To the Families: tough love

Families and friends are a really important part of the recovery journey for any addict. I know I was fortunate that my family had access to money and they were both willing and able to finance my rehab experience. It helped, it really did. My early learning days of recovery were vital for me to be where I am today, here and now. My family's support ensured that I had access to professional, private help to be certain that my recovery at least started off on the right foot. This is not always the case, but recovery is still possible without financial means if you set yourself out to go get it. Recovery is easily achieved through the rooms of all 12-Step recovery programmes with no financial cost at all. I know this because I've helped many men and women recover through the 12-Step process and by channelling them into the 12-Step Fellowships.

In today's economic environment, it is more often than not that families do not have the resources to provide for their loved ones quite the same level of residential rehab I was fortunate enough to experience. One of the things I am very proud of when it comes to my own journey is the residential rehabilitation chain I began building in 2006, which was designed specifically to attempt to address this situation and to finally manage to bring the costs down, making residential treatment far more affordable and thus accessible to the greater population. Working-class families can afford treatment now, whereas before you needed to be middle or upper-middle class. Now you can get a full treatment cycle that costs around £6,000 for a 12-week stay, rather than £30,000 to £40,000 for a 4-week stint.

This being said, clearly some families will still not have this sort of money. People in this position are reliant on support from the NHS but I would suggest that those of you seriously seeking help go straight into the Anonymous Fellowship scene where good treatment is offered for free. At this point, it may be worth pointing out that if you are considering getting some help, please go to my site [www.soberservices.co.uk] where I'll be able to assess your particulars and consider the best treatment option for you. One thing is certain, Sober Services will absolutely find the best facility for you around the world based upon many different factors and circumstances. We will not send you to the cheapest or the most expensive place simply because that's what you want. The cheapest place in the world is actually the most expensive if it doesn't work. So we fit the centre to the client.

RECOVERY – *onwards & upwards*

My family has been instrumental in so many ways throughout my recovery journey. They saw me walking into recovery a sick, grey bag of bones, and then they watched the transformation as I recovered. It is truly a beautiful thing to watch someone you love recover. They watched and supported me every step of the way, and I am a far better person because of it. I rebuilt my relationships with every member of my family and, when my father passed away 1st January 2007, I was able to hold on to many beautiful private moments we shared in the years before his passing.

The biggest obstacle for any addict is staring right back at them in the mirror. They really are their own worst enemy. But also, they alone can decide to set themselves free, though we can help them make that decision. If you are serious about wanting to recover, no one can stop you. If you want to change your life, you have to be willing to make the changes. It's not always easy, in fact more often than not it's really hard. But it is always rewarding and your life will be transformed in the process. The biggest obstacle I see with people trying to recover is when they are not willing to adopt abstinence as a theory and are not willing to change their lives sufficiently to truly make a difference. Changing habitual behaviour is hard, but it's the only way. Some people, however, are just not willing to do the hard work and make the changes.

My family was a long-suffering family who never knew where I was or what I was up to. But when I was ready for help, they were the first people to stand by my side. I'm sure my family suffered from fear and worry not knowing where I was or what I was doing for so much of my life, but they stayed out of it and, in so many ways, this was the right thing to do. Sometimes the biggest victims of a person's addictions are their family. I have watched families who continue to try to actively love the person back to wellness, failing, as they easily and eventually become victims to the addict's manipulations, lies and deceit. They are more often than not the first victims of theft and their quality of life becomes compromised as the addict rules the family home. The alcoholic who beats his wife, or doesn't come home or cheats on her will destroy the relationship and make his loved one suffer through his addiction. It is the family who suffers. I always try to encourage families to practise or at least consider 'tough love'. It's how my parents were with me, and it worked. It is the hardest thing to ask a family to do, but it can help. To ask a parent to let go of a child they love, to lay down the rules, to step back, despite the fact that this person is clearly destroying their lives is a very big ask, but the consequences of not engaging in tough love are far more devastating and more likely to lead to an early grave.

It's Not About Me!

When I first speak to family members, I tell them that they mustn't let the addict's life affect their own quality of life, and the stories I have heard have amazed me. Families will go to outrageous lengths and depths to support the addict and their intolerable behaviour. They do this out of love, but it isn't helping anyone. One of the decisions I made when I was an addict was that I would never use or abuse my family the way I used other people in my life. I say that I made this decision, but the reality was my father and mother made it clear to me. They drew a line in the sand and told me that they wouldn't support or tolerate me living like that. So, as long as a lived my life under such circumstances, I was largely left to my own devices. I stayed away from them. I left home at sixteen and did not communicate with them more than two or three times a year. But not every addict is like this. I have seen many people who see their families as a soft option, easy pickings. Stealing from their close family feels justified and they will take whatever money (or electrical items to pawn, etc.) they can get their hands on, whenever the need arises. I see that same family supporting that person, giving them money, a place to stay, accepting the behaviour and allowing them to use drugs in the home just to keep them happy and keep the peace. The addict/alcoholic kicks up such a fuss whenever the subject is mentioned that the family walks around as if treading on eggshells, trying to avoid such flamboyant, aggressive and fury-filled confrontations. Families buy their addicts alcohol and drugs, allowing them to control the family dynamic because they can see they are spiritually struggling. These families suffer so much pain and torture living with an erratic addict who will not only steal from them but also treat them and their home with little or no respect. Families go above and beyond to subdue their loved one, giving in to their every whim just to keep them under control. It's outrageous.

The first thing any family in this situation needs to do is kick the offender out of the house. Put down an ultimatum: "If you want to continue using drugs, if you want to continue your life of addiction I can't stop you, but you will do it in your own environment and you won't be bringing it into my life any longer!"

That's the first step as a family, and it is really hard. Families struggle desperately when I tell them that they have to sever all ties with their loved one until they are prepared to make the decision to do the right thing. More often than not families are not willing to cut off their loved one despite their bad behaviours and will continue to live a life of supporting chronic gamblers, drugs addicts and alcoholics because they are too scared to take the steps necessary to make the change. What I try and remind people is that addicts and alcoholics are survivors.

RECOVERY – *onwards & upwards*

We have a survival instinct in us. Although, you'll hear a lot of stories in the media how drugs have killed another celebrity, and I'm sure you've heard the stories about how drugs are killing many people in a particular year, but aside from King Alcohol and Brother Tobacco, it's actually not that prolific a killer in this country. Of all the people who die of illegal drug-related illnesses, 10 times more die from alcohol-related illnesses, and then another 100 times more people die of tobacco smoking-related illnesses. Heart disease, often associated with obesity from sugar addiction, is a much more powerful killer, but in the press drug deaths are viewed as 'sexy' and sell papers. I want people to move away from that perception. I understand that an addict in their midst is only going to get worse, but once you leave an addict to his or own devices, sooner or later they'll reach a base where they're ready to change.

We survive. We are survivors. You will hear in this industry and in this environment that you can't help a drug addict until they're ready to stop. Most practices will tell you to let the addict or alcoholic just get on with it and that was certainly my experience. I just kept going along with my life until finally my head popped out of my arse and I realised it was time to change.

Through Sober Services, we offer what is called an Intervention. We have built our reputation based upon, amongst other things, our success rate of Interventions, which are modelled on the North American style Interventions, as featured in the TV show 'Interventions', which runs shows every day on the A&E channel in the USA. We go into an Intervention to actively change someone's mind-set by bringing them to an emotional rock bottom and preparing them to accept our help. We do it by increasing the level of pain they're experiencing based on the problems they're causing themselves and others (who they know love them), getting them to an emotional state where they're ready to accept our help, and quit there and then. At that point, we'll whisk them straight off to a detoxing treatment facility or residential rehab.

We have to consider how we perform the Intervention on each individual case, because each person needs a different approach, but this is the most common method we've devised with incredible success rates. We have found to help an addict become ready for change, to help an addict admit to the need for change in their lives, they must be experiencing enough consequences. Our Interventions expose them to the possibilities of what those consequences may be, without them actually having them.

The old fashioned way, which is equally affective but takes many, many years, is just let them grow out of it, have a bunch of health, social, emotional and mental problems, run their own course and get themselves to a place where they're ready to pull their head out of their arse. This is the method that increases the chance of an early death - especially in the cases of alcoholism.

The old fashioned way of just growing out of it, is something that can be very difficult for families to accept. They ask me whether it happens and, of course, it does. I am an example in some sense; I came to my parents asking for a place to stay, having done my own detox first, and allowed them to lead me into the next step of my detox and the first step of my recovery. They ask if it happens a lot, and honestly I don't know. I have seen enough people for whom it does happen, particularly some of my old friends. Yet I'm sure there are far more people who never get around to addressing their problems, also shown to me by a vast array of my old friends. They never get to the point where anyone has shown them enough tough love that they're pushed into a corner and actually encouraged to stop and stay stopped. Sadly, so maybe not.

15. Crossing over the bridge to normal living – aka Life's in session and I'm showing up

Crossing over the bridge from recovery to normal living is a personal journey of discovery. Programmes like the one I run are designed to facilitate and aid this transition and help guide people to find their own pathway to a better and healthier life. The message to any recovering addict is that they can achieve whatever it is they want to achieve, so long as they're serious about doing so. If they are genuine about changing the very fabric of their own lives, then the world truly is their oyster. This is the very moment in our lives where we can seriously impact the quality of the rest of our lives - this is the Golden Ticket opportunity. This is winning the lottery and getting a new life!

There is no final goal here; there is no final result. The only result is that we stop using, and that comes right at the beginning. Everything else is a constant work in progress, because as we all know life changes every day. Things change, so people need to be prepared to be flexible, to move along, to make changes and to grow inside their own lives. When life changes and takes us in a new direction, things happen that inspire us to go further, to discover more, to want more. The hardest part is the very first step, to surrender and move into abstinence. Once we have that figured out and we have accepted that as our new lifestyle, everything that comes afterwards is a bonus. They say, "There's no destination, so enjoy the journey" and that's exactly the point of living a life in recovery from our addictions. We get to enjoy the journey once again.

I know that once I got into recovery my life evolved into new plains of existence, and I experienced an incredible sense of relief and freedom. I was free of my addiction, and I had the ability and desire to open myself up to the world and discover what was out there for me. It was as if I had been given a new pair of glasses and all of a sudden the world looked like a completely different place full of amazing possibilities. I became involved in other people's lives and I was welcomed back into the day-to-day life of my own family. I was given support and encouragement to build my life up again. I had a new set of Fellowship friends and I started to travel abroad again, build my businesses and work with people who inspired me. I moved house, I moved out of the City (London). I moved around the streets wherever I wanted to. I went anywhere I wanted without fear of arrest, or bumping into people I owed money, etc. These were luxuries I seldom experienced when I was using and dealing. There is a whole tapestry of opportunities out there when you just go for it. It is amazing how much can and, indeed, will change once you're back in healthy living and recovery.

It all depends on how much you want to gain and how far you want to take it. I never expected I would stop smoking on this journey after five years, aged thirty-four. I had been sober for five years when I stopped smoking, I had never really expected that I would, but I did. When I quit, my life headed in a new direction once again. I started going to the gym and exercising. Every little thing makes a difference. I don't know what people can expect from life after recovery, all I can say is that it will be more than you could possibly imagine now.

As I sit here writing I'm tempted to start listing everything I've achieved in my time since getting sober in 2001, but to do so feels inappropriate. It doesn't feel in line with the spiritual principles of humility. It's like I said, this book isn't really about me! It's actually about just how much can be achieved when you're willing to take responsibility for your life and take actions towards your own destiny. It's about changing the mind-set of society that people with addictions are doomed. It's about freeing addicts and alcoholics from their limiting belief that the world owes them a living, and coaching them to take the fruits of the world by contributing towards them.

"I learned long ago that those who are happiest
are those who do the most for others"

Booker T Washington

And so I simply don't think its a necessary part of this story for me to start going into the details of all the wonderful gifts my recovery has bought me, but rather to ask you to take it as a given. Have some faith. You don't need me to tell you all about all the great things I've experienced through hard work and faith over these past years. It's just not a requirement. I've written about some of them in this book, but to really get to know me, I'm afraid you're going to have to do it the old school way - you're simply going to have to get to know me. Is that reasonable? Come find me www.facebook.com/ianyoungfriends and subscribe to my personal site www.ianyoung.co

Suffice it to say, I'm a success today. I'm a successful human being. And, to top it all, I'm a happy successful human being. I haven't decided to stop seeking more success, more adventure, more fun and more life ...not yet anyways. I'm having far too much fun enjoying the journey!

16. My Mission Statement explained

Everyone has a purpose in life and there is no better place than recovery from addictions to discover this purpose, particularly when you understand that we've been given a second chance at life, so we must have been saved for a reason. I've had many moments of gratitude along my recovery journey and I've come to understand that my personal existence is about creating a mission for myself from the ashes of my addiction and into my own recovery. Every person, in recovery or not, should be encouraged to find out what their purpose, their meaning and their mission in life is.

Ask yourself some of life's most important questions. How have you come to be where you currently are? Why has God brought you this far? Who have you met along the way that has also impacted your life? What are you going to do with your life next? I realised quickly that my purpose was to help others, initially contributing to their recovery and then interacting with the larger population and in a more generic sense seeing how I can contribute to their overall well being, i.e. non-addiction specific. This is the thrust of one of my other businesses, Living Big - a coaching and mentoring network. In this business I truly believe we can make a real difference to people's mental, emotional and physical health, and to be a force for good. If you're looking for personal and private help for any kind of issue, then have a browse through all the Coaches, Therapists, Trainers, Counsellors and other amazing leaders offering their services through www.livingbig.co.uk It's a one-stop shop to get all the help you need to become the very best you possible – it requires will power.

You may have a different God than me and your God might direct you down a different path, and that's fine. But if you feel like you don't know what direction you are heading, you are very welcome to borrow my God and you are always welcome to join this pathway. My God has set me on a mission in life.

My mission is to:

'Co-create a green and harmonious world, through laughter and love, and to contribute towards the quality of the lives of other people.'

It is in doing exactly that, giving and committing my life to others, that I have received so much reward for myself personally and experienced so many positive changes in my own life.

I haven't achieved any of that through self-seeking behaviours. These amazing things just seem to happen to me, because I find that when I give, I get great stuff in return. In fact, the more I give, the greater I get in return. Nothing I can tangibly say is a direct result of doing this or that - but more and more coincidences occur in my life that seem to draw me down certain paths, bringing me new, exciting and life-changing experiences along my journey.

There's a saying in the 12-Step programme that goes, "You keep what you have, by giving it away." I know this is true and that it is actually an understatement. I keep what I have and I acquire new skills and experiences by continually giving them away.

"The value of a man should be seen in what he gives and not what he is able to receive"

Albert Einstein

17. Have I mentioned that it is not actually about me?

My most important beliefs about being sober I summarise by my two primary principle beliefs:

'Do unto others as I would like done unto myself'

And:

'Do for others what they cannot do for themselves'

I believe those are the two basic spiritual principles that guide me. These founding principles helped me change my life by simply changing my behaviour towards others. Being sober, for me, isn't just about not drinking and not using drugs; it is about conducting myself in a certain way, and it's an attitude, a lifestyle choice. I mentioned a classic phrase earlier about the drunken horse thief, do you remember? You can sober him up but you still have a horse thief. The thing about being sober for me is it has not just been about not drinking; it has been about no longer being a thief of horses or any other items that you could potentially steal.

Getting and staying sober is about no longer behaving like I did when I was using. It's about adopting positive behaviours that I can be proud of. Getting sober is about changing everything in my life, including all of my attitudes, and swapping the negative for the positive. Getting sober and staying sober is a journey towards inspiration, towards contribution and into generosity of spirit and mind. It's about transforming myself into a person who isn't scared of doing the right thing, or of hard work, or of expressing myself. I have changed from being a scared, selfish, arrogant addicted boy, into a man who is prepared to step up and participate, instead of running away from responsibility. There are a lot of wonderful attributes that can come from being sober. But the two primary rules I try to live my life by are always: 'Do unto others as I would like done unto myself' and 'Do for others what they cannot do for themselves'.

I hope you can begin to understand just how relevant the words 'It's not about me' are now. You see, as I understand things, the world simply no longer revolves around me. In fact, my world revolves around you! Or at least it revolves around those for whom I can make a difference somehow. I seek to find ways to improve the quality of your life.

The story of my journey into and out of addiction is a story of love, loss and self-discovery. My journey taught me about survival, and the path that I chose for recovery taught me about spirituality and peace both within myself and with the world around me. My understanding of God and my intense connection with Mother Earth 'Gaia', comes from a deep understanding and belief in living a peaceful existence full of harmony and unity in one world, on one planet. The spiritual journey I took to get sober - and then adopted as a code for living - has led me along this path. For anyone else who wishes to create a loving existence in their own life and on earth as a whole, I would love to support you and spend some of my excess energy making that possible. Remember, all it requires is will power and a desire to change. We can all support and bring about change on this planet, one person at a time, just like the Pay It Forward Foundation that I mentioned earlier in this book.

So as this book comes to an end, I would like to make the same promise and guarantee I make to all the people I work with...

18. My Promise

If you are still drinking or using, please indulge me in some fantasy thinking. I absolutely promise that once you stop and stay stopped, if you follow the principles in this book (or something similar), starting with abstinence and continuing with various forms of self-development, you'll be amazed at the results. What you're about to read will be unbelievable to you. I know this because I've been where you are and I've been down the path I'm encouraging you to take. I'm asking for your trust and I'm offering you a promise if you can trust me enough to put your faith in a future of abstinence and personal emotional and mental growth. Please, I beg of you, have some faith.

It's Not About Me!

If you're just at that point now where you've begun trying to stop, then you understand that the next step is to stay stopped. That's where the hard work begins. But when you start to feel yourself staying stopped, miracles will happen and your life will begin to evolve in ways you cannot possibly imagine right here, right now. I know this because I've been where you are right now, and I've found a way out. You may not believe me just yet, but please give yourself the chance to find out. Why don't you have a go at following some of the ideas I've shared in this book? I know that may seem so out of reach for you right now, but if you can just trust that you have in you the implicit knowledge of what it means to be a decent person as well as the ability to let go of the notion that you must remain bad, simply because that's all you know, then I promise you, things are going to get better. Things are going to be tough for a while, but they will definitely get better. This is where the magic begins. I promise.

Every single day of clean or sober time that you put together is the building block and foundation for what's to come. Always remember that you're on a quest to improve your lot, and no longer looking for ways to self-destruct. You're now seeking out a better way to live. Each day takes so long, but each day is a celebration of your new quest for a life worth living. I know, because I've been there. I've struggled at just the same places in my own recovery. It's tough, but it's absolutely achievable.

One **day** at a time, I promise you things will get better and things will get easier.

One **week** at a time, I promise you things will get better and things will get easier.

One **month** at a time, I promise you things will get better and things will get easier.

If you are 30 days sober today I promise you that by the time you reach 60 days you will be amazed by the things that have happened during the 30 days between then and now. Think back to where you were on day one; think about all the amazing things that happened in those first 30 days. I suspect you are already impressed by some of the changes you have begun to make in your life. I promise you, these amazements are just the beginning.

For those of you who are at 60 days, the same goes for you, and in just 30 more days you will reach the 90-day mark where you will be equally impressed at the amazing things you have just experienced. I know you will have experienced so much goodness already, but I promise you... the best is yet to come. I know that when I was 60 days sober my parents gave me a key to the front door of their house. When I was 90 days sober they gave me a code to the house alarm. Both of those were deeply emotional, spiritual breakthroughs for me along my road to recovery.

Massive change is right around the corner. Change that will take you down roads less travelled and paths set to offer you a fulfilling life of abundance. This is true for all of you. I promise.

Life will take on new meaning. To see others recover around you will be one of the highlights of your journey. But knowing the new way your own life is opening up will be the most powerful tool you have for continued success. I promise.

Here is the promise I will make to you. When you get to six months clean and sober, your life will be transformed. You will have a life that was unimaginable, just half a year earlier. It will literally be beyond your imagination. It will not be recognisable from the life you live today.

I promise that when you reach a year sober that your life will have transformed all over again. Amazing stuff is going to happen to you during the first year you are substance addiction free; amazing stuff that I can't even begin to foresee and tell you about. Amazing stuff that you can't even imagine yet, but it is sure to blow your mind. You will be living a life that was inconceivable just one year before.

In some cases, it takes much less than a year for your life to be absolutely unrecognizable. I know this because my life was already unrecognisable after just nine months. I know this because I see it time and time again in the people I work with. And then I get to see it in the people those people are working with (Grand Sponsees and clients of clients), and so it goes on.

I promise - everything just gets **better** and **better**.

It doesn't stop there. Living your life sober every year is full of amazing surprises. As each year goes by, my life takes on new meaning and new direction and new stuff happens that I never would have anticipated, even for a moment, not even in my wildest dreams. It just keeps getting better and better. Stick with it, never give up and see what incredible opportunities are waiting for you, just around the corner!

There are going to be some pitfalls, of course. There are going to be times that are tough. I lost my father to a brain tumour. I've had some disastrous business relationships, which have left me close to bankruptcy. I've witnessed tragic events such as September 11th, live before my very own eyes. Things happen in life. Life carries on being life. We learn how to live with such sadness, without finding it necessary to get pissed or wasted. I lost my father and it was very difficult. I watched him go downhill over a year with my family and I sitting by his side. I watched him slip away. Fortunately, however, I already had enough new ways of living that I was able to step up and become the oldest male member of the family, growing into this new role. My father watched my mother move out of the family home. He watched as both of my sisters got their first houses. He watched me move into my own house and then he let go. It was very appropriate that he hung on for as long as he did. He stuck around just long enough to see us all get settled. I have had the opportunity to help men I have sponsored with similar experiences of cancer in their families, particularly male members moving on, and I get to help my Fellowship friends with that sort of stuff. We will see where our experience can benefit others. This gift and many others, I promise will give you a life beyond your wildest dreams - no matter what is going on in the background.

I promise you as each year goes by, things will happen that will be hard, because that is just part of life. But I also promise you that spiritually we feel better and healthier. We feel more in tune and more aligned with the real world, as long as we maintain our sobriety, our spiritual growth and we find ourselves a mission. Go find yourself your mission. Find out why God got you sober and work your mission every day.

19. My Guarantee

Gratitude

When I was able to be grateful for my own life, there was no longer any justifiable reason to go back to using. Being able to tap into that gratitude every day made it easier to stay clean and helped me each day, even in those dark days, to maintain my recovery. Gratitude is not something I have seen manifested in everyone. But it is something I believe is inherent in every person. I do honestly believe that everyone can achieve that feeling of gratitude if they allow a power into their lives that fills them with a sense of fulfilment and purpose every day. My disciplines teach this very carefully because it is something I value so highly. It does not happen overnight; instead, it happens at the right time, as the consistent and continued result of doing the right thing over and over again, and feeling really good about it. When we start doing the right thing, and we stick with doing the right thing, life seems to take on new dynamics and new boundaries. It is as if we are in a different dimension. Some would say, "We have been rocketed into the fourth dimension."

For me gratitude really is the key to a successful recovery, and to a life that is happy, joyous and free. Without this inherent feeling within me, there is absolutely no guarantee of my sobriety. But with it, I am free to go about my day without any fear, anxiety or unnecessary stress.

My offer of a guarantee should not be taken lightly. The message I want to offer you is one of depth and weight. I can guarantee that staying sober is contingent upon your level of gratitude. What I mean by that is if you are able to feel grateful right here, right now, if you are able to sit still and breathe and feel truly grateful, I can guarantee that you will not use or drink today. I can absolutely guarantee it.

If, however, you are not feeling grateful for everything you have today, then I cannot guarantee your sobriety. If you are not feeling grateful, I can offer no such guarantee. Surely this is a warning sign. Therefore, I urge you to find that place within you that feels attached to the energy of love and begin by appreciating that. You'll then start to move into a place of gratitude.

I am so confident of this connection between gratitude and positive recovery, which I guarantee to you, that I promise you there is hope, abundance and all things will absolutely get better, so long as you appreciate what you've achieved so far.

Believe me, when I first entered my recovery journey with only one pair of shoes with a hole in the soles, it was snowing and I had no idea how my life was going to change, but even then I still felt grateful because I felt safe. You can always find a reason to feel grateful - if you want to. Now I have many, many pairs of really great shoes.

If you can feel grateful about anything whether it's that you have a roof over your head tonight or you know you will have a hot meal this evening, or if you can tap into that energy that comes with gratitude, I can guarantee that you will not need to drink or use today.

Now that's a pretty powerful guarantee, don't you agree?

20. Final reflections on the journey so far

I have had so many amazing experiences as part of my recovery journey so far. There have been many life lessons learnt; many new ways to change my direction have been offered to me. Some of the things that have happened to me are in the pages of this book and, yet, even as I finish typing this story the journey is continuing and there are already new things I could add. I'm still changing and evolving every day. I'm very keen to continue this journey that started as a 12-Step process and took me into many different fields of learning. I would like to encourage other people to go on that journey of personal development and see where they can take their lives. It doesn't have to stop with just discontinuing drug use. Let's get sober, let's change our attitudes and outlooks on life and let's head in a new direction. It's a great journey.

A couple of things I have learnt in the past twelve or so years are the power of faith and spirituality, and just how much courage I can tap into to help me through any situatiuon. When the chips are down, with everything going upside down and it looks like I'm about to fall, I draw in enough faith to give me the hope to get through whatever it is that's crushing me. I draw the courage and the strength to get through it. That faith initially was blind faith. I just had to believe that everything was going to be all right, that I'd come this far, so I could keep going and everything would be cool. Then over time that faith grew into evidence-based faith. I had enough evidence to know there was a power (I call God) that was giving me the reason and the courage and the hope and the expectation that everything was still going to be all right, no matter what. All I needed to do was keep doing the right thing and put one foot in front of another. What I learnt about myself was I have the courage to go through the hard times and I have the courage to stick to my convictions. I have the courage never to give up. Time and time again my convictions have been challenged and it has been my experience that when I stick with my convictions and face the challenges, everything turns out all right. To quote the great Spike Lee once again, "Always do the right thing!" and good stuff happens.

If you have read this book and you haven't yet started your journey to recovery, I urge you to find someone who has recovered to help guide you. Find someone who has recovered and stayed positive and uplifted. Find someone who truly inspires you and ask that person to show you the way. Put your trust in them, they are your new guiding light. Do what they suggest, follow their direction, allow someone to help you. Trust in those people when they turn you on to a life of abstinence. Permit them the right to work with you in the realm of spiritual healing as part of your recovery path. If it doesn't feel right, if you don't feel inspired to change, shift your direction slightly. Get yourself a circle of like-minded people. Get it today. Stop waiting for tomorrow. This group of people should all be on the same journey - a ship of fellows. Together you will become involved in each other's lives, you will forge relationships, care about each other, learn how to socialise without substances and take care of each other's health and emotional wellbeing. You are a family now. As a group you will need to find an emerging process that can work with you so you can learn how to recover. After recovery, you will continue with this group throughout your life on a journey of self-discovery and life improvements.

Give yourself a reason to get sober and stay sober - find a mission for your life, give yourself a meaningful goal. What is your life about if you are not using?

Give yourself a solid justification for not using anymore. Be happy with yourself, make sure you are happy and if you are not, do something about it, change it. I am always about making sure I'm having a good time and if I'm not having a good time I need to make some sort of change.

The world as it exists for you today can change, here and now.
It's your choice.

It's Not About Me!

EPILOGUE
– a final word from Ian

How do I see my story helping others? I am constantly reminded everyday of the people who need to read stories like this. People come to me for advice, and it's not just the addicts. There are parents who are concerned about their child, wives who are concerned about their husbands and vice versa, bosses who are concerned about their employees (and vice versa, no doubt!), close friends concerned about one another. The list goes on. This story is not just for the addicts, it is for the family members, the loved ones and the concerned friends, too.

For twelve years I have been telling my story to addicts and I think the biggest gift of all is telling this story to the families. Telling this story to the people who care. I can help the addicts in a hands-on way. I can help them get clean. But this story is a message of hope to those who have loved ones who seem to be drowning in their own addiction. This is a message of hope showing families that there is a way out for everyone. It's not over yet. Families worry and stress themselves out until they are sick and yet the addict will continue on, insensitive to the difficulties they're actually bringing to everyone around them, oblivious and in a state of denial. People who are not addicts cannot understand an addict's ability to survive no matter how bad the circumstances. In fact, the real danger for an addict is when they're not just permitted to indulge in their self destruction but actually aided by loved ones paying their debts, giving them money to buy booze and drugs, supporting their lifestyle and not actually giving the addict or alcoholic any genuine reason to stop. Families need to let go of their worry and understand that the addict needs to go through their own journey, rather than destroying their lives trying to protect and love the addict. I can tell you more about how far too often it's the family's love and kindness that's actually killing the very people they think they're loving, meanwhile absolutely destroying their own quality of life.

Addicts in recovery can read this story and reflect on their own journey through to the point they have reached today. Take my story and find inspiration, laughter and joy in seeing the parallels that most addicts experience throughout their journey. I'd love to hear from you, so please feel free to email me your thoughts and share with me your ideas ian@soberservices.co.uk

People who are still using can pick this book up and hopefully find inspiration in its pages. Inspiration that will help them discover what they need to stop. Inspiration and hope that there is a way out for them and an understanding that there are people, who will guide them, support them and educate them every step of the way. Hopefully, these people will see from my story that life has considerably more value once you stop using, and the world is just out there, waiting for them to get clean and experience the amazing web of opportunities just around the corner. Please get in touch if you're serious about changing your life. I'd be delighted to see how I can contribute towards your recovery. I'm happy to help. www.soberservices.co.uk

AFTERWORD
– the 12-Step Programme (formal explanation)

Introduction to 12-Step Fellowships

This information is important for people trying to find their way out of addiction and for families supporting an addict through their recovery. Understanding, awareness, acceptance and support are all key to success with this programme and a gateway to a better quality of life.

The 12-Step programme is taken from the original textbook entitled 'Alcoholics Anonymous', which is more commonly referred to as the 'Big Book'. This book was first printed in April 1939 and has been used to help alcoholics become sober for more than seventy years. It is simple but effective, using a set of 12-Steps (directions or suggestions) for living a rewarding life, free from the misery, terror and pain of addiction and leading towards long-term sustainable recovery.

Since the Big Book was originally written by and for recovering alcoholics, people with problems other than alcoholism (drugs, etc.) will find it useful to substitute the word 'alcohol' for 'drugs' and the word 'drinking' for 'using'. The 12-Step programme works for all addictions if applied appropriately. There are at least 130 different 12-Step Fellowships that exist within the USA. Here there are 55 that I've come across whilst researching that I've put into eight different categories:

1. **Alcoholism:** AA, (Alcoholics Anonymous), ACOA (Adult Children of Alcoholics), Al-Anon (for friends and family members of alcoholics) and Alateen (for teenaged friends and family members of alcoholics).

2. **Substance Addiction:** NA (Narcotics Anonymous), CA (Cocaine Anonymous), CAA (Cocaine Addicts Anonymous), AAA (All Addictions Anonymous), CDA (Chemically Dependent Anonymous), CMA (Crystal Meth Anonymous), MA (Marijuana Anonymous), NicA (Nicotine Anonymous), Co-Anon (for friends and family of Cocaine addicts) and Nar-Anon (for friends and family members of addicts).

3. **Gambling:** GA (Gamblers Anonymous), OLGA (On-Line Gamers Anonymous), Gam-Anon (for friends and families of problem gamblers) and /Gam-A-Teen (for Teenaged friends and families of problem gamblers)

4. **Sex addiction:** SAA (Sex Addicts Anonymous), SLAA (Sex and Love Addicts Anonymous), COSLAA (CoSex and Love Addicts Anonymous), SA (Sexaholics Anonymous), SCA (Sexual Compulsives Anonymous), SWA (Sex Workers Anonymous), SIS (Sex Industry Survivors), COSA (Codependents of Sex Addicts) and S-Anon (spouses and family members of Sexaholics).

5. **Psychiatric Disorders and Behaviours:** Dep-Anon (Depressed Anonymous), DDA (Dual Diagnosis Anonymous), DRA (Dual Recovery Anonymous), NAIL (Neurotics Anonymous), OCA (Obsessive Compulsive Anonymous), SA (Schizophrenics Anonymous), SMA (Self-Mutilators Anonymous), SPA (Social Phobics Anonymous), WA (Workaholics Anonymous), CLA (Clutterers Anonymous), DA (Debtors Anonymous), and SA (Spenders Anonymous).

6. **Eating disorders:** OA (Overeaters Anonymous) ABA (Anorexics and Bulimics Anonymous), CEA (Compulsive Eaters Anonymous), EAA (Eating Addictions Anonymous), EDA (Eating Disorders Anonymous), FA (Food Addicts in Recovery Anonymous), FAA (Food Addicts Anonymous), and GSA (GreySheeters Anonymous).

7. **Emotional issues:** CoDA (Co-Dependents Anonymous), EA (Emotions Anonymous), EHA (Emotional Health Anonymous), FA (Families Anonymous), RCA (Recovering Couples Anonymous), Chapter 9 (Couples in Recovery), and SIA (Survivors of Incest Anonymous).

8. **Others:** This category holds two that I can't easily fit in anywhere else – AA (Addictions Anonymous), and RA (Recoveries Anonymous; the Solution Focused 12-Step Fellowship)

Overview

The 12-Step process prepares individuals to have a 'spiritual awakening' or a 'psychological change'. These changes refer to the transformation in thinking, attitude, and outlook on life that occur during and after working the steps. This conversion allows them to free themselves from the compulsion and obsession to use and drink, and therefore from active addiction. It could also be considered a form of personal motivation and inspiration.

This alteration in thinking allows for a dramatic change in behaviour, which then permits the individual to feel better without the desire to return to damaging substances in order to attempt to elevate their mood.

The basis of the 12-Step recovery programme is firstly acceptance that addiction is an illness and secondly a desire to treat it through personal action, rather than self-medication. By letting go of the past and dealing with the problems as they arise in the 'here and now', combined with the self awareness they learn through this programme, the individuals can better identify their negative behaviours and celebrate their positive successes achieved each day.

Applying the principles of the steps within their daily lives enables addicts to establish and improve upon some form of conscious or unconscious contact with a God (good energy) of their own understanding or particular faith. The important part of this is not whether someone believes in God or not, but rather whether they believe it's possible that there is a power (non-human) that can help them, such as nature, or spirit or something else (anything that isn't them). This is commonly referred to as a 'Higher Power' or 'Power Greater than Yourself'.

It must be stressed that the 12-Step Fellowships are not allied with any particular religion, sect or denomination, and that the form of God the individual chooses is completely up to the individual to discover. Indeed there are many atheists and agnostics who have progressed through the 12-Step programme relying upon a God they refuse to understand. I am also aware of a number of 'Jedi Knights' who have used their understanding of the 'Force' to help them with their addiction (successfully). The key here is simply about keeping an open mind and being willing enough to consider other possibilities.

Many recovering alcoholics and addicts believe that the greatest safeguard in preventing relapse lies in consistent application of the 12-Steps and continuing to place their trust in a power greater than themselves (whatever their personal interpretation may be) and understanding that 'everything will be all right - if they choose not to use', and the knowledge that 'things will never improve, if they continue to use'.

STEP ONE

We admitted we were powerless over our addiction - that our lives had become unmanageable.

Two useful questions for deciding whether you or a loved one is really an alcoholic/addict are, 'Can they actually stop permanently if and when they choose to?' and, 'Can they control the amount they drink/use once they begin?' If the answer to either question is 'no', then they probably have an addiction problem that requires addressing.

The most important aspect behind this Step is honesty. The intention of this Step is to expose any denial that may remain in the client's thinking - the idea that they may be able to drink or use safely again. Step one is the statement that summarizes their problem and the reason for seeking help, whether it is professional treatment or any other peer on peer support.

Powerlessness is the concept that drugs and drink have such a hold on someone they are powerless in their ability to choose not do it anymore, i.e., they've lost the power of choice.

It operates on three levels:
1. A physical allergy to alcohol and drugs - known as the phenomenon of craving, which makes it virtually impossible for them to stop drinking and/or using once they start;
2. A mental obsession, which makes it unlikely that they will remain sober or straight permanently on their own; and
3. A spiritual malady, which separates them from their friends and family in their ability to become sober and maintain their sobriety, through their own self-centred thinking and behaviour. The World Health Organisation and the United Nations has recognised this as a disease, although chronic and potentially crippling, one may recover from.

People may assume that Step one means that they couldn't get high anymore because they could no longer handle it. In fact, it really means that barring some sort of intervention, they are unable to stay away from that first drink, hit, line or smoke and that they will drink and/or use again and again, no matter how much they wish to stay clean. Lack of power against the first drink or drug is actually their dilemma. This person is typically drinking/using against their own willpower and they are powerless to stop themselves.

The second part of Step one refers to how they are unable to manage their own lives, even when they are sober. One example of this unmanageability is being restless, irritable, and discontent. Many recovering addicts and alcoholics are of the opinion that they were unmanageable before they began using substances and drink, and that their addiction initially removed the fear of feeling inferior and anxious around other people, places or situations.

STEP TWO

Came to believe that a Power greater than ourselves could restore us to sanity.

Step two is the summary of the solution to the identified problem outlined in Step one.

Coming to believe in a power other than themselves and this power's ability to restore them to sanity (to becoming manageable again) does not require that they believe in a God. However, it is vital they have an open mind and find the willingness to believe there is a power greater than themselves - that they are not God, and that other people, places and situations produce their own actions and consequences.

Some people may find it useful to simply step aside from being the God of their own universe temporarily, while going through the Steps, with the idea that they can step back into their preferred role afterwards. This temporary measure has permitted many people to recover who may never have done so due to their fixed beliefs about God or the lack of the universe and everything else. It really is useful to have an open mind and be flexible. Remember, if getting sober were easy, then they'd have done it already without our help.

Many people in today's recovering Fellowships did not have any religious or spiritual experience prior to their sobriety. However, once they were able to make a start towards what the concept of a Higher Power might mean to them, then they began to find some direction to their sobriety. Many of them use the Fellowship itself as a Power greater than themselves. Some call it 'Group of Drunks' or 'Gang of Druggies'. Others choose to put an extra 'o' in the word and consider it 'Good Energy' as opposed to 'Bad energy'. Some people have aspired to become 'Good Guys' instead of remaining 'Bad Boys'. Any concept, no matter how inadequate we believe it to be at the time, is enough to make a start with Step two. Even agnostics and atheists have found this step easy enough to master once they understand that the Higher Power can be anything, as long as it's not them. So, they are able to develop their entirely unique and understandable concept.

This is a Step about hope. Hope that there is a bright and beautiful future ahead of them if they are prepared to put the appropriate work into changing themselves. Much of this hope is found by seeing how other members of the group have changed and grown as a result of working this programme in their individual lives.

The insanity referred to in Step two is the part of their thinking that allows them to convince themselves that they can successfully drink/use again, often fooling themselves into the idea that they can do it without a negative reaction. Once this 'mental obsession' takes hold, they become compelled to use over and over again, regardless of the consequences that they know will follow. It is the consideration of this vicious cycle that helps them become willing to believe that perhaps a power greater than themselves may restore them to sanity. It is often said that insanity is repeating the same behaviour and expecting a different result. Or not learning from previous behaviours or conclusions and still making the same mistakes.

STEP THREE

Made a decision to turn our will and our lives over to the care of God as we understood Him.

In Step three, a decision is made to turn their will (thoughts) and their lives (actions) over to the care of whatever their concept of God is at that time. The first requirement is becoming convinced that anyone who runs his or her addictive life through self-will (selfishly, self-centred, self-obsessed, etc.) could hardly be a success. One of the ways to illustrate the meaning of a life run on self-will is by describing the behaviour of an actor who wants to run the whole theatrical show, and therefore falls short on the lighting, stage props, production, direction, ticket sales, etc. Many people may find it useful to substitute themselves into this idea and ask themselves honestly whether this scenario doesn't sound similar to the way they are currently running their lives. We then suggest to them that these kinds of self-centred thoughts and behaviours are the root cause behind many of their troubles.

Step three is the understanding that if one is able to change the way one thinks, then one is able to change the way one behaves, resulting in feeling differently about oneself because of the different reaction received to one's new way of dealing with things.

It is also about placing trust in the future and finding the faith that they can get well (recover), through the various professional treatment programmes around the world and within the established 12-Step Fellowships of recovering alcoholics and addicts such as those mentioned previously in the 'Introduction to 12-Step Fellowships' chapter.

The third Step also helps our clients get a grasp of the 'One day at a time' principle. This is the idea that if an alcoholic/addict can just stay sober/clean for a day, and get into this practice, then they have a much better chance of long term and permanent recovery.

STEP FOUR

Made a searching and fearless moral inventory of ourselves.

In the fourth Step, people are asked to examine the places in their lives that have had negative consequences, often accumulating from their behaviour while intoxicated. By completing and analysing their own moral inventory, they are able to see where their natural instincts for alcohol, drugs, money, sex, power, and prestige may have gone out of control, as they attempted to satisfy themselves in selfish and self-centred behaviours. The inventory involves looking at the people they have issues with, or resentments towards, the things they are afraid of, and the people they have harmed through their misconduct.

Step four enables them to realise their own methods of thinking and behaving, then to own these as previous ways of living, and begin to feel freedom from their addiction and selfishness by knowing that they are about to make some great changes to the negativity in their lives.

This Step takes a great deal of courage to do, since it involves looking deeply at themselves and taking responsibility for their own thoughts, feelings, actions and behaviours. It requires a high level of self examination, vulnerability and courage. But we have seen this type of courage displayed time and time again by people serious about healing from their addictions. They may find this courage through other members of their 12-Step group, who share their experiences of this Step and point out the benefits they have received as a result of completing it. This change is miraculous and a beautiful thing to witness.

STEP FIVE

Admitted to God, to ourselves, and to another human being the exact nature of our wrongs

In Step five, they share their fourth-step inventory and continue to discover 'the exact nature of their wrongs'.

Step five should be done immediately after having written and completed their fourth Step. This is usually on the same day. By taking this Step, they are able to identify areas where they may have allowed their addiction, their selfishness, their instincts, and their fears to control their thinking and emotions. Sharing this inventory with another person allows them to examine problems that they may have been unable to understand alone and offers them personal integrity.

It is at this Step that people begin to feel free from the shame, guilt and pain they may have experienced and been carrying with them throughout their lives. They are encouraged to trust this process and, as a result, they begin to taste a genuine prospect of a hopeful future.

STEP SIX

Were entirely ready to have God remove all these defects of character.

In reviewing these 'shortcomings', which became highlighted in the fourth and fifth Steps, the clients ask themselves whether they find these defects of character are undesirable and whether they are ready to believe that a God of their own understanding (whatever their interpretation of the word God) may be able to help remove them.

In most cases, there will be some outstanding defects of their characters that they are not willing to let go of yet. By allowing them to feel these shortcomings (feelings) before moving them on to Step seven, most people find the willingness to have them removed within a few days, often hours. It is always a privilege watching the lights come on in their eyes and this is a very powerful moment for both the alcoholic/addict and their family.

STEP SEVEN

Humbly asked Him to remove our shortcomings.

Step seven focuses on the things that cause our clients problems in life on general terms. Writing a balanced inventory of things they like about themselves is, of course, as important as writing down the negatives, particularly for those who may have lost a sense of self worth. It's been my experience that people I've worked with have often found it genuinely difficult to balance their negative self-assessment with their own positive assessments.

We have also found that continuous attendance at 12-Step Fellowship meetings to be a particularly useful method of counterbalancing these defects of character, especially when someone 'becomes of service' or rather volunteers their time and energy towards the success of their meeting, or Fellowship. It is when people become active and involved in such a way, that their recovery and their commitment to it, shows up as their success becomes a genuine part of their lives. This is because these groups work in a 'self-less' way, completely the opposite to an addict's usual selfishness and self-centredness. So by someone joining that culture of contribution, generosity and selflessness, real genuine life-changing character traits are very positively displayed. This newfound attitude and this charitable behaviour will also help deal with patience, tolerance, compassion, understanding, love and humility. It's very beautiful to watch a loved one undergo this transformation, which can only have a positive impact on everyone's lives.

STEP EIGHT

Made a list of all persons we had harmed and became willing to make amends to them all.

In Step eight, all the people who have been harmed by the alcoholic's drinking and the addict's using careers are considered. This list was originally drafted in Step four, although it's likely to have further additional names added to the list before it's ready to work from.

They will discuss possible methods of making amends to them all and search for the willingness to accomplish this. Most of the amends they need to make have been disclosed in their fourth Step 'resentment' inventory, their 'harms to others' inventory and their 'sexual' inventory. They also update this list to include anyone else they have come to realise was harmed as a result of their shortcomings, but was previously overlooked.

People are encouraged to discover love for their fellow humans and to display this love through interaction with the outside world. The important part of this Step is the willingness to accept their part in their past transgressions and the willingness to make things right. Willingness is the key, for if someone is still not willing to make right their wrongs, they may still be holding on to their selfish, self-centred view of the world, which doesn't fit with the recovery concepts of selfishness, contribution and generosity of spirit.

STEP NINE

Made direct amends to such people wherever possible, except, when to do so would injure them or others.

AFTERWORD

In Step nine, the recovering addicts/alcoholics begin to actually make amends to the people they have harmed and considered in the list of amends they made in Step eight. It is through Step nine that they become truly free from the guilt, fear, shame, and remorse that result from the harm they may have caused others.

This is the most forgiving Step. Not just of other people, but more importantly of themselves. By forgiving themselves of their past lives of chaos, deceit, cheating, lying, stealing, etc. they become freed from their addiction's prison. It has been compared to re-balancing one's karma.

Step nine may well be the most challenging of all the Steps, but by planning and working it thoroughly it has been seen to be the single most important part of the programme in establishing long-term sobriety and a healthy future.

Some of these amends may be worked directly by contacting the person face-to-face. Many of them are indirect amends, such as volunteering to work for a charity organisation. But most immediate amends are conducted as living amends - by living differently and no longer repeating their previous behaviours.

STEP TEN

Continued to take personal inventory and when we were wrong, promptly admitted it.

Although the 12-Steps are designed to be taken in order, it is suggested that Steps ten, eleven and twelve are continuously taken on a daily basis. These are often referred to as the 'maintenance Steps' and they encompass much of the first nine Steps in their structure and application.

Step ten involves continuing to take a personal inventory and setting right any new wrongs as one goes along. Step ten is basically a way of practising Steps three through to nine on a daily basis. In this way, whenever their recovery programme goes slightly off track, the client has the tools to re-balance themselves and their karma, making sure they recalibrate themselves before going to bed at night. Through this method, permanent recovery is possible and, indeed, probable.

In Step ten they will constructively review their day and they will be able to notice when they were resentful, selfish, dishonest or afraid. They will consider to whom do they need to apologise? Is there anything they may have kept to themselves that ought to have been discussed with another person? Were they kind and generous towards everyone? What could they have done differently? Were they thinking about themselves most of the day, or were they considering how they could improve the quality of other people's lives? And then they make it right as promptly as possible.

It has been said that any tenth Step amends need to be addressed immediately so that the client does not return to, or remain in, unhealthy thinking or behaving. It is common knowledge that those who do not take this Step seriously may lose all the good work they have already done in the previous nine Steps. It is for this reason that the clients are encouraged to find a sponsor (mentor) from the Fellowships. Step ten is worked daily with their sponsor, until such a time as they feel strong enough to manage their daily routines alone, at which point they'll check in with their sponsor on a less frequent basis.

It is at this point that true freedom from their obsession around drink and drugs can be experienced. Strangely enough, this freedom comes through the disciplines that they find and practise in this Step. Freedom through discipline, despite being a contradiction, is often a statement particularly unfamiliar to recovering addicts and alcoholics. But we witness this new way of life embraced time and time again.

STEP ELEVEN

Sought through prayer and meditation to improve our conscious contact with God as we understood Him, praying only for knowledge of His will for us and the power to carry that out.

Step eleven is a revitalising Step, and is there to encourage meditation and reflection. Because so many addicts and alcoholics were previously perfectly able to go to any lengths to secure their drugs or drinks, many of them find this eleventh Step where they are encouraged to be still and often silent, the most difficult of daily practices. This Step requires discipline, patience and practice.

Because Step eleven follows ten, once they have constructively reviewed their day, that they are able to seek through prayer and meditation God's forgiveness and different ways of correcting their behaviours. The results are often surprisingly simple and effective, particularly after a few weeks of practising this discipline.

There are many definitions of prayer and meditation, and we'd encourage active debate from the recovering alcoholic or addict on this subject. They are encouraged to explore all types of religions and spiritual practices and decide if there is one, or parts of some, that feel more comfortable than others. Alternatively many of them decide to use a method of their own fabrication. It is down to their personal choice. There is no dogma attached to this.

It could be considered that prayer and meditation is a private and personal moment with a Higher Power of their own understanding, saying, "Please keep me clean and sober today" in the morning, and "Thank you for keeping me clean and sober today" at night. There is no reason to be shy about this matter of prayer, or meditation. There are people around the world using it constantly. We find that when our clients develop an honest and genuine attitude around it that it works.

As the clients go through each new day and address new problems, we ask them to pause whenever doubtful or agitated and ask whichever power greater than themselves they have chosen to tap into, to provide them with the correct thought or action. They are reminded constantly that they are no longer running the show, and humbly say to themselves, "Thy will be done". They are therefore in much less of a danger from over-excitement, fear, anger, worry, self-pity or poor life choices.

This Step is an on-going Step as it asks them only to improve their awareness as their recovery programme develops, particularly as they deal with life on life's terms within society and the world.

STEP TWELVE

Having had a spiritual awakening as the result of these Steps, we tried to carry this message to alcoholics/addicts, and to practise these principles in all our affairs

Having taken the first eleven Steps, they are now at Step twelve and are ready to carry the programme of recovery in some form or another to other addicts and alcoholics. Every time they work with another addict they are reminded just how bad it was for them when they first came into the programme. When a new alcoholic/addict arrives in the Fellowships, they will all recognise the same trembling hands, weight loss, the look of desperation and sheer terror that they themselves may have previously had. They all come face-to-face with the newcomer's unmanageability in terms of depression, misery, and unhappiness (whether openly expressed or feebly concealed) and they witness the staggering destruction they may have caused everyone and everything around them. They are reminded of their own past troubles with personal relationships, as they see the new members struggle with theirs.

The therapeutic value at this point of one alcoholic/addict reaching out and helping another is truly incredible. It is at this point in the programme that the obsession and compulsion to use drugs and drink has been removed and a physical change is visible for everyone to witness.

Finally, their faith in the God of their own understanding's ability to restore them to sanity is reinforced, as they see how this programme begins to transform the life of the new prospect, right before their eyes.

In addition to carrying the message of recovery to other addicts, Step twelve involves practising these principles in all areas of their lives. When we've seen addicts or alcoholics who, unfortunately, relapse but are fortunate enough to return to seek help again from the 12-Step community and practitioners, once beginning the programme again it becomes clear that once they've analysed what happened, that they'd stopped practising these principles in some or all of their affairs, they were no longer examining their motives, reviewing their days, caring for others, or carrying the message of hope and recovery to newcomers.

A summary of how to behave from a perspective of spiritual awareness could be in two complementary ways. Firstly, doing unto others what one would like done to oneself. And, secondly, doing for others that which they cannot do for themselves.

This Step is about being of service to society, the world and all those around them. The complete opposite to the way they would have thought, acted and considered behaving previously. Selfless as opposed to selfish.

How it works

If there were one watchword to describe how these Steps should be practised, it would be 'continuously', for it is only through constant application of these principles that our recovering and recovered addicts/alcoholics can be assured of the promises of freedom from addiction offered within these 12-Step programmes. That said, by the time most recovering addicts and alcoholics have completed the 12-Step programme, these principles have become a new way of life, and effectively the programme begins to work as if on autopilot.

Compare this programme to exercise. If, in your first year, you exercised a great deal, you'd (hopefully) get into a much better state physically. Then, if you kept up a regular discipline of a few times each week, you would maintain that for the rest of your life. However, if you stopped exercising, you would lose all that you gained from it in the first year and revert back to the way you were before you even started (or in some cases even worse). A very similar parable can be said for recovery. Despite how much good effort you put into it at the beginning, you will always need to ensure that you're living your life upon these newfound principles and you'll always need some interaction with the Steps. To not do so is likely to lead you back to previous ways.

This 12-Step programme is a design for living we hope our clients will continue to make use of, long after they have graduated and put down their drugs of choice (and any other substances, behaviours and procedures that cause them pain). The fact that recovering and recovered alcoholics and addicts alike keep attending Fellowship meetings in later years is often interpreted as a developing dependency upon the 12-Step Fellowships. But this interpretation is debatable, as the most poignant part of an individual's choice to 'keep coming back' is the continued reinforcement of the learning process, which strengthens a personal commitment to change and can so easily be challenged in daily life by pubs, clubs, casinos, etc. So, the Fellowships encourage their members to return to their communities and become involved in local meetings and maybe start their own groups wherever needed and encourage others by carrying the message of recovery. Furthermore, once someone has recovered from their previously considered hopeless state of mind and body, they return to the Fellowship meetings, not so that they can receive help from others, but more so that they can contribute towards helping the newcomers. And so the circle of recovery continues.

Contact us:

Do you know someone who is struggling or suffering from untreated addiction? Would you like our help?

Please go to www.soberservices.co.uk and email me ian@soberservices.co.uk

I'd be happy to see how I could help.

"There's a way. There's always a way. It just requires desire."

IAN YOUNG

24th November 2012

To discover more about some of the other projects I'm involved in, go to www.ianyoung.co

IAN YOUNG

It's Not About Me!

Biography of the Author
– *Ian Young*

Ian Young has successfully touched the lives of thousands of addicted people and their families, showing them a new way to live and encouraging them to rebuild their lives without their destructive patterns or influences once and for all.

Ian is the founder of two large rehabilitation facilities still operating within the European Treatment Industry and currently runs Sober Services ltd; another of his dynamic and influential business within the addiction treatment industry.

But it wasn't always like that...

Early 2001, aged 29, after 13 years of chronic drug addiction, alcoholism, homelessness and unemployment, Ian discovered a permanent way out of his debilitating lifestyle, and through hard work built himself a world filled with the riches and royalties that life really does has to offer – addiction free.

Ian is a multiple business owner, including Senior Director of the popular LivingBig – an 'On and Offline' network and training academy for Coaches and Mentors.

Ian is both honoured and proud to be one of 35 founding members of the Association of Transformation Leaders, Europe, qualification for membership of which involves positively affecting the lives of over 6000 people.

Ian is a homeowner living in a quiet part of Northern Hertfordshire with his wife, two dogs, two cats and a horse.

Ian's personal mission is to co-create harmony through laughter and love, and to help others improve the quality of their lives.

Connect with Ian at www.ianyoung.co or www.soberservices.co.uk

Profile photography courtesy of Joel Dyer at www.peterdyerphotos.com 0208-363-2456